CLEANLINESS AND GODLINESS

Cleanliness

✄ and ✄

Godliness

or

THE FURTHER METAMORPHOSIS

A Discussion of the Problems of Sanitation
raised by SIR JOHN HARINGTON,
together with Reflections upon Further
Progress recorded since that Excellent
Knight, by his Invention of the
Metamorphosed

AJAX

Father of Conveniences

revolutionised the System of Sanitation
in this country but raised
at the same time fresh
PROBLEMS FOR POSTERITY
which are discussed in all their implications,
with numerous digressions upon all aspects
of Cleanliness by the author

REGINALD REYNOLDS

NIHIL OBSTAT

DOUBLEDAY AND COMPANY, INC.

Garden City 1946 New York

DEDICATION TO AJAX

Midas to gold transmuted,
Medusa turned to stone;
The learnèd Muse of Ovid traces
Innumerable classic cases
Of altered forms and changing faces,
With testimony shewn.

The poisoned cup of Circe
Still at our feasts is seen;
The water changes not to wine,
But wine to water when we dine,
And we (as like as not) to swine,
Gargantuan, Gadarene.

But you, immortal Ajax,
Sexton of meat and wine,
Hospitably content to house
Transmuted relics of carouse,
Shall feed the field that feeds the cows
And fertilise the vine.

Contents

CLEANLINESS AND GODLINESS

CLEANLINESS AND GODLINESS

CAPUT I

A General Introduction to the Subject

The New Order is shewn to begin with the Closet.—It may be thought that a man must have a small mind who, at such a time as the present, can concern himself with the subject I have chosen. One may read much of New Orders, of the Defence of Civilisation, of the means to destroy whole cities and populations, together with Blue Prints for our rehabilitation when the destruction shall be at an end. Where, you may ask, is there room in such a world for the discussions I would seek to initiate? How can Cloacina, the unheroic guardian of public sanitation, compete with Mars for the favour of your attention?

I should be but a poor fool if I put on the gloves when, like a Japanese wrestler, I can defeat my opponent by his own weight. Briefly, my thesis is that though the whole is greater than the part, the part is a component of the whole. Or, to paraphrase an old saying, take care of sanitation, and civilisation will take care of itself. Then, surely, even as charity still begins at home, so sanitation begins at the close-stool, and a good closet is the microcosm of the New Order. Therefore I put it to the architects of Utopia that there is no good architecture without sound detail and no sound detail without proper specifications for the plumber. For whatever danger there may be that a man may fail to see the wood for the multitude of trees, the reverse is an equal catastrophe; and it is of the individual trees that the planter must think first.

It is but of recent years that cleanliness has discovered its place next to godliness. The blessed St. Catherine of Siena was not of that opinion when she drank filthy water and withheld from the stool *ad majorem dei gloriam*. Nor was St. Francis of Assisi, who considered dirt to be among the proper humiliations and mortifications of the flesh, and appeared after his death (according to Thomas of Eccleston, *De Adventu Fratrum Minorum*) to commend certain friars minor in this country for the filthiness of the room in which they lodged. Even the innovations of the past century were still strenuously opposed by those who saw Mr. Henry Doulton as the Devil himself, the clergy declaring openly the impiety of all attempts to abolish infectious diseases, which they regarded as plainly the Will of God.

Wisdom from the East.—Sanitation is therefore properly to be considered as part of the New Order, and let it not be imagined that little remains here to be achieved. For the consideration of cleanliness alone we have as yet some way to go, and I hope to shew that this problem does not end with a few chains and flushes, as any Brahmin is at liberty to inform you. For when I was in India I recall that a pious Hindu once asked me what was the Christian teaching on the subject of personal hygiene? Why, none, said I. But that, said he, is impossible, for every religion has a code for the closet, how cleansing is to be performed, when and in what manner the hands shall be washed, also concerning baths and the cleaning of the teeth. Nevertheless, I told him, though these would seem to me more proper subjects for religious teaching than the orientation of the priest in his offices, we have none such. How so, then, says he, have you no teachings at all in these matters? To which I replied that our priests taught theology, but left hygiene to the individual conscience.

For this reason there were those who had hopes, when the first New Order was proclaimed by the Muscovites, under the title of the Union of the Socialist Soviet Republics, that where priests had neglected their duty, commissars might perform it. But after near twenty years of their dispensation a traveller from Moscow to Turkestan found their privies to be so noisome that they were remembered as the hardiest portion of her adventure; and it is said of one librarian that he classified Miss Ethel Mannin's *South to Samarkand* under the general category of Closets, upon this account. From this it may be observed that I have no *odium theologicum*.

Hygiene and Civilised Behaviour begin in the Bowels.— But let not the reader imagine that we speak only of hygiene, and that in so narrow a sense. Who knows but that Hitler himself, had he been more fortunate in his habits, would have been a happy and (in consequence) a harmless person? For I have heard it said, even of our own countrymen, that their habits of feeding induced a lethargy in their bowels, which in turn so irritated and inflamed their constitutions that they were induced to subdue one-fifth of the globe to their dominion; when for the cost of a few figs each day they might have lived in peace, with their household gods. Therefore, if history be properly understood, it may prove to be the case that our present calamities began, not at Munich or at Versailles, but in an empty closet in Austria, where a dismal failure was unrecorded for which even the empire of the world could not atone.

And end with the proper Disposal of Sewage.—Or if you will bear with me I hope to shew that there are even greater issues at stake than those which have made Europe a battlefield. Civilisation, being a selective process, has both negative and positive requirements, of which hygiene represents those that are negative. Sterility and fertility describe our needs—the destruction, elimination and safe removal of that which is undesirable, and the encouragement, promotion and creation of that which is desired. If, then, I may speak (as the fashion is) dialectically, I would say that sewage may be considered from either end, and that the greatest errors with regard to it arise from a formal or scholastic approach, in which S is always P and things are considered as static entities. To speak plainly (and it is time I should) dung is foul matter in an animal, for which reason nature conspires to be rid of it; and if it remains in some ill-considered closet it remains only as a pollution and a source of infection. But those who treat of these affairs only as matters of hygiene have neglected the dialectic antithesis, which is that dung is a link in the chain of life, the source of vegetable fertility, the means whereby we make payment to nature for that which we have from her. And of this I will say more hereafter in defence of my programme, *sterility in the closet, fertility in the fields,* lest in our anxiety for sanitation we bankrupt Mother Ceres.

Magnitude of the Subject.—Whoever, indeed, would study this subject with a knowledge worthy of its magnitude must consider it from so many angles and with such a wealth of learning that I cannot without pretentiousness claim to do more than write a primer or introductory thesis upon it. Sanitation has its history, its archaeology, its literature and its science. Most religions concern themselves with it, sociology includes it within its sphere, and its study is imperative to social ethics. Some knowledge of psychology is necessary to understand its development and retardation, an aesthetic sense is required for its full appreciation, economics determine, to a large degree, its growth and extent, while the ultimate disposal of sewage must be viewed in the light of biology.

Inadequacy of available Writings.—It is, then, surprising that so little has been written to lighten our darkness and to create some body of knowledge relating to a subject in which so many arts and sciences are in conjunction. In recent years but two slight volumes have appeared among popular literature to deal with isolated facets of our subject, the one an account of a maker of earth-closets, locally celebrated and now known to the world as *The Specialist,* and the other entitled *For Your Convenience,* an account of the facilities afforded to the wayfarer in the metropolis. Not since the great Sir John Harington published his *Metamorphosis of Ajax* has any attempt been made at a comprehensive work on sanitary matters, though I must acknowledge more than a little to the fruitful researches of Mr. Desmond Eyles, who dealt with the technical side of the matter in the *Official Architect,* under the title *Sanitation Through the Ages,* and to other technical writers.

Let us now praise famous Men.—Harington was the great revolutionary of his age, the most practical Utopian of the Renaissance, the true prophet of what little progress we can claim. He made modern hygiene an achievement so predominantly British that (as Mr. John Lindsay justly remarks) the French to this day have burdened their language with a word they cannot hope to pronounce, and pay us a delicate tribute every time they direct us, with simplicity we in turn might envy, to *le vatercloset.* But we should shew ourselves unworthy of such a compliment if we failed to appreciate the labours of earlier ages, though so little of these survived the empire of Rome. The very mention of that empire should remind us that Roman armies, though they may have marched, like those of Napoleon, upon their bellies, stabilised their conquests upon a basis of good drainage. Rome grew with sanita-

tion and declined with its decline; and we may speculate
profitably as to which was the cause and which the effect.
Had the Supreme Pontiff continued in this respect the
best traditions of the Caesars, there would have been less
reason to regret the fatal gift of Constantine or the decline of his successors. Instead of this there was a great
hunting for heretics while the *Cloaca Maxima* filled up
and choked; and not until England began to export water-
closets did the Vatican become a shining light in matters
temporal and secular. Then, if tradition may be credited,
the first of these English innovations being installed in the
Papal Palace, His Holiness himself (was it Pio Nono?)
was the first to enter, while the higher clergy sang litanies
on the further side of the door. But the same tradition
will have it that there came at last a pause in the singing
and a voice was heard from within, faint and dispirited,
pronouncing the words *Non possumus.* Others say, however, that this story was maliciously invented by Schis-
matics in a contemptible effort to prove papal fallibility,
and it may even be found upon exhaustive researches that
this is but a legend, arising from the name of the throne
upon which the popes once sat. This throne, which is still
to be seen in the Vatican Museum, is known as the *Ster-
coraria;* but the reason is not as you might suppose, for the
name arose from the anthem, *De stercore erigens pau-
perem,* which was sung at the enthronement of a new
pope.

A pious Exhortation to the Churches.—Be that as it may,
I regard the most important revolution since Sir John's
Ajax, that pioneer of water-closets, as the conversion of
the Churches to a belief in hygiene; for there is no doubt
that to make an idea imperative it is of the first importance to give it a religious sanction. Moses was a wise man
who had trouble enough with a stiff-necked people, but
armed with the tablets of Sinai he could make them do

what reason, persuasion and threats failed to achieve. The Church, finding the gospels inadequate for its requirements, invented the creeds and took over enough paganism to provide itself with a theology which the evangelists had neglected to supply. In a later age the Society of Jesus carried adoption to such a point that some Jesuit missionaries in Cathay, finding the pig to be there considered a sacred animal and the lamb held in contempt, adapted the symbolism of the gospels to these weaker China vessels. Bearing such previous metamorphoses in mind, we may anticipate some amendments to Christian theology and ritual, in which doctrines of hygiene could play an appropriate part in the professions and observances of the Church. Such a process should be less difficult on account of the importance given to this subject by the ancient Hebrews; and the Biblical quotations with which the new movement could be supported are, indeed, remarkably sound in almost every particular, as I hope to demonstrate.

Of Prudery and Progress—Distress of Dean Swift.—This last reflection calls to mind the singular fact that, whereas the natural functions of man were in previous ages a matter for open comment and discussion, as they are today among most nations other than our own, we suffer from this impediment in discussing these important matters, that among the English all relating to excretion is made a matter of euphemism. Hence it may be observed that those things which it is most proper for us to consider are considered most improper to discuss; which is indeed the reverse of what is reasonable. It was said by the celebrated Venetian, Alvise da Ca'da Mosto, who made many voyages in the fifteenth century to countries of the Blacks, that there was a strange tribe whom he calls the Azanaghi, who covered their mouths with a handkerchief. And this, says he, they do because they say that the mouth is a brutish thing, that is always uttering wind and bad odours so that it should be kept covered. And I doubt not that Mr. Samuel Butler knew or had read of these same Azanaghi when he wrote of a people who ate in secret and made great shame of what went into them. Yet these savages seem to my understanding no less rational than those who eat openly and make much talk of their food, what they shall eat and what they shall drink (contrary to the teaching of the gospels), but would have us believe that they are incinerators that burn their own rubbish. Then when they are discovered of a sudden to be men and women with animal requirements, there is a great to-do, and such an intelligent man as the Very Rev. Dean Swift, on discovering that his mistress is possessed of a close-stool, must needs cry out in a passion—as though (that dour critic the late Mr. Lawrence has more recently remarked) it would not have been the true catastrophe if Celia had not needed it.

Be sure we will return to this matter at greater length; for here, if anywhere, is our true Barbarism, as though by keeping mum upon foul matter we could dispose of it. And I will warrant that Bishop Berkeley, for all his theories, found that his closet did not void itself for lack of his regard; and had he lived longer might have added a rider to his propositions, that so long as a thing smelt it had existence. Nature will not conspire with our silences to pretend our problems do not exist, but answers the prude with noxious vapours and forces our attention in spite of our prejudices, as a man may now learn by stepping into a Tube station of an early morning.

A Parable of the Present Times.—Enough, then, of prudery. If we are minded to live, like our ancestors, in caves, squeamish scruples will no longer serve. It will profit us but little if we save ourselves from starvation to die of disease, and this will not be avoided without plain speaking.

The population is now so congregated or dispersed that new problems force themselves upon us, and sanitation should be among the first for our consideration. Is there not to this day one half of a school settled in a town within a few miles of London while the other half is in Cornwall; and all because the near half was in a coach that had no corridor to it, necessitating this uncovenanted dumping? Here is a parable for those who will not discuss such matters, for in plain language the want of a water-closet upon this occasion was of historical importance and changed the course of some forty lives.

Let the reader judge, then, whether we speak *ad rem* or *non ad rem*. Whether this be a war for civilisation or no, there is still a war for sanitation, and Ajax girds on his armour once more. *Business as Usual* shall be our motto, and for those who think to read more than I have intended I will add the familiar tag—*Honi soit qui mal y pense.*

CAPUT II

Mainly Concerning Prehistoric Privies

THOSE OF MY READERS who have perused (as I will warrant the greater part have not) the work of Sir John Marshall and his fellow-labourers upon *Mohenjo-Daro and the Indus Civilisation,* may know that a certain Mr. Banerji began about twenty years past to dig by the banks of the Indus in the country of Sind. And here Mr. Banerji and those who followed him discovered, as it might be termed, a pile of buried cities, each superimposed upon the last, thus earning the name of Mohenjo-Daro, or *The Mound of the Dead*.

Now these cities were of brick, and, if Sir John's calculations may be credited, were built between 3250 and 2750 years before the birth of Our Lord by a people of whom little is known and much speculated. Their civilisation is termed Chalcolithic and doubtless lasted longer than the five hundred years which Sir John allows for the life of these ruins.

Concerning Chalcolithic Drains—The Dustbins of Dead Man Lane.—Of sanitation in general among these people Sir John Marshall says that bathrooms and drains are common to their buildings. The former, says he, are invariably well paved and usually connected with the drains in their streets. In private houses these baths appear to have been made both upon upper and lower floors, with horizontal drains, commonly of brick, also vertical drains from the upper chambers, fashioned of terra-cotta pipes, cunningly fitted together with spigot and faucet joints, and protected by brickwork or by the thickness of the walls. There were also, says Sir John, rubbish chutes or flues, descending from the upper storeys through hollows in their broad walls, and disgorging in some instances into a bin, where scavengers from the street might remove the household filth. And at convenient places by the roadside were public bins in addition to these household dumps, as for example in the street which Sir John calls *Dead Man Lane*. So that whoever passed down Dead Man Lane in The Mound of the Dead need have seen no garbish by the wayside, but all neatly packed away and, as we may imagine, removed with regularity by Chalcolithic dustmen. And their drains, Sir John tells us, were constructed with as much care in the street as in their houses, shewing these men of the Indus to have been persons of a profound civic sensibility.

In one matter only were these people lacking in sanitary intelligence, that being their failure to carry their drains beyond the town; for they preferred to let their filth collect within their own walls in soak-pits, where the fluids would become absorbed into the earth and the solid residue would be removed by scavengers. In this they were ill advised, but in most matters they were persons worthy of our admiration in all that pertains to public health. Even the poorest quarters of their city were found to possess an excellent and elaborate system of drainage, with covers of brick or stone that could be removed with ease for the purpose of clearance. These drains were laid some two feet or less below the level of the street, being fashioned for the most part of moulded bricks, cemented with a mortar of mud; but within the houses better materials were used, and in one instance we read of drain pipes made of pottery, turned upon the wheel, and embedded in gypsum plaster against the possibility of leakage.

Contentions of Mr. Ernest Mackay regarding the Drains of Mohenjo-Daro.—It is the opinion of Mr. Ernest Mackay, the eminent archaeologist, that these drains were not used for the disposal of sewage, and as evidence of this he cites us the *Charaka-Samhita,* a work of the second century A.D., as nearly as can be computed, in which it is said that latrines are intended only for the sick and infirm; and for the rest that a man should proceed a bow-shot from his house to do his business. But such an authority is no more competent to describe the ways of the Chalcolithic Age than a statute of Edward III to provide a picture of the Romans in Britain, and for the rest the arguments of Mr. Mackay are of little weight. *Item* that the waters were suffered on occasion to run down the walls of the house, which he says would have been a noxious custom if these waters had contained sewage. But he omits to remind us that the contrary proposition, which is the absence of sewage disposal, would have been, in a city, even more noxious than an open drain; and since there were both open water-chutes and closed drains in these houses, it were more reasonable to suppose that these two systems served separate purposes, the one to carry off rain water and bath water, the other to dispose of sewage.

Furthermore, Mr. Mackay informs us that the soak-pits were of inadequate size for such a purpose, so that constant clearing of these would have been necessary. But in so industrious a society constant clearing may well have been the custom; and if I must suffer a soak-pit near my threshold, I had rather it were a small pit, constantly emptied, than a large one where refuse would long remain and stink. Also Mr. Mackay will have it that the structure of the drains was not suited to such a task, these being of rough brickwork with joints at a right angle. But, as he has been careful to inform us of their movable covers, he has replied to his own argument that there would be a settlement of solid matter; for these drains could be opened up in the manner of a man-hole for the purpose of clearage. And lastly he argues from the close proximity of the wells to these drains and the danger of infiltration; but whoever has seen a heap of British manure or a cesspool, set close to a country well of drinking water, will more easily believe that such things were possible three thousand years before Christ.

Refuted on the Authority of Sir John Marshall.—Indeed, Mr. Mackay admits the very case that he would refute, for he speaks of *a single exception*. This *single exception* is described by Rai Bahadur D. R. Sahni, Superintendent of the Archaeological Survey of India, when he writes of two well-built privies in a house of the later period. These, he says, were emptied by outlets in the wall conducting the sewage to a drain in the street; and if this could be the case in one house it is not too presumptuous to suppose, in despite of Mr. Mackay's arguments, that it might have been common or even general in others. Of these two closets Sir John Marshall observes both that they are *privies with seats, as to the character of which there can be no question* and that the drains to which they connect *must therefore have been designed for sewage of any kind, solid or fluid.*

I therefore make bold to suggest that, on this question of privies, I have Sir John on my side. Moreover, on Sir John's evidence there is more than a *single exception,* as Mr. Mackay terms it, to his contention that *no latrines have been satisfactorily identified*. For Sir John Marshall, whilst referring to these two privies (if two privies can be one exception), also makes mention explicitly of a third in another building, from which a drain ran to a soak-pit in the street, and of a vertical drain in the wall of this

latrine, which he presumes to have descended from
another latrine on an upper floor. From the small size of
this vertical drain he concludes this hypothetical or conjectured latrine to have been no more than a urinal; but
even such a supposition disposes further of many points
in Mr. Mackay's argument. And in yet another house Sir
John records the presence of a drain which he says must
have connected an upstair privy with an earthenware
vessel, sunk beneath the courtyard pavement and having
no outlet. To this he adds that the contents of the sunk
vessel must of necessity have been cleared and conveyed
by hand to some neighbouring street-drain or soak-pit.
Thus, once more, we cannot escape the supposition that
the drains were (notwithstanding objections to such a
practice based upon structural grounds) employed for the
disposal of sewage.

Chalcolithic Hygiene vindicated.—For these reasons I
prefer, in the absence of conclusive evidence to the contrary, to imagine that those who knew so much of drainage and were such able and industrious sanitary engineers,
did not suffer themselves to be incommoded by sewage
when they were at such pains to be rid—as Mr. Mackay
would have it—of rain water. But this at least is beyond
dispute concerning those who inhabited The Mound of
the Dead, that they were possessed of well-appointed bathrooms, together with the system of drainage that I have
described in brief, and at least a few latrines attached to
that system; so that they may for this cause alone be considered (with the inhabitants of Harappa in the Punjab,
of whom I could say much the same) as part of the Sanitary Vanguard of Mankind.

Of the Egyptians.—Of the ancient Egyptians we know
more, because their writings have been preserved for us.
Dr. Jamieson Hurry, in his monograph on Imhotep, one
of the earliest physicians known to history, observes that

the Egyptians boasted themselves the healthiest of mortals. They regulated, he says, the sanitation of the town, of the dwelling and even of the person, while the priests maintained a high standard of cleanliness by their frequent ablutions and the immaculate purity of their clothing. That they might the better preserve the purity of their bodies he records that these priests washed themselves from head to foot in cold water twice every day and twice every night. The homes of the people were fumigated from time to time to preserve their sweetness, and provision was made to prevent annoyance by insects. Also he says that there was among the Egyptians some knowledge of antiseptics, since the virtues of extreme dryness and of certain chemicals such as nitre, common salt and alcohol, as preservatives, were recognised. To this he adds that the value of preventive medicine was well recognised and that the Egyptians appreciated the superiority of *prophylaxis* to *therapeutics*. And this writer cites Diodorus, who observed that among the Egyptians the whole manner of life was so evenly ordered that it would appear as though it had been arranged according to the rules of health by a learned physician rather than by a law-giver. Which may indeed have been the case, for this Doctor Imhotep of Egypt was Vizier to King Zoser some 2900 years before Christ, and of such renown that he was translated to be God of Medicine when his body was maturely mummified.

A Sumptuous Jakes of the Eighteenth Dynasty.—Also Sir G. Maspero, sometime Director-General of the Service of Antiquities in Egypt, speaks of the indications which bear witness to the excellent hygienic and sanitary arrangements known in ancient Egypt, of which he mentions the elaborate bath discovered at Tell el-Amarneh, in the house of a high official of the Eighteenth Dynasty. And he observes that in the midst of their paved streets they provided a channel of stone to carry off water and drainage. And in this same bathroom at Tell el-Amarneh there was discovered a well-preserved closet behind a screen wall, this closet being provided with a seat of limestone, elegantly shaped. At the ancient city of Kahun, also, the most delectable system of drainage was discovered and much information regarding the Egyptian latrines of the Second Dynasty will be found in the British Association Report for the year 1914.

Alas that I must add here a familiar story; for the excavations of Professor Peet and Mr. C. M. Woolley shew that sanitary provisions at Tell el-Amarneh were only for the nobles, priests and *commissars* of this age, no such arrangements being discovered in the crowded quarters of the poor. And the same was observed in the town of Illahun, providing a thesis more eloquent than *Das Kapital;* for here, indeed, are sermons in stones.

Curious Customs described by Herodotus.—It was nevertheless the opinion of Herodotus that these Egyptians were of all nations the most healthy; for he found them distinguished from other peoples by the singularity of their institutions and their manners; and if in some of these peculiarities we can find no reason for his praise, in others we shall find much. Thus in the thirty-fifth chapter of his second book, called *Euterpe,* he tells us that women stand erect to make water, while men squat; a custom as little deserving special praise as that credited to the Turks, of whom the anonymous author of *Ulysses Upon Ajax* tells us that *among the Turks it is an heresy to p——s standing.* But the offices of nature, says Herodotus, are performed at home, though they eat their meals publicly in the streets. Of these habits, both contrary to Greek custom, Herodotus tells us that the Egyptians asserted in vindication of them that those things which, though necessary, are unseemly, are best done in private; but whatever has no shame attached to it should be done openly. The

Egyptians also (like the Pythagoreans, who imitated them) abstained from beans, which they held to be unclean, for which I can give no good explanation; though some say that Pythagoras was in this matter misunderstood by Aristotle.

But as to their closets, if in these they used earth rather than water for the most part, we have yet to see whether we are wiser than the Pharaohs; for sanitation is not to be confused with any popular notion or prevalent system, but must be considered in relation to the best and most expeditious disposal of sewage, the abatement of nuisances and causes of infection, the fertility of the soil, and many other matters, such as the climate and the means at human disposal. But we know from these general observations that the priest-physicians who directed the public hygiene of Egypt found cleanliness next to godliness, and were concerned to keep at least the upper-class quarters of their cities wholesome.

The Egyptians knew even the art of making drains of hammered copper, of which one was found, fully 450 yards in length, at the temple of Sahû-ra, though this drain served only for rain water. And that their supply of water was considered a matter of great importance, for the attention of the highest officer of the State, we know from an inscription concerning the duties of the Vizier under the Eighteenth Dynasty. For this inscription says of the Vizier, *It is he who dispatches the official staff to attend to the water supply in the whole land;* and again the inscription reads that *It is he who inspects the water supply on the first of every ten-day period.* This will be found in the second volume of the *Ancient Records of Egypt,* edited by Mr. Breasted.

A Digression into Philology.—Also the late and very learned Dr. Rendel Harris will have it that the very words *swab* and *swabber* derive from the Egyptian lan-

guage and are of the greatest antiquity. For in a lecture
delivered on his seventy-ninth birthday at Woodbrooke,
Birmingham, in January of 1931, the doctor followed this
line of reasoning. *Wāb,* he says, among the Ancient Egyptians signified *pure,* and from this word he would trace
the name of the *Wahabis,* who are the Puritans of Islam
today. Also the letter S, he says, expresses causation, so
that *ankh* being the word meaning *life, S-ankh* signifies *to
make alive.* From this he concludes that, if *wāb* be *pure,*
S-wāb would be *to make pure;* that is to say, to cleanse or
to swab. And since it was among the opinions strongly
held by Dr. Harris that the Egyptians were a great seafaring people, he contends that this word *swab* came into
our language through the ancient intercourse of seamen,
whose language may be in parts older than any now
spoken in Europe. For the seafaring use of the word he
invokes Shakespeare, who wrote of

The master, the swabber, the boatswain and I,

and, as to the seafaring habits of the Egyptians, it is beyond dispute that they had great fleets of ships, which
they will scarcely have used for pleasure trips on the Nile.

Now from this word *swab* Dr. Harris will have us believe that the word soap is in turn derived, making it to
mean *that which makes clean.* So that he would have the
very symbol of modern hygiene to be wearing an Egyptian
name out of antiquity; and to prove this he gives us variations in the word, such as *swope* and *soope,* shewing also
that the most erudite philologists have no certainty as to
the origin of this word.

The Waters of Babylon.—Next we will consider Babylon, where among the ancient ruins, beneath the mounds
of Nippur, there were found by excavators a series of
drain pipes laid in vaulted tunnels, these being of great

antiquity. And of the excavations by Dr. Banks at Bismya, a city of southern Babylonia, it is mentioned by Dr. Morris Jastrow in *The Civilisation of Babylonia and Assyria* that vertical drains leading down to the foundations were found in several rooms, suggesting their use as bathrooms and shewing at least some attempts at sanitation in very early days.

Venerable Privies of the Sumerians.—As to the Assyrians, we are told that they knew the use of the enema, for internal cleansing, which demonstrates their sagacity. For these people learned much from the Egyptians, whose sanitary arrangements and ideas of hygiene they imitated, continuing their efforts at sanitary engineering (as the records prove) even at a time when His Gracious Majesty King Nebuchadrezzar had reverted to four legs and a diet of grass. Among the oldest achievements of these people, before the days of Babylon, are the drains which they built of cemented tiles in the dim, prehistoric dawn, which drains were discovered (together with a great swimming-pool) among the ruins of Kish, on the Euphrates. The Sumerians also left us three privies at Tell Asman, which they called Ashnunnak; and these may well be the oldest of all those yet discovered. Also of six privies found in a palace, built in the days of the great Sargon, King of Kings, about 4500 years before Christ, I learn at second hand that Professor Henri Frankfort (of the University of Chicago) writes that they were of the most western design, with high seats, and not of the oriental kind, which is level with the floor.

The Water-closet of Mrs. Minos.—Then we may consider those old sea-kings at Knossos who ruled there some 2800 years before the birth of our Saviour; and of their ways Mr. Wells says briefly that they had water-pipes, bathrooms *and the like conveniences,* such as have hitherto been regarded as *the latest refinements of modern life*. (Whereat the Greeks so marvelled that they made of Minoan sewers a *labyrinth* to which their fancy added a monster whom they called the minotaur.) Here Sir Arthur Evans discovered an excellent water-closet, which must have been fashioned with a seat of wood and was made to be flushed in the modern manner, having water always in the pan, as Mr. Wells delicately hints. And such closets, it would seem, were flushed with rain water when it was plentiful, but at other times with water from a cistern. Also these kings, whom the Cretans called *Minos,* could bathe themselves in baths of pottery, and their pipes of this material were cunningly devised with tapering sections, to fit end to end.

For those who would know but a little of these marvels there is a clue to Sir Arthur's *Palace of Minos,* like that of Ariadne, in a slender handbook by Mr. Pendlebury, the Curator. From him you may learn briefly of the drains and pipes of the first Middle Minoan period, between 2200 and 2000 years before Christ, and how these pipes are believed to have run upward as well as downward. And you may learn of the drains in Middle Minoan II, which signifies 2000 to 1800 B.C., how these are of stone and cement; of this closet, the eighth wonder of the world, in the toilet room of the Queen; of man-holes for the inspection of sewers; of the Queen's bathroom; and of foot-baths and tubs for the weary traveller at the caravanserai. And if the late battles have left a few stones to see, that survived so many centuries, we may yet behold these things for ourselves.

Concerning the water supply in this ancient kingdom, Professor Gustave Glotz has written with eloquence in *The Aegean Civilisation,* calling it a very monument of hydraulic science. This system he describes in some detail, concluding that not one of the laws which should be observed in order to check and clarify a flow of water seems to have escaped the builder of these water-works.

Lastly, as to their disposal of garbage, or *dry refuse,* as it is called, Sir Arthur Evans discovered many large pits that were employed for this purpose, called *Kouloura;* and from what he tells us of their construction it may well be that these Minoans (like the ancient Chinese) understood the art of *composting* putrescible matter and making of it good humus for their fields, of which we shall have more to say later.

The Jews called the Privy The House of Honour.— Next we will consider the Jews, who were at all times greatly concerned with matters of hygiene, and scorned not to speak openly of such things in their holy scriptures, in very plain language, so that one is astounded at the squeamish stomachs of modern puritans, who make so much of these writings, when they would die rather than use such terms themselves, holding as unspeakably obscene the very words and images that the prophets so freely employed. Their privies were held in such esteem by these Children of Israel that they were known by a name signifying *The House of Honour,* and their ancient books contain the most minute instructions regarding the disposal of sewage, how it should be dug into the soil and not suffered to accumulate.

Of these and other sanitary measures, ordained by Moses for a nomadic people, My Lord Raglan writes in *Jocasta's Crime* that it has been alleged that Moses was a great Sanitarian; that a great part of his code was deliberately enacted from hygienic motives, and that he pretended to have obtained Divine Sanction for laws which were either based on the results of his own scientific researches or extracted from the regulations issued by the Egyptian Ministry of Health. But My Lord pours scorn upon such suppositions, observing that there is not the slightest justification for basing the Mosaic code upon scientific knowledge, or believing that it was inspired by other than religious ideas.

If this be so, it is more to the credit of religion that the inspirations of the heart should so often and so closely have followed the path of truth and reached the goal before Science had girded up her loins. But I mistrust this division of ideas into *scientific* and *religious,* holding that human knowledge and experience, from the sublime to the ridiculous, are of one essence and wholeness, whether we consider the doctrine of transubstantiation, the metabolism of the body, the logos becoming flesh, or a dunghill becoming a vegetable marrow, *in nomine patris,* etc., and all to the glory of God.

Speculations of Sir John Harington regarding Saul and David.—Whoever will search the scriptures at this time will find that Sir John Harington has been there before him and claimed this whole Empire for Ajax, planting his flag alike upon both testaments with all reverence. Thus he observes of the translations then available that the first Book of Samuel tells how David in a certain cave did cut off the lap of Saul's coat, and leaves not to tell what Saul was then doing. To which my Authorised Version makes answer that Saul *went in to cover his feet;* which I can scarcely believe, and find more sense in the words of the Vulgate, *ut purgaret ventrem,* wherein Sir John finds the true explanation.

Murder of Eglon.—But what was it that I remember to have read concerning Eglon, that very fat man, as the chronicler tells us, who was King of Moab? Bring me the Book of Judges, and we will read of his most treacherous assassination by the lefthanded Ehud, when he talked privily with the King in his Summer Parlour. Here we have it, in the third chapter: *and the haft also went in after the blade; and the fat closed upon the blade, so that he could not draw the dagger out of his belly; and the dirt came out.* Surely this is a very foul murder, but what is the Special Branch doing all this time? Ehud has made off, locking the door behind him, and up they come in plain clothes to see what is afoot. *And when they saw that, behold, the doors of the parlour were locked, they said, surely he covereth his feet in his summer chamber.* Tut, tut; that was only their habitual reticence, as they would have said: May it please Your Worship, he was washing his hands or behaving in a certain manner; or, The Accused made a certain gesture; or, Proceeding upon my beat, I observed that King Eglon had been interfered with. For in the margin I find this gloss: *doeth his easement;* and the Vulgate says *forsitan purgat alvum in aestivo cubiculo.*

So, like King Edmund Ironside, he may have been killed in a jakes, where, being a King of Moab, he no doubt had an altar to Baal-Peor or Bel-phegor, to whom the Israelites also made sacrifices when they were in Shittim, as recorded in Numbers, in the twenty-fifth chapter; of which the Rabbi Solomon Jarchi wrote in comment *Eo quod distendebant coram illo foramen podicis et stercus offerebant.* But we will say more of such gods in another place and pass on now to other business. The Book of Nehemiah shall be our guide: *And I went out by night by the gate of the valley, even before the Dragon Well, and to the dung port, and viewed the walls of Jerusalem.* To this verse and those that follow Sir John shewed me the way, this from the second chapter, and the next from the third: *The valley gate repaired Hanu, and the inhabitants of Zanoah; they built it, and set up the doors thereof, the locks thereof, and the bars thereof, and a thousand cubits on the wall unto the dung gate.*

The Dung Gate of Jerusalem led to Gehenna.—But the dung gate repaired Malchiah the son of Rechab; and thereafter follows more talk of locks and bars. Now, what was this *Porta Stercoris,* asks Sir John, but that through which the rain water *and all other conveyances ran, as they do out of the City of London into the Thames?* And he observes also that the place called Gehenna was used for this same purpose, from which it came about that this valley, which the Jews defiled in penance for the abominations committed there, came to be regarded among them as *Hell,* a place of punishment and torment and (above all) of a most horrid stench, *where their worm dieth not, and the fire is not quenched.*

The Hebrews were the First Puritans.—Of the curious customs of this people in later days Fabyan tells us an example which is proper to our subject. For it happened that in the year A.D. 1259 a Jew of Tewkesbury fell into a *gonge,* that is to say, a privy, on a Saturday and would not (says the chronicler) be plucked out for reverence of his Sabbath Day. The Earl of Gloucester, being told of this, determined that the Jew should be kept in this place throughout Sunday, in order that he might do a like reverence to the Christian Sabbath; and this was done to such effect that on the Monday the Jew was discovered dead. But whether the moral of this story belongs to the Pentateuch or to the age of which it is recorded I am unable to say. These customs are of great antiquity, shewing the Hebrews to have been the first Puritans in their nice observance of law, and particularly of all laws relating to the exposure of the body, the sexual and other natural functions. Indeed, I find in Heinrich Bullinger's *Sermonum Decades* (Dec. III, Serm. V) this most interesting account of the apparel worn by their priests. First (he says) their privities are hidden with linen breeches coming down to their knees and hams, to the end that, if they should chance to fall, while they were busy with their sacrifices, or in bearing burdens to and fro, the parts should not appear which shame bids us to cover. (Which shews an admirable foresight.)

To a people so essentially modest the most shameful diseases appeared to be the worst, and it was appropriate to the fullest satisfaction of their rancour that their enemies were afflicted by the God of Israel *with emerods in their secret parts,* that is to say, with piles; as you will find in the fifth chapter of the first Book of Samuel, where the chronicler cannot refrain from savouring this disgrace done to the Philistines by continual repetition. But how the *five golden emerods* were fashioned I cannot imagine, or what purpose they served.

Moab was their Wash-pot.—These ancient Hebrews called Moab their wash-pot, or such (at least) was the term employed by the Psalmist, of whom Dr. Rendel Harris observes that there is here no mention of soap, and certainly not of soft soap, but an anticipation of *Deutschland über alles.* Certainly the Jews did not go as far as Moab to wash themselves, but looked to nearer supplies with diligence. For Hezekiah (2 Kings xx, 20) *made the pool and the conduit, and brought water into the city,* which is also mentioned in the second Book of Chronicles, xxxii, 30. And many tunnels of the ancient Israelites are to be found, one leading through rock to a place above the brook Kidron, this tunnel being made (it is believed) for fetching water from a spring. Another tunnel brought water to the Upper Pool of Siloam, within the walls of Jerusalem. Also, in later times, an aqueduct was made, over forty miles in length, to bring water to Jerusalem from distant reservoirs; and this is believed to have been done in the time of Herod the Great, the aqueduct being still used to this day. There was also another, and older, aqueduct of great length which is now used no longer.

Of Neolithic Privies in the Orkneys.—Of the habits of these people, enjoined by their religion, we shall speak later, as also of the Muslims from the time of their prophet and the Hindus and other peoples among whom the traditions of religion have concerned themselves with the practice of hygiene. And here I must lament my ignorance of the customs and provision made among the ancient Chinese, of whom I can discover little save this, that persons of rank among them have at all times allowed great importance to washing and bathing their bodies and to the immaculate cleanliness of their attire. But of their manner of employing sewage much is known, and of this I shall have more to say in another place. Also of the Neolithic inhabitants of our own island we know little; but in one of their villages, dug up at Skara Brae in the Orkneys, there were observed small oblong enclosures, let into the thickness of their stone walls, from which primitive drains led to the beach; so that these enclosures are supposed to have been Neolithic privies. Then at Meschers in the Gironde there are prehistoric caves with privies of great antiquity, and in Cornwall, near to Gunnard's Head, an ancient Celtic village with a drainage system. But of the ancient Norsemen I can find nothing that relates to their natural functions, but only that they were a cleanly people in the matter of bathing, which they did in a common bath-hut by means of steam, which they generated by pouring water upon stones heated over a great fire.

A fair Warning to the Reader.—So much, then, for the baths, aqueducts, drains, privies and hygienic customs of man in the earliest ages where such things are to be discovered. If the reader has found it wearisome, I promise him better fare among the historians than we have had among the archaeologists. But if, like that Philostilpnos, Lover of Cleanliness, for whom Sir John Harington wrote his *Metamorphosis of Ajax,* the present reader is truly devoted to the goddess Hygieia, then he will bear my industry in this matter with as much patience as (I hope) he will have of tolerance for some foulness yet to be plumbed. I say this because, when we have disposed of Greece and Rome, we have the Middle Ages, as they are called, still ahead of us; and if we are to be good plumbers, there are some grim jakes to be explored, yielding (as Sir John would have it) a whorson saucy stink. But whether the reader has a stomach for this or no, for my own part I am under contract to go right to the bottom of this matter, and have taken to myself for consolation the excellent precept of Philostilpnos in his letter to Misacmos, Hater of Filthiness: *Pens may blot, but they cannot blush.*

Of the Greeks and Romans

The Greeks built noble Temples for their Gods, but housed themselves meanly.—The cities of the Greeks were, for the most part, ill-planned, for all the beauty of their best achievements, for they built the noblest temples for their gods and housed themselves meanly. Something must have come down to them from the civilisation of Mycenae (a Cretan colony), but they never equalled Crete, nor yet Egypt, in their understanding of health and of what things appertained to their goddess Hygieia. Nevertheless they had, in each city, hot shower baths and cold, with bathrooms in their houses (and who does not remember Diogenes in his cynic tub?), though, for the most part, they held the use of hot water to be effeminate. And closets they had in certain houses, of a simple contrivance, draining into a sewer beneath the street, which it would seem was kept wholesome by waste water, and in certain streets the sewer was provided with a shaft for ventilation. Of these privies some were found at Priene, greatly resembling our modern water-closets. Also they were careful in the matter of water, and laid great aqueducts, some as much as sixty feet below the earth, to bring water from the mountains or other clean sources.

Moreover, the philosophers of Greece did not disdain to discuss the right planning of a city, and on this head both

Plato and Aristotle, heathens and blackguards though they were, discoursed long and learnedly. And one of these learned men, named Hippodamus, not only planned how things should be, but saw his planning accomplished; for Aristotle tells us that he planned the Piraeus, which may not be doubted. And in their colonies abroad the Greeks remembered what Plato and Aristotle had told them too late for their use in Hellas, building their colonial cities with great care and thought, not only for beauty and for defence, but for the health of the public.

The Heroes of Homer understood Plumbing.—In his book *Tiryns,* where Dr. Schliemann tells of his excavations in that ancient Homeric city, he speaks of the bathroom which he found in the palace of prehistoric kings as certainly one of the most interesting discoveries; and this place he describes in great detail, together with the square drain-pipes of terra-cotta, like those discovered in the famous aqueduct of Eupalinos at Samos. From this we know the great antiquity of such things among the Greeks, and that the heroes of Homer did indeed use baths, in which we may hope that they were, for the most part, more fortunate than Agamemnon. But I will say no more of the Greeks, for to speak truth I am in all haste to be in Rome, where I am confident of good hunting.

On the furthest frontier of Roman Britain, where Hadrian built his wall to hold off the marauding Picts, excavations at Housesteads have revealed that even in this distant outpost of empire latrines were built, flushed by surface water. The extraordinary progress of the Romans in matters of hygiene and sanitation was not unknown to succeeding ages, and the decline in such matters since the days of ancient Rome was by many profoundly regretted. Montaigne speaks of it with awe, and a certain Dr. Clarke, in a work published in the year 1810, to which we shall return later, cites the lament of Bacon at this decline, and himself observes that, among the ancients, baths were public edifices, under the immediate inspection of the government. They were considered, he says, as institutions which owed their origin to absolute necessity, as well as to decency and cleanliness.

Roman Baths the Envy and Admiration of later Generations—A convivial Jakes.—In contrast to the general absence of baths in England at the time when he wrote, Dr. Clarke observes with wonder and admiration that Rome had near a thousand such buildings, though he speaks not of their drains and privies. Throughout the empire of Rome such marvels were to be seen, so that in the city of Pompeii there were discovered well-built sewers, though these would appear to have been intended for surface water, since cesspools were provided for household sewage. The private houses in this city were well supplied with water, which was conveyed by pipes of sheet lead, folded together and the flow controlled by stopcocks. Public latrines, also, were common in the cities of the Romans, of which an example is to be seen at Timgad, in Northern Africa, where five and twenty stone seats, each separated from the next by a carved dolphin, are grouped around three sides of a large room, in the middle of which a fountain once played; thus shewing that in those days natural necessities of this kind were considered to make a social occasion, like eating and drinking, to be performed in decorous surroundings. Indeed, their most learned scholars did not disdain to occupy themselves with privy matters, as you will find in Pliny's *Natural History,* where he discusses such things as enemas, saying of seawater (as Philemon Holland renders it) that clysterised hot it allayeth the wrings and grindings of the belly.

The Author moralises.—That the Romans were not entirely free from prejudice in this matter may be observed, however, in the story of those Roman soldiers in the reign of Tarquin I, who, thinking themselves disgraced by being ordered to make common sewers, committed suicide in 606 B.C. Also it is notable that the sewers of the Romans were kept clean by the labour of *convicts,* and those who for this purpose employed them as contractors were held in contempt, like the Untouchables of India and for a reason which bears comparison. For man, when he is most particular to be clean, will despise those by whose labours cleanliness is maintained, even as those who most enjoy wealth are the most contemptuous of those who create it. And if, for that matter, you would know how little the nature of man has changed, I commend the writings of Seneca. For he, having taken lodgings over a bathing establishment, complains of the distractions suffered in his studies; and among these distractions he mentions the noise of those who love to hear their own voices in the bathroom, and the amateurs of swimming, who plunge with a furious noise of splashing.

Seneca says that Scipio stank of Heroism.—Seneca took no pride in the baths of his time and despised their luxury. For he says of their heat that a slave condemned for crime should be bathed alive, and he upbraids the luxury with which they were devised. But he commends the bathroom of Scipio, which was small and dark, saying that the Romans of old bathed but once a week, and upon other days washed only their arms and their legs. But if one should say that such persons must have stunk, he observes that they stank of the camp, of the farm and of heroism. From this we may conjecture as much of the habits of his time as we may learn of the character of Seneca.

Two Gods for the Privy.—But to return, as the French say, to our sheep, or rather to our sewers; in spite of the dishonour attached to those who cleaned them or contracted for that purpose, the office of Curator of the City

Sewers was considered honourable, and numbered among those who held it the younger Pliny. For Master Walter Pater says of the Romans that *salus,* or salvation, came, for them, to mean bodily sanity, that is to say, health. And, like the Greeks, when they planted their colonies abroad, they planned their cities with great care, leaving no matter to chance, but considered all things in advance of building to make their cities secure and healthy, for which purpose very specific deities were invoked. Such deities were *Stercutius* and *Cloacina,* of whose functions you will find considerable discussion in Juan de Torquemada's *Monarchia Indiana.* According to this learned Franciscan, the Romans borrowed their goddess Cloacina from the Egyptians, of whom he asserts that they used to *adore* (as St. Clement wrote to St. James the Less) stinking and filthy privies and latrines; and, what is even more vile and abominable (says he) and an occasion for our tears and not to be tolerated or so much as mentioned by name, they adored the noise and wind of the stomach when it expels from itself any cold or flatulence.

Discussed by the Early Fathers and Others.—That such adoration was common among the ancients we have already shewn and can demonstrate from many examples; for of the Moabites and their God Bel-phegor, Dulaure wrote in *Des Divinités Génératrices* that *l'adorateur présentait devant l'autel son postérior nu, soulageait ses entrailles et faisait à l'idole une offrande de sa puante déjection.* Such, indeed, were the gods for whom the Israelites so often jilted Jehovah, and to whom reference is made by Hosea and the Psalmist, and in the Book of Deuteronomy, where it is written: *And ye have seen their abominations and their idols.* And it was perhaps for this reason that the Hebrews were so careful to avoid any semblance of such customs in their worship of the God of Israel; for (as Picart says in his work on *Coutûmes et*

Cérémonies, concerning the manner of prayer used by a child of Israel) *Il doit éviter autant qu'il se peut de bâiller, de cracher, de se moucher, de laisser aller des vents.* He must avoid an inadvertent *pujah* to Baal.

I will leave it to others to discuss whether the Romans inherited their privy gods from Egypt or Moab, and whether Cloacina was in actual fact none other than Venus (for they were ever neighbours, and a statue of Venus, called by some the *Venus Cloacina,* was found in the Cloaca Maxima), but St. Clement and St. Augustine have given us some account of these gods, and Fra. Torquemada, writing in the year 1615, mentioned also Lactantius, Eusebius, Lucian, Cicero and Pliny among his authorities. However, I will now return to Sir John Harington, who has much to say on this matter in his *Metamorphosis of Ajax.*

The Genealogy of Ajax, from Stercutius.—As to Cloacina, she was the goddess of the *Cloacae,* or sewers; but Stercutius (if Sir John is to be credited) must have been the oldest of all the gods, for upon the authority of the blessed St. Augustine, *De Civitate Dei,* this great Elizabethan claims that Stercutius was none other than Saturn himself; as well he might be, seeing that he presided over the manuring of the fields and therefore (as I shall later demonstrate beyond dispute) he was the true father of life. And if you will pardon me I will give here the genealogy of Ajax as recorded by Sir John upon the authority of Augustine and Ovid, seeing that Ajax was metamorphosed into privy, which the good knight has explained better than I can:

> Saturn-Stercutius begat Jupiter,
> Jupiter begat Aeacus,
> Aeacus begat Telamon,
> Telamon begat Ajax.

Which being so, this metamorphosis was no such marvel; and I find on consulting the Bishop of Hippo that Stercutius was the son of Sterces, which will be discovered in the fifteenth chapter of Lib. xxviii, *De Civitate Dei,* with a plain statement that Saturn was either Sterces or Stercutius. But the learned Joannes Ludovicus Vives in his commentary says that, according to Pliny, Stercutius was the son of Saturn, which is good enough.

A facetious Digression, to enrage the Critics.—Now as to these planned colonies of the Romans, this city of Timgad, of which we have spoken, was such a one, built for old soldiers, whom we may well imagine seated in that convivial latrine and entertaining one another with stories of old campaigns. But to consider a pleasanter matter, the water drunk in Rome by these builders of empire was conveyed by aqueducts (such as the Porta Maggiore) from the Alban and Sabine mountains (and such an aqueduct may be seen at Pont du Gard across the Gardon at Nîmes, also). For all purposes of public health these Romans divided their city into districts, each under an *aedile,* and much that pertained to health, including the filtering of this water supply, was understood by them; for they were not so ignorant as that wretched hack who, describing the scene witnessed at the dedication of Westminster Cathedral, wrote that the Cardinal was robed in his *cloaca maxima.*

Like the Greeks, the ancient Romans, before the time of Pliny, had no knowledge of soap, but by means of great heat in their vapour baths and the use of the *strigil* or skin-scraper they cleansed their bodies. And it is believed by some that such implements were in use among Neolithic man, whose *flintscrapers,* as they are called, may have been employed for such a purpose.

But it is possible (and, indeed, common in some quarters) to value too highly the progress of Rome in these matters: for it has been observed that, though the Roman sewers were built to endure for ever, and much attention paid to their condition, they disgorged their filth into the Tiber, making a cesspool of it.

Such, indeed, was the practice in many English towns until recent years, for they ran their sewers into the greater rivers and still make such a use of the sea; but we cannot commend such habits, even when the supply of household water is fetched from a distance, as was the case in Rome. Indeed, the objections to such practices are not only those of a sanitary origin, but Baron von Liebig wrote of the Romans that the sewers of the immense metropolis of the Ancient World *engulfed in the course of centuries the prosperity of the Roman peasants,* and that when the fields of the latter (he said) would no longer yield the means of feeding her population, *these same sewers devoured the wealth of Sicily, Sardinia, and the fertile lands on the coast of Africa.* To this alarming subject we shall return at the end of this book, but content ourselves for the moment to minute a proviso in our praise of sanitary systems—viz. that for more than one reason they should not use rivers as cesspools.

Some nasty Habits among the Romans.—In the case of the Romans, moreover, since their sewers were made to receive both sewage and rain water, there were openings in the street to receive the flood from the gutters, but also (we may be sure) to return a stench in good measure. And in their houses they placed the *latrina* close to the kitchen, using the same *cloaca* for the kitchen sink and the next-door necessities. But in Rome, because of the steep descent from their hills to the river, they were able to lay their drains at such an incline, flooding them with such great quantities of water, that some of the evils arising from their system must have been overcome by the violence of passage in the *cloacae*.

The Decline of Rome was politico-hygienic.—The neglect of sanitation in the declining days of Rome, also of
Greece, without doubt led to the general increase of
malaria among these people and to the depopulation of
cities, the debilitation of those that remained alive. For
where men are herded together in great towns and cities,
and their life in these conditions made possible only by
attention to public hygiene and sanitation, the neglect of
that which alone has made such a civilisation possible
must speedily bring about its ruin. But the corruption of
Roman society made it subservient to an emperor; and
when the court itself was corrupted by its own power of
oppression, public works declined, from which it followed
that malaria was the scourge that did as much as all the
Huns, Goths and Vandals to destroy the achievements of
the past, while the Tiber devoured their agricultural
wealth. But of these achievements Gibbon speaks in his
Decline and Fall of the Roman Empire with a justifiable
use of the superlative, giving the aqueducts their due,
though he ignores the sewers and condemns the baths.
For of these aqueducts, which he ranks among the noblest
monuments of Roman genius and power, he observes that
the curious traveller, who, without the light of history,
should examine those of Spoleto, of Metz or of Segovia,
would very naturally conclude that those provincial towns
had formerly been the residence of some potent monarch.
In very truth they had been the abode of a goddess, whose
name is Hygieia, not to mention other deities to whom we
have made reference.

The public Urinals of Vespasian.—Among the curious
things mentioned by Sir John Harington is the interest
shewn by great emperors in the details of public sanitation. For Vespasian, he says, who had been himself an
aedile, and not too careful in the performance of his
duties, on becoming emperor thought it not beneath his

dignity to concern himself with the lack of public urinals
in the city, of which he caused a number to be constructed,
in which the precious liquid was stored in cisterns so that
it might afterwards be sold to the dyers, for the emperor's
own profit. Other stories also are told by Sir John of this
Vespasian, and one concerning Claudius, less proper to
the austerities of this more sober volume.

Fascinated by the discovery of this curious enterprise of
a Roman emperor, I recalled the word *vespasienne,* which
signifies, in the French language of today, a street urinal.
And a search in Littré's *Dictionnaire de la Langue Fran-
çaise* revealed this further information: *Vespasienne, s.f.
1°) Grands vases en terre cuite, hauts comme une
amphore, semblables à un tonneau coupé, que Vespasien
établit comme urinoirs à Rome, et pour lesquels il perçut
une taxe. 2° Par imitations, urinoirs publics établis dans
Paris, sous forme de petites guérites ou de colonnes.*

Curious Roman Customs.—Ah, Monsieur Littré, you
have betrayed me. What I had hoped to learn above all
things was the age of this word, trusting to find it of great
antiquity in your language. For I had imagined it to be a
word used by the Roman legionaries, who left behind
them the *argot* of the army and a good crop of Roman
noses in the rising generation, as evidence of their peaceful
penetration. Let us at least, then, suppose this to have
been the case; for it is a pleasant thought to assume that
those old veterans named these places after their emperor,
of the Saturnine or *Stercutian* countenance, and told the
tale all over Gaul of how the people were taxed to build
urinals which the emperor then turned to his further
profit by selling the proceeds. And from that, I have no
doubt, they would pass to other matters, astonishing the
lasses with strange tales of Roman life. Were not the
laundrymen known by the whiteness of their feet,
through dabbling so much in the urine they used to

bleach the clothes? And does not Pliny say in his *Naturalis Historia* (Book xxviii, ch. 18) that Roman fullers were, for this reason, untroubled by gout?

But old Pliny has failed me no less than M. Littré; for I have read where he says much concerning sponges and their uses, in Book ix, ch. 69, and in Book xxxi, ch. 47, and I cannot find what I am seeking, which is the authority Montaigne had for certain observations which he made. As Florio reads him, he says that the Romans were wont to wipe their tails (this vain superstition of words must be left unto women) with a sponge; and that (he says) is the reason why *spongia* in Latin is counted an obscene word. These sponges were tied for the purpose to the end of a stick, and Montaigne tells of one who, being condemned to be devoured by wild beasts, asked leave to visit a privy before attending this banquet (as well he might) and there found a more agreeable death by choking himself. The same authority tells us that some, the rich as I suppose, used perfumed wool for the same purpose; and though he says nothing of Vespasian's buildings he tells of tubs for the use of wayfarers in every street, upon which matter he quotes Lucretius very learnedly.

Well, as to this word *vespasienne,* though I have searched in vain for a clue in the *Glossarium Mediae et Infimae Latinitatis* of the Sieur Du Cange, I will never believe that it was dug up by some modern antiquarian and popularised among the vulgar, who know nothing of Vespasian and care less. So when next you see the patent name *vespa* upon a closet you may meditate profitably upon its origin. But to return to our Roman emperors, there is a story which Sir John tells of the Emperor Trajan which shews us how justly this man was called the pattern of all princely qualities and earned the prayers even of the Christians whom he persecuted. For the younger Pliny having written to his emperor that the city of the Ames-

trians was spoilt and fouled by a brook that had become
an open sewer, Trajan replied to him most affectionately
addressing his servant as *carissime,* and said *Permittit con-*
fornicari cloacam, adding that he could safely trust all matters of expense to Pliny's discretion. And for the rest of
the story, I leave Sir John to do the translation.

Sir John Harington searches the Dictionary.—(*Haring-*
ton loquitur) Look it, sirra, there in the Dictionary. *Con,*
con. Tush, what, dost thou look in the French? Thou wilt
make a sweet piece of looking, to look for *con fornicar* in
the French; look in the Latin for *fornicor. F. fa, fe, fi, fo*
foramē, forfex, forica, forma, fornicator (now I think I am
near it), *fornix, fornicor, aris, are.* There, what is it? A
vault, to vault or arch anything with a compass. Well said,
carry away the book again, now I have it; then thus it is.
He alloweth the vaulting or arching over the jakes.

And digresses very sweetly in praise of Trajan.—Now
it is here that Sir John does such honour to Trajan that I
(who would have equal honour done to Sir John for as
good a reason) must needs give you more of his wisdom,
though it little concerns our subject (as little as it did his
own), lest you should think that only a lewd fellow without a soul would write of privies. For what does he say
of Trajan in his panegyric? Having extolled his qualities
(and here was a prince paragon indeed, that would attend
to such things), he asked what were his sins, and answers
his accusers in these words: *For that same sweet sin of*
lechery, I would say as the friar said, a young man and a
young woman in a green arbour in a May morning; if God
do not forgive it, I would. Will you tell me now that a
poet may not write of *cloacae* as well as an emperor can
attend to their construction or a pontiff make use of them?
Besides (says he of Trajan), *no doubt his sin was the less*
in that he ever loved his wife most dearly, and used her
most respectively; for I have ever maintained this paradox,

it is better to love two too many than one too few. Here is more than a poet, for herein speaks a philosopher and a very bold moralist. But lastly, see what he says concerning the soul of the great Trajan, as to whether it was delivered from Hell by the prayers of St. Gregory: *Yet as in love* (says he) *I had rather love too many than too few, so in charity I had rather believe too much than too little.* Bravely spoken; for this is more than philosophy and morals, ranging into high metaphysics and mysticism. But take the words as they are intended, in praise of Trajan, and we will leave the alchemist of Ajax till we shall come to him, except that he must be our guide a little further, on account of his great learning.

Tarquin abused for his building of a Sewer.—Here, then, are three more Roman rulers from among those kings who first reigned upon the seven hills, in whom the diligence of Sir John discovered a proper interest in our subject. The first was Titus Tacius, who ruled with Romulus, and according to Lactantius erected a statue of the goddess Cloacina in a great privy which he had built, as a fitting shrine for such a deity. And the second was Tarquinius Priscus, whom we have mentioned before, and those who would know more may find it in Livy. The third was the second Tarquin, whose rape of Lucrece so obnebulated the harsh judgement of history that this is remembered alone, while his building of sewers is forgotten; for he caused to be made in his days a stately temple *cloacamque maximum receptaculum omnium purgamentorum urbis;* that is to say, in the words of Sir John, and a mighty great vault to receive all the filth of the city, which won praise even from the republican historian of his crimes. But such is the nature of man, who will never give his due to the Devil and will for ever hang the dog with a bad name, that even in his time Tarquin could get no credit for this undertaking; and Brutus, not content with abusing the king for his faults (of which the worst was surely in his being a king, and therefore *ipso facto,* leaving little more to be said), must needs inveigh against him for tiring out the people *in exhauriendis cloacis.* For this Sir John very soundly chastises the *manes* of the first Brutus, that he should rail against a prince for making so sumptuous a jakes; and he shews at great length how he would plead the case of Tarquin before the Court of Star Chamber, if the prince would give him a fee, to convict Brutus under the Statute of Unlawful Assemblies. But this Brutus was a wise man who is known to have feigned stupidity for the same reason (as I believe) that has led me to my present studies.

Concerning the Ordure of Chivalry and Other Matters

The Odour of Sanctity was not always the Smell of Soap.
—In its first embraces with Roman civilisation, the Christian Church would appear to have done little to preserve, and a great deal to undermine, the standards of cleanliness among the people. Thus we read of the Blessed St. Jerome rebuking the dames who followed him *for too much washing.* And it may be doubted if cleanliness had any part in Christianity until the return of Paganism, at the end of what we term the Middle Ages, together with the return of Judaism (which was announced as the Reformation), corrected the laxity of Christendom with a strong mixture from the Ancients of Rome, Greece and Palestine. Was not St. Agnes canonised primarily for her refusal to bathe? And did not St. Francis of Assisi consider dirt among the proper insignia of Holy Poverty? And was it not accounted a most creditable *act of renunciation* in Adalbert, Archbishop of Bremen in the eleventh century, that he abstained from bathing, or in Archbishop Bruno of Cologne, that he did likewise? Let us write it to the credit of Gregory the Great that he rebuked those preachers of his time who sought to forbid bathing on Sundays; but that such a rebuke should have been necessary is still of some interest.

But Salerno taught that bad Drains bred Infection.—
There was, none the less, some plain sense on such questions that survived throughout these times, and notably I
must mention the school of medicine at Salerno, whence
issued that famous *Regimen Sanitatis Salernitanum,* a
treatise supposed to have been written for the use of Robert, Duke of Normandy, whom the author or authors call
Anglorum Rex. This famous duke, the son of England's
Conqueror, having visited Salerno in the year 1096, and
wintering there on his way to the Crusades, was presented
with the *Regimen,* which became a handbook for centuries
to come, until our own Sir John Harington did it into
English verse, calling it *The Englishman's Doctor, or The
School of Salerne.* We shall consider later, in discoursing
of other matters, some excellent precepts to be found in
this work concerning the use of the closet; but one I will
set down here as Sir John construes it, to shew that there
was a little light in these dark days:

> *A builder that will follow wise direction*
> *Must first foresee, before his house he makes,*
> *That the air be clear and free from all infection*
> *And not annoyed with stench of any Jakes.*

But in the matter of baths I find this authority very equiv-
ocal, for:

> *Wine, Women, Baths, by art or Nature warm,*
> *Used or abused do men much good or harm.*

Or so Sir John has it, and this I find somewhat cautious.
Concerning the Physicians of Myddvai.—Some knowledge of hygiene would appear to have been preserved
among the Welsh, for Giraldus Cambrensis observes of
these people, in the twelfth century, that they paid great
attention to cleaning their teeth, rubbing them with the
leaves or the bark of the hazel; so that (he says) their teeth

were of a dazzling whiteness. For medicine, which the Welsh call *meddyginiaeth,* was said to have been practised among them a thousand years before Christ. And about the middle of the thirteenth century A.D. there was a celebrated physician of Myddvai in Caermarthenshire, whose name was Rhiwallon. This physician and his sons practised medicine and wrote many recipes for specific ailments, also for general health. Among these last I find instructions on the manner of rising in the morning; for the physicians of Myddvai ordain a cold bath at this time in the summer months and then (they say) *array yourself in fair garments, for a man's mind delights in fair things, and his heart is rendered lighter. Then clean the teeth with the dry bark of the hazel.* And many other things these physicians say, concerning the general conduct of one who would be healthy, in eating and drinking, in sleeping and waking, so that I am astonished at their wisdom, for they ordain all the things most conducive to health for reasons which appear to be absurd.

It is also upon record (and the digression will surely pass among so many) that inoculation for the smallpox was practised in Wales from the most ancient times, long before the introduction of that practice by Lady Wortley Montagu, who learned it from the Turks. This practice of inoculation the Welsh called *buying the smallpox,* for it was their custom to purchase the matter from one who had the disease.

In the Middle Ages habits of cleanliness were held in such low esteem among most of the peoples of Europe that to wash in hot water, and more particularly to immerse the body in it, was considered a manner of sinfully indulging the flesh. But that they were not utterly ignorant of certain causes of disease among insanitary conditions we may surmise from the fact that the Jews were accused of spreading the Black Death *by poisoning the drinking*

water. For, like the ancients, they believed water to be a
great source of infection, and that plagues were spread by

Pois'ning the Standing lakes and pools impure

as Virgil has it, or Dryden if you will.

Of Secret Passages and their Uses.—Moreover, in certain
of their castles, as that of Conway, it is clear that the men
of the Middle Ages applied some knowledge of the principles of sanitation. And those *secret passages* which commonly lead to a stream were without doubt the sewers of
these castles and monasteries. Such a secret passage was
used by the person who, in the year 1836, wrote to the Di-
rectors of the Bank of England, offering to meet them at
their convenience in their Bullion Room. And this he did,
coming up from the middle of the floor, which was over
an old sewer from Dowgate. Also in Exeter today there
are so many of these sewers or, as they are called, underground passages, that the land upon which roads and
houses stand is in danger of subsidence; and in Croydon
also, where I was as a boy, such a passage was discovered
by a road beginning to fall in; and in many other towns
and cities these things are known.

In the *Ancient Rites and Monuments of the Monastical
and Cathedral Church of Durham,* compiled in A.D. 1662
by a Mr. Davies of Kidwelly, there is an account of a very
worthy establishment in a monastery. Within the Cloister-
garth (writes Mr. Davies) over the Frater-house door, was
a fair Laver, or conduit, for the Monks to wash their hands
and faces, being round, covered with lead, and all of Marble, saving the outermost walls, within which they might
walk about the Laver. It had many spouts of Brass, with
twenty-four Brass Cocks round about it, having in it
seven fair windows of stone work, and over it a Dove-cote,
covered with lead, finely wrought; as appears (he said) to
this day.

Adjoining to the East-side of the Conduit-door hung a Bell to call the Monks at eleven of the clock, to come and wash before dinner, having their Closets or Ambries on either side of the Frater-house door on the outside within the Cloister, kept always with clean Towels to dry their hands.

Concerning monastic Privies, of which too little is known.—There was also a large and decent place, adjoining to the West-side of the said Dorter, towards the water, for the Monks and the Novices to resort to, called the Privies, two great Pillars of Stone bearing up the whole floor thereof. Every Seat and Partition was of Wainscott, close on either side, so that they could not see one another when they were in that place. There were as many seats on either side as there were little Windows in the Wall to give light to the said Seats; which afterwards were walled up to make the House more close. At the West-end of it there were three fair glass Windows, which Windows gave light to the whole House.

Such is the elegance described by Mr. J. Davies, and we know at least that these monks had the means to wash themselves, though little is to be learnt of the state of their privies, which may have pleased the nose less than the eye. Of such provision for ablutions we have frequent evidence, as in the ancient plans of the London Charterhouse, described by Mr. W. H. St. John Hope in *The London Charterhouse and its Water Supply* (*Archaeologia,* 58, Part I). But of their privies, which the monks called *rere-dorter* or *necessaria,* we know less. Of these I learn from Mr. H. A. J. Lamb, in an article to be found in the *Architects' Journal* for March 4th, 1937, that they were often attached to the dorter or dormitories, from which fact this name of *rere-dorter* is derived. But on account, we may suppose, of their unsavoury nature, they were commonly approached by a bridge.

The Answer to some debated Questions is found at St. Albans.—This Mr. Lamb tells us that at Furness the seats of the necessarium were placed back to back in a row; but more commonly they were arranged as described in the case of Durham. Below, he says, there would be a walled-in drain, which might be artificially fashioned or made by the diversion of some stream. And of excavations at St. Albans in the year 1924 he says that these revealed a deep pit used by the Benedictines when casting aside the things of this world; in which pit were found fragments of coarse cloth, believed to be from old gowns that were torn up in the days before toilet paper was known; also seeds of the buckthorn, known as a powerful aperient. Of the provisions for ablutions among these Benedictines Mr. Lamb makes no mention, but we may suppose them to have been meagre, since the Blessed St. Benedict himself had said: *To those who are well, and especially to the young, baths shall seldom be permitted.* Among certain orders, however, a minimum of cleanliness was prescribed in an injunction that the feet should be washed once in a week; and in general the monks would appear to have cared more than the laity for cleanliness and decency in these times, though that is to say very little.

The sanitary system at Fountains Abbey I have heard commended by some, though I have not seen it and can find no written record of it; also at Tintern, where the River Severn, being tidal at this point, was ingeniously employed to effect a complete flushing of the monastic dykes that must surely have swept them from their seats when the tide was at its highest. I have also heard of ingenious *garderobes* at St. Nicholas Priory, Exeter, and at Cleeve Abbey in Somerset, of the drains at Beaulieu and Netley and at the Augustinian Priory of Bristol.

Of the Tower of London and its ill-constructed Garderobes.—The castles of the Barons nowhere compete with such a system, nor do those of the Kings, as you may have observed in the closets of the Tower of London. These closets, called *garderobes* (for already they must make pretence that this was a place to hang up your clothes, or, as we should say, a cloak-room), are exceedingly crude in design, one of them being placed so near to the banqueting-hall that some guests must have sat within a few feet of a privy. The *garderobes* in the Tower are built in the thickness of the wall, having their outlets so contrived that their filth ran down the outside wall into the moat. Such careless closets are to be found among the old border castles of Northumberland and the Scottish Lowlands; though I learn that Langley Castle, in Northumberland, shews some small improvement in design; and the same is said of Southwell Palace in Nottinghamshire, where later mediaeval builders planned more discreetly, as may be seen with detailed plans in *Domestic Architecture of the Middle Ages,* by Mr. Turner and Mr. Parker. At Langley the principal tower was devoted entirely to privies, four upon each floor, and every privy had its own flue, emptying into a stream. Ludlow Castle in like manner preserved its walls from contamination by the use of shafts, which led to the moat.

Like those kings and emperors of Rome, who were not too proud to concern themselves with such things, the great Bruce of Scotland (who learnt perseverance from a spider, as every schoolmarm knows) seems to have combined regularity with modesty and a regard for the hygienic code of Deuteronomy. For we learn this much from John Barbour, in the fifth Book of *The Bruce:*

> *That the King had in custum ay*
> *For to riss airly euirilk day,*
> *And pas weill fer fra his menze*
> *Quhen he vold pas to the preue.*

Which scarce needs translation into English. Indeed, it was upon one of these morning excursions that the Bruce was near killed by treachery, for three men whom an English knight had bribed (I am sure the chronicler will not lie) lay in wait for him, knowing this custom. But the King seems to have carried *si vis pacem* to its logical conclusions, and, being armed, he disposed of all three before doing what he set out to do; from which (if any moral is to be drawn) I suppose it would be that there are dangers attending even regular habits and that one should always be prepared for emergencies; to which it might be possible to add some new variant of

Uneasy lies the head that wears a crown.

A Royal Writ to make a Jakes.—Where Bruce met the spider may now be conjectured with recollections of Saul at Engedi; but I must pass on. For next you will find it upon record that our English king, Henry III, made the construction of a privy the occasion of a Royal Writ to the Sheriff of Surrey; and Mr. Lamb, in his article already mentioned, says that at the Tower of London the Constable was ordered to *cause the drain of our private chamber to be made in the fashion of a hollow column.* Also he tells us that this same king ordered the Sheriff of Southampton to make, in Winchester Castle, a fireplace and a privy within a certain chamber.

Of a sumptuous Jakes made by a Shah for his Harem. —In general, however, sanitation was so alien to Gothic architecture that I remember an American visitor, after being shewn all the most magnificent buildings in our oldest university, asking of his guide *whether there was not a urinal in Oxford College;* a question which I consider as apt as it was (in another sense) barbarous. And in no Christian capital (unless it were in Constantinople) was there to be found, at any time in the Middle

Ages, a closet to equal those marble latrines which were made for the Harem of the Shah Jehren at Agra, in the fifteenth century. Of these there is a fair picture in a book by Mr. Bertram Hellyer, commemorating the two hundred years in which the firm of Dent and Hellyer has served our most intimate needs. To this book, which is entitled *Under Eight Reigns,* I am in debt for much of my information on mediaeval practices, and especially for this view of Indian latrines. These are so beautifully fashioned and made to be flushed (so Mr. Hellyer says) with water perfumed by otto of roses, so convivially arranged for the harem to enjoy its comforts communally, that I do not doubt they forgave the square shape of the seats and (the climate being what it is) the chill affront of marble. Adjoining these latrines was a sumptuous marble bath and a fountain, and I cannot believe that any Christian king at that time did as much for one wife as this Shah did for the whole troop, though the royal owner of the Amber Palace at Jaipur could boast of a very similar equipment, the art of building good baths and well-appointed privies being better understood and appreciated in India.

Miseries of Prisoners and the Poor.—However, I perceive that I begin to lead you upon a rambling discourse, like the idle thoughts of a man *covering his feet;* or whatever you choose to call it. Our next consideration must be: What became of all this mediaeval sewage? That is answered simply enough, for where it did not flow into a castle moat or pollute the streams and rivers, it massed in great wells and cesses. These had, perforce, to be emptied at times; and of the cesspit at Newgate Jail Mr. Lamb says that in the year 1281 it required the labour of thirteen men for five nights to clean it (which puts me in mind of those calculations in which I wasted so much of my youth, so that I reflect as to how long it might have required for 2 men to accomplish the task, or 7 maids with 7 brooms;

or I suppose it would be buckets). These men earned 7d. each night, which I hope was then considered a good wage. As for the dyke at the Fleet Prison, it became so choked that when Edward III ordered an enquiry into its conditions, in the year 1355, the ordure was found to be sufficiently deep to float a boat, though the ditch was 10 feet in width. It was of the odours from the Fleet ditch that the White Friars complained bitterly in the twelfth century; but rarely were complaints made in the interest of those who suffered most. For those who protested against beggars saw only *miserable people lying in the street, offending every clean person passing by the way with their filthy and nasty savours.* And so little was thought of prisoners that the sewage of Rochester Castle was allowed to flow through the dungeons to its outlet.

Next, as to the commonality, those who did not live in castles, monasteries or prisons had little choice but to use such public latrines as were provided or to use none, for this provision was very meagre. In London there was one such place in the ward of Cripplegate and one to the south of Fleet Street built over the Thames at Temple Bridge. One was at Queenshithe, mentioned by Harington in his *Metamorphosis,* and there was a large one at London Bridge. The author of that instructive work (of which more anon), *For Your Convenience,* would certainly have had little to write of had he lived at this time; and as a private closet was in those days something of a luxury, I shrewdly suspect the greater part of London's citizens made what shift they could without their benefit. Mr. Lamb tells of one woman who made herself a privy with an outflow by means of a wooden pipe to the rain-water gutter. But when this pipe became blocked her arrangements caused offence to her neighbours, who invoked against her the penalties of the law. Of the closets made upon boards over deep pits he says that the boards were often known to rot, from which there arose many accidents, in which persons were *literally drowned in their own filth*. Of such sad cases, including that of Richard the Raker, who met his end in the year 1326, you will find some record in an article by Ernest L. Sabine on *Latrines and Cesspools of Mediaeval London,* which will be discovered in the American journal of mediaeval studies known as *Speculum,* July 1934.

Horrid Death of Eight Princes and many Knights and Nobles—Chapel of Cloacina attributed in Error to Christian Devotion.—But the most celebrated instance of such a tragedy was the fate suffered by eight ruling princes and a large company of knights and nobles, all of whom died miserably in a vast cesspool beneath the Great Hall at Erfurt in the year 1183. For the Emperor Frederick I having summoned a Diet at this place, the weight of the guests broke down the floor, and fortunate indeed were those who escaped the horrid death that lay below. Such places invited the attention of inventive minds, which were not found lacking even in these early days. Mr. Sabine tells us of cosy privies built in chimneys, and of one, Thomas Brightfield, of the parish of St. Martin, who, about A.D. 1449 to 1450, constructed some kind of a water-closet, flushed by pipe water (though without a valve) a century and a half before the historic invention of Sir John Harington, which we shall consider in the next chapter. And there is also in this article by Mr. Sabine much useful information concerning the public latrines, such as that at London Bridge, with two doors, from one of which a debtor escaped while his creditor was waiting at the other, as recorded in the year 1306. Also he tells us of the contracts for cleaning the city privies, and how one, John Lovegold, petitioned the authorities for a monopoly of this work, which he was granted, and paid at the rate of two shillings and twopence per ton. But among the most

curious things I have read regarding early English privies
is the theory of Mr. Lamb that many places to which Romance has attached the names of *oratories* or *hiding-holes*
were intended and used for a homelier purpose; and as
examples he mentions the *chapel,* as it was believed to be,
at Aydon Castle, in Northumberland, and the *altar slab* at
Abington Pigotts, which had a hole in it to fit over a shaft.

We have next to consider further (for a little bathing
comes not amiss after so much time spent in these places)
what provision was made for washing the body in these
times. As to this, we may say that, apart from certain
castles, monasteries and large houses, there was little or
none, but to the privileged orders the bath was not unknown. The German Romances of Tristram and Parsifal
and that concerning Guy of Warwick mention baths, and
in the Romance of Merlin, which will be found in the British Museum, this manuscript of the thirteenth century
shews us in a very charming picture a lady bathing in a
round tub, assisted by her knight in full armour and
watched with suspicion by a donkey. Froissart also describes the ceremony of becoming a *Knight of the Bath,*
where each squire to be knighted *had his chamber and his
bath in which he bathed,* and an authority cited by Mr.
Bertram Hellyer says that in the numerous stories of
amorous intrigues, the two lovers usually begin their in-
terview by bathing together. There is, however, no reason
to believe that bathing was a frequent or regular habit
among the Christian peoples in these days, even among
those who enjoyed sufficient leisure and wealth to make
such habits possible; and as to the baths themselves, they
in no way compared with the sumptuous *thermae* of the
Romans, being mere wooden tubs; though I learn that
there existed at Cambridge certain Roman baths which
were actually in use as late as the eleventh century, and
Dan Chaucer speaks in his *Second Nun's Tale* of a bath

which must have been of metal, for a fire to be lit beneath
it. Chaucer tells us also of bath-water scented with herbs,
and the French *Romance of the Rose* commends cleanliness to young men.

But the contempt of the Moslems for such poor pro-
vision is shewn in the comments of an Arabic writer in the
fourteenth century, who speaks of the numerous baths in
Cairo, which he describes, and contrasts the cleanliness of
True Believers with the dirtiness of the *Franks,* as he calls
them, that is to say, the Western Christians. But of the
Eastern Christians in the Byzantine Empire and of the
Moors in Spain we shall have more to say presently.

*A Mediaeval Encouragement to Bathing which was nev-
ertheless spurned by Parsifal.*—It is also necessary to observe that in the Middle Ages the use of baths among
Christians was perhaps less for purposes of cleanliness
than for certain other purposes, which are detailed in the
chapter entitled *The Alchemy of Love* in the *Encyclopaedia of Sexual Knowledge,* edited by Dr. Norman Haire.
Thus, in Germany, where public baths were more common than in most parts of Europe, and pious foundations
even provided baths for the poor, it was customary for
persons to be attended always by others of the opposite sex
in their ablutions; and in the Romance of Parsifal, to
which we have already referred, the young knight is
offered the use of a bath by Gurnemanz of Graharz, with
maidens to tend him, whom (however) he dismisses from
his presence; which I suppose to have been unusual and
a proof of exceptional purity. Of communal baths at
Baden, the great spa of the later Middle Ages, Gian Fran-
cesco Poggio Bracciolini said that *there could be no better
baths for ladies desiring children.* Such practices, however, were not approved by the Church, as may be seen in
the prohibition of mixed bathing by St. Boniface in the
year 745. They nevertheless continued, until the end of the

fifteenth century, to bathe communally, the baths being eventually closed from terror of epidemic diseases.

Dugdale in his *Monasticon Anglicanum* shews that monks called baths *Seminaria Venenata,* hot-beds of vice. And Haire's *Encyclopaedia* further reminds us that perfumes were used because of their stimulating properties and *to hide the odour of the natural secretions, which assailed the nostrils disagreeably*. And indeed it has often been the case that scents have been used rather as an alternative to cleanliness than as an ornament to it, which may be observed as late in our history as the eighteenth century.

Among other curious things, Dr. Rendel Harris affirms (I know not from what source he quotes) that King John had in his employ a servant called *Aquarius,* whose duty it was to give the King a bath three times a year, at the principal festivals. But if, says Dr. Harris, the King was in need of further baths, these could be arranged upon payment of twopence to the *Aquarius*. Such was royal example.

The mention of *Aquarius* serves to remind us that water was distributed in the city of London at this time (and even many centuries later) by the agency of water-carriers, who would fill from some well or from the Thames two tubs or *tyne's,* which they carried upon a yoke, over their shoulders. Such men were of necessity very numerous and had their own guild. We read that Henry III for the profit of the city and good of the whole realm, *for poor to drink and the rich to dress their meat,* granted to the citizens and their successors liberty to convey water from the town of Tybourne *by pipes of lead* into their city. From which it may be observed that the rich had not many uses for water and the poor but one, for lack (one may suppose) of meat to dress or anything better to drink; and there is no mention of ablutions. But such water continued for long to be distributed by carriers, and a petition was presented as late as *circa* 1600 by the Company of Water-Tankard Bearers to the House of Commons, in which they say that they and their families number 4000 persons. Among the complaints of the Tankard Bearers at this time we learn that one was the growing practice of wealthy persons, having houses near the conduits of the city, to obtain by permission a *quill,* as it was called, into their houses; which may be regarded as the beginning of the household water supply, as it is known today.

Passing of a Sanitary Act.—We read of a law passed in the year 1388 imposing a penalty upon such as cast garbage, dung, entrails or any other ordure into the ditches, rivers, waters and other places within and about the cities, boroughs and towns of the realm. For this Act (of which a copy will be found in Mr. Coulton's work on *Social Life in Britain from the Conquest to the Reformation*) states plainly that the air in these towns and boroughs is greatly corrupt and infect, and many maladies and other intolerable diseases do daily happen. Therefore it was ordered that these places aforesaid should be cleansed of such filth, and it was the opinion of Mr. B. G. Bannington, in his account of *English Public Health Administration,* that such laws were maintained. But I observe that his examples belong to a later age than that with which I am concerned, and shall therefore turn to them in discussing the sixteenth century.

To consider, therefore, a time more relevant to our present consideration, we have a grim account of the town of Hythe at the beginning of the fifteenth century presented by a jury. Streets were choken with stable refuse, all manner of waste and filth making them nigh impassable; the smells being so bad and abominable that even the jury took cognizance of them. Two wells they described as choked with refuse, and the water, *by which* (they say) *the whole community is refreshed,* was corrupted by this filth.

Putrid and Unclean Food given to the Sick and to Lepers.—That something was known of the purification of water by boiling is shewn by Trevisa (*De Prop. Rer.*) where the boiling of water is commended in spring-time *because it is infect with frogs and other worms that then breed.* But how little account was taken of putrefaction may be known from the fact that an agreement was made in the year 1356 giving power to the Chancellor of the University of Oxford over all flesh and fish that should be found to be putrid, unclean, vicious or otherwise unfit. Such rotten food was to be held forfeit and given to the Hospital of St. John. So also in Scotland and Berwick corrupt flesh was forfeited to the lepers.

Concerning the city of London in the fourteenth century, there was one, Fitz Stephen, whom Sir Walter Besant cites in his great work on *The History of London,* and this writer would have it that London in his day was a fine and healthy city. For he speaks of its wells, Holy Well, Clerkenwell and St. Clement's Well, *Sweet, wholesome and clear, streaming forth among the glistening Pebble Stones.* Also he speaks of the wholesomeness of the air, of which he makes this strange observation, that the Calmness of the Air doth mollify Men's Minds, not corrupting them with Veneral Lusts, but preserving them from Savage and rude Behaviour, and seasoning their Inclinations with a more kind and free Temper. But if that is how he names a damp river mist (for our fog at least was spared them) then I will have none of him. The Black Death caught him lying.

A Chronological Digression on the Subject of Fog.— And while we speak of this matter, lest any reader should imagine our sooty skies to be any very new thing in London, I commend to his attention a passage in *Fumifugium,*

a work written by the diarist John Evelyn, and published
in 1661. For, so early as that, this observer of men and
their ways could write of his indignation that London
*should wrap her stately head in clouds of smoke and sul-
phur, so full of stink and darkness.* And he speaks of the
immoderate use of sea-coal, and that not from the culinary
fires, *but from some few particular tunnels and issues, be-
longing only to brewers, dyers, lime-burners, salt and soap
boilers, and some other private trades.* So then, he speaks
of industrial smoke and an industrial fog, which was no
small matter by his reckoning, for he likens London,
where such smoke belches from the sooty jaws of industry,
to Mount Aetna, the Court of Vulcan, Stromboli or the
Suburbs of Hell. And he says that when in all other places
the air is pure and serene, in London the sun is hardly able
to penetrate this gloom and impart daylight; also that the
traveller can smell the city before ever he sees it.

The Evidence of Boccaccio.—But to return to the fourteenth century, whoever would see a true picture of sanitation and notions of cleanliness at this time may find it in
the *Decameron.* For in the fifth story of the second day,
told by the lady Fiammetta, there is, in the first place, an
account of a privy, of which the contrivance is thus described: *A narrow and blind alley, such as we commonly
see between two houses, was spanned by planks supported
by joists on either side, and on the planks was the stool.*
This story concerns a young man named Andreuccio; and
among his adventures one is told in which he falls from
his contrivance of planks into the alley, sousing himself
from head to food with ordure; from all of which one may
conclude that the alley was made an open sewer by the
houses that bordered it. And, being in this condition,
Andreuccio falls in company with two men who purpose
to rob a tomb, in which enterprise he agrees to accompany them, so that they set out together until one of

Andreuccio's companions asks of the other, *Can we not contrive that he somehow wash himself a little that he stink not so shrewdly?* This being agreed, Andreuccio is next let down into a well for this purpose; and that this well is commonly used by persons for drawing of water to quench their thirst is made clear from what follows. Yet there is not, either in the expressions used by Andreuccio and his companions, or in any comment by the narrator of this story, any suggestion of *disgust* that a man should use the potable water of others to cleanse himself of such filthiness, which offends nothing but their sense of smell.

If such, then, were the contrivances for sewage at this time and the notions of cleanliness, the circumstances which produced the stories in the *Decameron* are the less remarkable, namely, that certain young men and women sought refuge from a deadly pestilence (which we in England knew as the Black Death). This scourge is known to have destroyed three persons out of every five in the city of Florence; and those who read such matters as I have related, or consider the general practices of the time (in which such things were not considered extraordinary), will marvel at the language used by Boccaccio. For in Florence, he says, *despite all that human wisdom and forethought could devise to avert it,* as the cleansing of the city from many impurities by officials appointed for the purpose, the refusal of entrance to all sick folk, and the adoption of *many precautions for the preservation of health;* despite also humble supplications addressed to God, and often repeated both in public procession and otherwise by the devout, the doleful effects of the pestilence began to be horribly apparent.

That the sick were barbarously treated and left to die without succour, we know well enough, and can credit this part of the story, as also the account of prayers and supplications. But what were the extraordinary measures devised in addition, by human wisdom and forethought, Signor Boccaccio does not tell us, and we may doubt with good reason whether either drainage or the purity of the water supply received great attention among persons so devoid of the first elements of hygiene in their common way of living. And Boccaccio, who wrote from experience of this pestilence, gives testimony against the precautions of which he tells us when he records that those who walked abroad carried flowers, fragrant herbs and spices, from which they breathed the perfume, because (he says) the air seemed to be everywhere laden and reeking with the stench emitted by the dead and the dying, and the odour of drugs.

Further Evidence to be considered in camera.—There is also in the *Heptameron* of Marguerite, Queen of Navarre, a tale so nasty concerning a privy used by the Grey Friars that I take no joy in repeating it and will only say that such stories shew us the exceeding filthiness of these times; not that such a tale should have been told, but that it should have been credible, to which fact there is later witness among the paintings of the elder Pieter Breughel, and, indeed, even later, in those of Rembrandt, shewing the nasty habits of the people as authors and artists viewed them.

Of sauve qui peut *and some Royal Examples*.—But what will you? The physicians, so far from commending cleanliness, were often known to worship dirt more ardently than St. Agnes, of which truth we shall provide examples as late as the seventeenth century and after. Flight from disease was the only remedy understood by all; and in this sovereign prophylaxis royalty and the rich, as the leaders of the community, neglected not to set an example, being the first to fly from disease, even as they are the first fugitives from war. From the town of Auxonne, where Margaret, Duchess of Bavaria, had fled from pestilence, in the year 1414, she writes to the rulers of Dijon her *will and order* concerning the inhabitants of that town, *that none of them should presume to come to Auxonne, to which place we, together with our children, have repaired to escape the plague.* Truly these were good foster-parents of their people; for even in religion, which was their last hope, they gave the example of *sauve qui peut,* which was the only strategy known to medicine. Thus also Louis XI, threatened by the plague at Auxerre in the year 1479, bids the monks at Dijon to pray for himself, the Dauphin and the Queen, *and let prayers be said* (he adds, since one cannot ask too much on these occasions) *for the good digestion of our stomachs and that neither wine nor meat may cause us indigestion and that we may be preserved in good health.* Well, there were two pagan deities who might have given some attention to this prayer, but their names are not mentioned. And having considered all that is proper and relevant to the question, I cannot wonder at those who, seeing the simplicity of certain people in the Pyrenees, said these must be true Christians to be as they were; for which cause they are called Chrétiens, or *Cretins,* to this day.

Concerning the Comforts of Constantinople.—Throughout this time we do well to remember that the city of Constantinople enjoyed, under the Christian rulers of the Byzantine Empire, such convenience and comfort in all matters of hygiene and sanitation as were almost unknown throughout the rest of Europe. In addition to a regular system of sanitation and an abundant supply of water, brought to the city by means of aqueducts, the people of Constantinople had the use of such baths as ancient Rome provided; for these baths were common in the city and in general use among the populace during the whole life of Constantinople, from its foundation by the imperial proselyte to its capture by the Ottomans, when *Roman* baths became *Turkish*. Of these baths Burton tells us in his *Anatomy of Melancholy,* on the authority of Gillius, that there were 155 at that time, under the rule of the Turks. At Dorylaion, also, in the Levant, it is said that baths were constructed under the Byzantines where at the same time 7000 men might be cleansed.

And of the hospitals of these Byzantines we read that they were well equipped with elaborate preparations for washing, that they knew the use of soap, which was supplied to the patients when they bathed, twice in the week; also, concerning their provision for natural necessities, the Justinian Code had a special section under Lib. VIII, tit. 10, *de aedificiis privatis,* which seems to have been adequate and hygienic. And as to that scurrilous writer who rendered the Justinian maxim *Cuicum jus tribuere* as meaning *To every one his own juice,* I say he lied.

But whilst the Christian light shone beneath a bushel at Byzantium, that of the Moors in Spain gave to the European continent such light as it could receive. We read of the University of Cordoba as the ornament of the world, to which students would travel from the furthest lands of Christendom. And men have said that the age of the New Learning begins with the overthrow of the Byzantines, as though the scholars of Constantinople had all walked out of the back door with their books. But as well might a man say it began when the Moors were chased from Spain and the Inquisitors sat in their seats of judgement. I will warrant no *New Learning* ever came by Turks sacking a Christian city or by Christians looting a Moorish university; but if a man will dig deeper he will find this same *New Learning* was pursued by Frederick Hohenstaufen, King of Sicily and Emperor of Almaine, whom they called *Stupor Mundi*. This Frederick learnt from the Moors and Saracens and fostered many arts and sciences; and I doubt not a trickle of wisdom began to run into the system of

Europe out of Arabia, Egypt and other lands of the Saracens through this opening in Sicily more than two hundred years before Constantinople fell to the Ottomans.
For what we call the Middle Ages long had the Renaissance in its belly.

*The Civilisation of the Moors in Spain and the Wisdom
of their Physicians.*—Among these Moors there were many
famous physicians, and of these Ibn Zohr was the most
famous. This Ibn Zohr was a greedy eater of green figs,
and it is written that on a certain occasion his brother
physician, Al Far, reproached his greed, saying that so
many figs would cause an abscess in his stomach. But Ibn
Zohr answered that Al Far, through abstaining from figs,
would die of fever and constipation. And how wise these
physicians were may be known from the fact that Ibn
Zohr died of an abscess and Al Far of fever and constipation, each justifying the other.

In the city of Cordoba were 300 public baths, and the
purest water was conveyed from the mountains, which
water was distributed among the houses of the people by
means of leaden pipes. In these houses of the citizens there
were to be found bathrooms with water, both hot and
cold. And the art of cleansing fabrics was studied, for the
courtier Zaryab, besides being a very learned man, a great
musician, an amateur gardener, a leader of fashion, an inventor of great genius and an epicure skilled in culinary
matters, did not disdain to attend to washingday. From
him the Moors learnt, in the time of Charlemagne, the art
of bringing linen to a perfect whiteness, and for this he
was much praised, for the Arabs at that time were called
the cleanest people upon earth. And these things I learn
from the work of Lady Lugard, which she calls *A Tropi-
cal Dependency;* for she says that such was the reputation
of the Arabs in all that related to their persons, dress, beds
and the interior of their houses. And it was said of them

that they carried cleanliness so far that it was not an uncommon thing for a man of the lower orders to spend his last coin on soap rather than to buy food for his daily consumption, and thus he would go without his dinner rather than appear in public in dirty clothes. But of their system of sanitation I can find no record, though I doubt little that among such people it was worthy of so high a civilisation.

Their Baths are pulled down by the Christians.—While much· of Moorish building remains to bear witness to a cultured society that lasted fully seven hundred years, the Christians in the first fury of victory pulled down their baths as temples of the body which they abhorred; for their rulers issued orders to this purport for the reformation, as they said, of the Moriscos. And in these orders it was commanded that neither themselves, their women nor any other persons, *should be permitted to wash or bathe themselves either at home or elsewhere;* and that all their bathing-houses should be pulled down and destroyed. That this zeal against cleanliness was not always found among the Christians of Spain is nevertheless shewn by the laws of Teruel, in Aragon, in the twelfth century. For in this Christian town there was a public bath at that time, such as few Christian towns possessed; and it was enacted that for three days of the week it should be used by Christian men, two days being set aside for their women and one (which was Friday) for both Jews and Moslems, male and female. But upon Sundays, in reverence (they said) to the resurrection of our Lord, the Bath was not to be heated. This bath was cheap to all and free to servants or children.

Apologia pro libello meo.—This shall suffice for our account of the Middle Ages, concerning which much more might be written, but rather to nauseate you than to elevate your minds to certain purposes which I have in my own, which is my present intention. For believe me, you shall find in this record the very mirror of human evolution, viz. the progress of man from the primitive to the artificial, with all the attendant problems, crises, neuroses, nemesis and what have you that are to be found in the march of civilisation itself. And if you will continue to bear with me while we build up our historical pyramid, there will be things worth seeing from its summit; all of which I shall shew forth in good time if the bombs do not begin to fall on London before I am ready for them. But as things are, I can thank God and the Chelsea Borough for three pounds ten a week, and all for sitting in an A.R.P. depot writing of baths and lavatories; and in this I hope to continue without interruption till my purpose is achieved, though every critic should say that I have made an Ivory Tower of Ajax and buried my head in worse than sand.

CAPUT V

Of the Coming of Ajax

Now upon the College of St. Mark and St. John, where I have my lodging, Phoebus Apollo, in glittering shafts of October benediction, sheds his silent blessing. The air is still, and sleepers in Whitehall stir in their dreams to wake and mutter: *Has Moscow fallen?* But still no shrieking siren rends the illusion of security. They sleep again, and I resume my story in an Indian Summer of deceptive peace.

Reflections upon the Seat of a Privy, discovered by the Author.—But yesterday, what time I shovelled the wreckage of some Chelsea citizen, a nameless and forgotten victim, into his own cellar, I found among the mounds of refuse a lavatory seat, anonymous as its owner. Alas, poor Yorick! Perchance it was the handiwork of Thomas Crapper, auspiciously named the leading sanitary engineer of the Borough, but there was no mark upon it; symbol of the useful arts, destroyed by the diabolical sciences, we threw it to the flames. And there, as the fire consumed it, this seat that had ministered, it may be, to the comfort of generations, set me pondering once more the unheroic history of man, written in sanitary progress. But, musing thus, there came to my mind the excellent precept, adapted from Terence, which you will find cited by Sir John, or (as he would have us believe) by his accomplished servant, in the margin of his *Metamorphosis*:

Humani nihil a me alienum puto.

A Purple Passage, by no means to be skipped.—Oh, Great Age, that had room and scope of spirit to nourish an *Avatar* upon the banks of Avon and epic piracy on Devon's double shores; to give us a whole nest of poets and play-writers, almost our only music, and the men who scattered an Armada; to fortify our souls with boisterous prose and the trumpet of a heroic pentameter, to comfort our poor bodies by reviving the Minoan miracle, the flushed water-closet! Here indeed were men whose genius, though nurtured in the perils of war, scorned not to be the servant of human happiness nor turned from the homelier task. In these pages shall names as forgotten as those of the owner and the maker of the seat I but recently excavated live once more for your admiration; but first we will consider their fathers, those earlier Tudor gallants, and their great contemporaries, not forgetting the discoverers of a New World, the illustrious Dagoes.

Behold, then, the England of Bluff King Hal, with a redrobed Cardinal mounted on his three-seated jakes. Against the stinks and infections of the courts he carries the customary—what did they call the things?—an orange skin, stuffed with scents; ah, a *pomander*. Bad cess to him, I shall always imagine he wore woollen underwear beneath those great robes of his, the scheming bourgeois. The successor whose ambition he nourished deserves an even harsher censure, for no man did more than Thomas Cromwell to destroy the records of earlier ages, and that is to say nothing of heads that fell from the block.

Ignominious Fate of many ancient Manuscripts.—Now, if there is one bigger falsehood than the story of culture diffused by the capture of Constantinople, it is the notion that the monks sat tight upon all learning, which the Reformers dispensed to the commonwealth at the dissolution of the monasteries. John Leland lived at this time, our first antiquary, and he was so disturbed by the wholesale

destruction of these same valuable documents by those to
whom Thomas Cromwell was giving the religious houses,
that he wrote to Cromwell in the year 1535, begging to be
permitted to collect all manuscripts for the King's Library.
Some, indeed, were saved by Leland in this manner, while
others (according to Leland) were filched by German
scholars—aha, the omnipresent Hun in history!—but of
the rest Bishop Bale, old Bilious Bale, wrote as follows in
his preface to *The Laborious Journey and Search of J. Ley-
lande for England's Antiquities,* an edition published in
1549: *A great number of them which purchased these
superstitious mansions reserved of those Library books,
some to serve their jakes, some to scour their candlesticks.*

So, then, that was no doubt the true fate of the knowledge long stored by mediaeval monks and delivered by
Cromwell to the keeping of the Protestant *nouveaux
riches.* But here is a Dutchman who should tell us something of the country, having seen it as the onlooker views
the game.

Erasmus condemns our Houses.—Of the houses in England in the time of the eighth Henry, that shrewd observer
Erasmus wrote that Englishmen built their chambers in
such a way as to admit of no ventilation. And that he
speaks here of the houses of the rich may be seen from
what follows, namely, that a great part of the walls of the
house, he says, is occupied with glass casements, which
admit light but exclude the air. As to the floors, he says
they are in general laid with white clay and covered with
rushes, occasionally removed, but that so imperfectly that
the bottom layer is undisturbed sometimes for twenty
years, *harbouring abominations not to be mentioned.* To
these observations Erasmus adds certain proposals for the
improvement of English houses to make them more
healthy, and in these he shews an understanding of both
deficiencies and remedies.

That there was some small interest in the public health may be judged from certain prosecutions at this time. For in the year 1512 the Mayor of Nottingham was summoned for selling herrings unfit for consumption and for beginning a muck-hill. Also the father of William Shakespeare was later (*an.* 1552) fined for depositing refuse in the street, and again in 1558 for failing to keep clean his gutters. But Mr. Jack Lindsay, in his introduction to a modern edition of Harington's *Metamorphosis,* cites two accounts of the foul conditions which made the labours of Sir John so timely, necessary and praiseworthy. The first of these is Stow's account of Petty France, where there was in his time a ditch filled up (he says) with unsavoury things, to the danger of empoisoning the whole city. And secondly, Mr. Lindsay gives items for complaints brought before the Manor Court of Castle Combe in Wiltshire, *an.* 1590; when it was necessary to forbid soiling in the churchyard and streets, and to order the removal of dung or filth from the house of one, John Davis.

The Dearth of Privies continues.—Such, indeed, was what we should expect to find; for it is upon record that in the year 1579 there were but three privies in Tower Street, in the Parish of All Hallows, supplying the needs of near sixty houses and eighty-five people. Which may, I suppose, be tabled as an improvement upon the state of certain rents in the Basinghall Ward in the previous century; for these were altogether without privies, and the householders were constrained to throw all their filth into the street. This method of sewage disposal was common enough and long remained in vogue.

Amerigo Vespucci expresses his Disapproval of certain Islanders.—It may be observed that Europeans at this time, whilst they allowed but little importance to matters of sanitation, made much of appearances. For the great Florentine, Amerigo Vespucci, in his account of his voyages, says of the islanders whom he found at the beginning of his first voyage that they were a people of neat exterior and clean of body, because of so continually washing themselves as they did. And when, says he, saving your reverence, they evacuate the stomach, they do their utmost not to be observed; and as much as in this they are cleanly and bashful, so much the more are they filthy and shameless in making water; since, while standing speaking to us, without turning around or shewing any shame, they let go their nastiness, for in this they have no shame.

And Sir Thomas More, who with so much wit and wisdom described his *Utopia,* had no more to say concerning the cruder problems of sanitation in that country than a few words for the debasement of precious metals, lest men should covet them. For he says that of gold and silver (in that country) they commonly make chamber-pots and other vessels that serve for most vile uses, not only in their common halls but in every man's private house. And this he says in despite of gold, not for the honour of sanitation and greater care thereto. So also my lord Verulam, when he writes *Of Buildings,* for all his cunning in things of a practical character, makes only an ambiguous mention of *offices,* whereof he treats not in detail. Nevertheless he may be called a martyr of hygiene who caught his death experimenting in refrigeration, an art known in ancient India for the preservation of corruptible matter, but long lost to the world.

Of the Contempt in which the Tartars held the Christians.—But one, Richard Johnson, writes of a voyage which he made (*an.* 1556) as servant to Master Richard Chancelour. And he speaks of the Tartarians, which be Mahumetans, and live in tents and wagons, and keep in herds and companies; and they hold it not good, he says, to abide long in one place, for they will say, when they curse any of their children, I would thou mightest tarry so long in a place *that thou mightest smell thine own dung, as the Christians do;* and this is the greatest curse that they have. This is written among the *Principal Navigations, Voyages, Traffics and Discoveries of the English Nation,* compiled by the indefatigable Hakluyt, and shows the contempt which a civilised nomad might feel for those that dwell in cities, if these be not kept sweet. Thus the Essenes in ancient times avoided the cities of the Jews; for they said that just as foul air breeds disease, so the soul contracts disease from bad associations.

Of the thrifty Use of Excrement by the Chinese.—And here I will mention another matter recorded among Hakluyt's *Principal Navigations,* concerning the excellent practice of the Chinese in the use of dung, which we shall consider in its proper place *in extenso* as one of the problems of our age. In a report on China, done out of Italian into English by one, Richard Willes, you will find these words: Here (he says) be sold the voidings of close stools, although there wanteth not the dung of beasts, *and the excrements of man are good merchandise throughout all China.* The dung farmers seek in every street by exchange to buy this dirty ware for herbs and wood. *The custom is very good for keeping the city clean.*

How good it was for other purposes also we have yet to discuss; but I may mention here that this custom of the Chinese still obtains; and that commercial gentleman who was sent to Cathay by a company of merchants engaged in the sale of chemical fertilisers, found that for this reason he could do no business. Insomuch that when he received an urgent request for information, after six months of silence, he was constrained to cable to his employers that he had 400,000,000 competitors.

But we must return to Tudor England. As to the cleanliness of the body, it is said with reason in the *Novum Organum* that this has always been allowed to proceed from moral modesty and reverence; first, towards God, whose creatures we are, next, towards society, wherein we live, and lastly, towards ourselves, whom we ought to reverence still more than others. But when this was written it was but a hope for the future and no picture of the present. Thus Sir Walter Besant makes mention, in his *History of London,* of the diseases that scourged the city of London in the thirty-eight years while Henry VIII reigned in England. (For there was in that time a return of the Plague from the year 1517 to 1522 and of the Sweating Sickness in 1518 and again in 1528, with the Plague once more in 1543.) And it seems, he observes, a strange thing that no physician spied the true cause of these diseases, the foulness of the narrow streets, the cesspools without number, the refuse and the putrefying blood of slaughtered beasts.

Concerning Sir Francis Drake and the Uses of Parliamentary Privilege.—A little was done by the Elizabethans for the better provision of water in certain towns, and notably in Plymouth, where to this day (for all that I know) the Mayor and Corporation inspect their ancient works and drink in water *to the pious memory of Sir Francis Drake;* after which toast they have been wont to drink in wine to his descendants (of which he left none), saying, *may the descendants of him who brought us water never lack wine.* But this custom is not of such antiquity as some have thought it to be, and it may be doubted if those who knew that old pirate thought so well of him. For Sir Francis (when not upon the high seas) sat in Parliament in those days for the borough of Bussiney; and being on a Select Committee of the House to consider the Plymouth Water Bill, he may be suspected of having had some hand in amending it to his advantage. This we know, that the Bill being drawn up by the burgesses of Plymouth, to fetch water from the River Meavy, with much talk of ships that harboured at Plymouth, this Bill was amended with some mention of water mills. So that where the burgesses spoke of their own need and those of the ships, more especially in time of war, the amendment made it to include a proviso concerning the erection of mills and the appropriation of water for that purpose. Let the reader judge the meaning of this from the fact that Sir Francis was the sole member of that Committee which so amended the Bill who had any interest in the matter, or in Plymouth, and that he even then leased the Corporation Manor Mills at Millbay. Sir Francis therefore established a sound interest in this matter, beyond the sum of £100 paid to him in compensation for land and £200 for work which he is supposed to have done in furtherance of the plan, or, as the records say, for *bringing in the water*.

The *Leat* which they made for this purpose was full seventeen miles in length and some six to seven feet in width, passing through mighty rocks which had been thought an impassable barrier to this enterprise. And within six months of completion we find that Sir Francis built upon the Leat six new mills, in accordance with the proviso in the amendment, from which he made enviable profits. Also we find that in the next year a further Bill was put forward in the Commons that these mills should be removed, and that Sir Francis was Chairman of the Committee which sat upon it, to such effect that it was heard of no more. Nevertheless, this matter of the Leat was a great undertaking, worthy of the enterprise of the Elizabethans; and many conduits they made from the Leat, of which one bore the motto *Redigit desertum in stagnum*. But the men of Plymouth would suffer those of Devonport, whom they called *Dockers,* to have none of their water; and Boswell records the language used by Doctor Johnson in this matter. For he, while on a visit to Plymouth (*an.* 1762), affected, says Boswell, to entertain the passions of the place, exclaiming, No, no, I am a Plymouth man. Rogues, let them die of thirst. They shall not have a drop.

Thus Plymouth, on account of its importance to our ships in a great age of seamen, was among the first towns to supply itself with wholesome water from a distance (though Hull can claim the first honour by a long lead), and as it is today, so it was then, we find a man profiting from the matter in such a way that what was undertaken for public use was made the occasion of private gain.

Queen Bess is shewn to have bathed more frequently than King John.—As to baths, these remained a rarity. But Gloriana had bathrooms installed at Windsor, and there (as a contemporary informs us) she bathed herself once a month *whether she required it or not*. This, as I suppose, shewed some advancement since the time of King John; but the speed of such progress would hardly even have alarmed the Fabian Society or that deceased apostle of Gradualism whose policies still govern the desperate revolutionaries of our time. Mr. H. A. J. Lamb, it is true, has reproduced in the *Architects' Journal* for March 4th, 1937, a drawing from a sixteenth-century manuscript shewing that about this time promiscuous bathing was practised to the accompaniment of music, in which some must have indulged their fancy. But for the most part such practices were unknown. Wash your hands often, your feet seldom, your head never, ran the English proverb of the period, scorning even to mention the chance of other parts being washed; and the most we can hope is that at least the first instruction carried a little weight with it. Few indeed can have been so fastidious as that criminal of whom Montaigne tells us, who on the scaffold would not so much as share a cup with the hangman, for fear he caught the pox; and does not Montaigne himself remark upon the foul stenches of Paris in his essay on smells and odours?

The excellent Precepts of Dr. Andrew Boorde.—Among the first to shew an empirical understanding of the principles of health was Andrew Boorde, who was born in the year 1490 and died in 1549, having learnt medicine in the universities of Europe and practised in this country. This man was learned in much that has escaped the attention of physicians until the present time, for he said that a good cook is half a physician and that the chief physic (the counsel of the physician excepted) doth come from the kitchen. For this cause he ordained that the physician and the cook should consult together; also he held that a man should be his own best physician, to consider the thing which did him good.

And in the principles of psychology this Andrew Boorde shewed himself a master, for in his *Breviary of Health* he praises mirth, because (he says) there is nothing that doth comfort the heart so much, beside God, as honest mirth and good company. Thus he considers the state of mind as of first importance to the preservation of health, for he says that the heart doth vivi Gate all other members and is the ground and foundation of all the vital spirits in man. Also in his book called *The Dietary of Health* he says that if the eye be not satisfied, the mind cannot be contented, which being so, the heart cannot be pleased. If the heart (he says) and mind be not pleased, nature doth abhor, and if nature do abhor, mortification of the vital and animal and spiritual powers do consequently follow. In this book he says, moreover, that mirth and rejoicing do lengthen a man's life and expel sickness.

But enough of this, for once more we digress from the true object of our passion. Let us return to fundamentals and resurrect among the Elizabethan giants the figure of Ajax, but for whose appearance at this time the title of this book would have no meaning and my book itself would never have been brought to birth. Lend force and sweetness to my words, Stercutius and Cloacina, Baal-Peor and Tlaçolteotl, deities of sanitation and fertility; and rise, ye genii, banished from Mohammed's paradise, who frequent the smallest chambers of our houses; for I would pay the neglected tribute of an ungrateful nation to the greatest of its sons, the foremost of its inventors, the most accomplished and versatile genius since the Moorish Zaryab, saving only Leonardo da Vinci.

The Royal Descent of Sir John Harington.—A royal bar sinister missed the house of Harington by no more than a hair's breadth. Lightly dispersed in bastardy, the seed of lusty Henry, amid the changing fortunes of marriage, had begotten without benefit of wedlock the lady who became the first wife of Harington *père*. Alas, she died barren, like so many of those dried-up tender shoots, and Harington *fils* was the fruit of a second marriage. If his conception was not immaculate, surely no mortal man could have been nearer to such honour, with a Virgin Queen for his godmother. Posterity alone, his legitimate heir and assign, neglects with the ingratitude of oblivion the sanitary messiah for whom the far-seeing fates decreed the spiritual motherhood of Great Elizabeth.

His Upbringing and Accomplishments.—A father also was provided for this prodigy by the eugenics of predestination who shared the spoils of the monks and at Kelston observed the rules of hygiene with untimely zeal. Did he not forbid the making of water within either of his courtyards on pain of a fine, namely, the sum of one penny? And was not this one-quarter of the sum mulcted from those who *toyed with the maids?* Such rules, with one that forbade the teaching of *any unhonest speech or bawdy word* to the children, you will find in the *Nugae Antiquae,* compiled by the labours of the Rev. Henry Harington from the dusty manuscripts of the period. Trained in such a tradition of cleanliness and decency, John Harington grew to the stature of manhood to find himself all that an Elizabethan aspired, or was required, to be: a wit, a soldier, a courtier and a poet. But not content with such trivial plumes, the royal blood in his veins demanded no less distinction than *Supremacy;* and this he discovered as an *inventor*.

Where is the man today who, with rank and beauty waiting upon his ready tongue, a queen for his audience, a court for his auditorium, and an archbishopric for his ambition, will turn aside from such fripperies, go to the bottom of things, and concern his mind with a sanitary convenience? Where is the inventor who, having devised such a thing of utility, will write you a book full of wit and wisdom to advertise his product with all the rich store of classical scholarship and the entertainment of a jester's tongue? Such a man was Sir John, such a book *The Metamorphosis of Ajax,* published in 1596, which carried with it a complete plan of *the first modern valve watercloset.*

Sir John held to scorn in Ulysses Upon Ajax.—There is a book which you will find among the curious works of the age which is called *Ulysses Upon Ajax,* a criticism of Sir John and his book, though some believe that Harington himself wrote it—a custom not uncommon at the time and in later years, before the late Joynson-Hicks and James Douglas were sent into the world to do for authors what they had formerly to do for themselves. The unknown author of *Ulysses* certainly shared Sir John's taste for a certain type of literature, especially the works of the Sieur de Brocourt; for he knew his way through the *Sérées de Guillaume Bouchet*. But whether he was in fact Sir John himself, or look we for another, he said plainly that Harington's metamorphosed Ajax was a notion cribbed from Vitruvius, or else (he said) *taken from a traveller's mouth*

who hath seen the Cardinal of Ferrara's buildings at Tivoli.
As to that, no life of Sir John has yet been written to consult upon this point, and for my part I have other matters
to consider; so the point shall remain in dispute until I
have leisure to turn biographer or a better man steps in before me. All that I know is, if Sir John was not in fact the
inventor, he was the first in this country to imitate the
invention; and how rare a spirit was his may be seen from
the small number of those who followed his example,
though inspired by a book of such great worth and charm.
But I am inclined myself to think that Sir John wrote
Ulysses himself in self-deprecation, to stir up controversy;
and among the many similarities of style and vocabulary
I have noticed that both Sir John and the anonymous
author use the term *Bocardo* to denote a jakes, a use of
that word which I have not found in any other writings,
and unknown to such dictionaries as I have consulted,
wherein its secondary uses are confined to jail-houses.

*Gloriana honoured him, but his Name was writ in
Water.*—Peace be to his bones. The Queen herself, a practical woman if ever there was, is said to have caused a
model of the invention to be installed at Richmond Palace,
with a copy of her godson's book hanging upon the wall.
But to his contemporaries Sir John's invention was a jest,
and he a prophet without honour in his own country. Succeeding generations forgot both; and when the water-
closet made its appearance once more in our houses, the
very name of the genius to whom this most beneficial of
all inventions is due had passed from human memory.
Too truly had it been writ in water. Even the *Dictionary of
National Biography* does him no justice, the edition of
1890 recording that his style resembled *Sterne at his worst.*

*Devices considered by Sir John for the Reformation of
Privies.*—The great Harington in his book sets forth the

many reflections and experiments which preceded the metamorphosis. Thus he tells us that one taught an excellent rule to keep a chimney from smoking and a privy from stinking, viz. to make your fire in your privy and to set the close-stool in the chimney. But this method he rejects. And other ways he discusses, notably that used in his house at Lincoln's Inn, where vents drew off the evil odours; but this too failed to satisfy him, because he found the wind so unruly, it would at times drive the ill airs down his vents, and not draw them up.

Therefore Sir John devised a privy where water should be employed to carry away the filth, for which reason he offered to be Admiral of such projects. And in his sudden discovery of this excellent device this rear-admiral likened himself to Archimedes (as well he might, being at least as deserving an engineer) but protested that he did not imitate Archimedes in leaving his employment (for we may conjecture what he was at) to cry *Eureka* about the town with his hose about his heels. Rather did this apostle of Sanitation soberly set down with plans, costs and the most complete instructions the manner in which a valve water-closet (such as he caused to be made in his own house at Kelston, near Bath) was to be made and flushed from a tank.

This, then, was the Haringtonian revelation; and we, who have yet to consider the filthiness of physicians in the time of the Plague, with all the dirt and disease to which we are still the heirs, may well marvel at this man's sagacity. For he sets it down that many physicians held in his time (though surely these must have been the exceptions) that the plague, the measles, the haemorrhoids, the smallpox, and perhaps the great ones too, with the *fistula in ano,* and many of those inward diseases, are no way sooner gotten than by favour of other excrements upon

unwholesome privies. To this testimony he adds that of
the *School of Salerno,* which we have already noticed.

New Laurels for Old Ajax.—A later age has but begun
to do scant justice to this neglected genius. Mr. Gerald
Heard, writing of a multitude of things under the title
Narcissus, An Anatomy of Clothes, has proclaimed the
use of a flush system of drainage by the men of Crete a
great invention, fit to rank beside the steam engine. And
in Sir John he observes his *almost Minoan figure,* calling
him a typical Elizabethan (which he was not, for he far
outstripped them all, and they did not so much as follow
where he had led). But it is none the less of note to find
even a bare mention of Harington and his achievement,
which Mr. Heard rightly describes as the re-invention of
the Minoan's masterpiece.

Or let the curious examine the story of Sir Ferdinando
in that excellent novel *Chrome Yellow,* by Mr. Huxley,
and he will find in this book a very pretty picture of an
Elizabethan gentleman who invented a privy, to be flushed
by water, and wrote on this subject a work (now said to
be rare) entitled *Certaine Privy Counsels* by *One of Her
Majestie's Honourable Privy Counsel.* Who is here indicated but our old friend Sir John, the true original of the
fictitious Ferdinando? But alas, few who read Mr. Huxley
are privy to this secret.

That the great Harington concerned his mind generally
with health we know from his translation of *The School
of Salerne,* setting forth the precepts of that famous College of Medicine, such as the cleansing of the teeth after
eating, as a protection against the worms which our forefathers believed to be the cause of the toothache. Therefore let no man say he was but a jester who was so widely
concerned with these matters, and, not content (like myself) to be a writer on sanitary matters, both invented and
caused to be fashioned the most useful of all innovations

in architecture. I will drink the Plymouth toast to him backwards: in wine to his memory and in water to his descendants; may their cisterns never lack it.

Campanella has Nothing to say of the Jakes used in the City of the Sun.—Now as to others who concerned themselves with hygiene, Thomas Campanella, who lived about the same time as Sir John and lightened the miseries of a dungeon by considering the attributes of an ideal society, says of the inhabitants of the *Civitas Solis* that they used baths, and, moreover, they had warm ones, according to the custom of Rome, also that they had discovered many secret remedies for the preservation of cleanliness and health; but of their privies he tells us nothing, from which we may conclude that he had no more to say upon this matter than other *Utopians,* such as Sir Thomas More or my Lord Verulam.

But Lilliput had at the least One Hygienic Statute.—Lilliput was no Utopia, but we may at this point observe that the court of that kingdom was protected by laws similar to those devised by the elder Harington for his household, though more drastic in the penalties which they imposed. For there was a statute in this country by which it was enacted that whoever should make water within the precincts of the royal palace should be liable to the pains and penalties of high treason. Therefore the first article of impeachment against Gulliver was that in open breach of the said law, under colour of extinguishing the fire kindled in the apartment of the queen, he did maliciously, traitorously and devilishly, by discharge of his urine, put out the said fire kindled in the said apartment. But I seem to have strayed into a later age, which, by your leave, we will consider in the next chapter.

The Author is tempted to fall between Two Stools.—Much sewage has flowed into the sea since Sir John wrote his memorable but unremembered work; and, like all great inventions, the water-closet (no less than the aeroplane) is used rather for destruction than for human welfare. This we shall discuss in good time; but first we have other things to consider and to these we will devote an undivided attention, lest in the words of the French proverb, *Entre deux arcouns chet cul à terre.*

CAPUT VI

Of Periwigs and Perfumed Corruption

Now AT AN EASY PACE we may amble through the succeeding centuries; and if it please you we will pause only to survey what is instructive to the mind, having first damped our handkerchiefs with eau-de-Cologne and inoculated our astral bodies with knowledge and courage to descend into these cesses of Modern History.

A vain Search for the Commode of Louis XIV—Mais où sont les neiges d'antan?—Here in distant India the Shah Jahangir holds his audiences in magnificent baths. Not so will you find the Court of Versailles, where there is great filthiness, and I am credibly informed that no privies existed even in the time of the Grand Monarque; but *commodes* are here in use, and upon one such sits Louis XIV, with his courtiers about him. In the pale hope of setting eyes upon that celebrated throne, the seat of such formidable majesty, I journeyed but recently to the Victoria and Albert Museum, where (as I had been told) it was still to be found. Others shall verify and write learned footnotes for future generations, exposing the vanity of my quest or justifying it, according to the decree of the Weird Sisters. All that I know is, I found the Victoria and Albert almost as bare and uninhabited as our mortuary at St. Mark's, and pray God that this war, which has emptied one museum, will yet fail to fill the other. Where then are now buried those treasures of the past? Where, if it exists, is that *reductio ad absurdum* of Bourbon arrogance? Where is the *pot de chambre* Great Louis carried in his coach of state, if another rumour be true? Never, surely, did the pick and shovel of research function in such a black-out, or learning contend with such barbarism; the very Reading Room of the British Museum is closed, and has been so these many months, a mishap lamented by every scholar in the Tramps' University, the free school of all the arts and sciences where once I sat among my peers, those ragged buccaneers of Pallas Athene.

Of an elusive Privy upon Wheels.—*Facilis descensus Averno,* but by God's help we will pull out; for, as Antonio said, my fortunes are not in one Bottom trusted. There are still books to be had—the more readily if I had the money—and above all, there is my memory, that should not lead you too far astray. For example, in Madrid, about this time, the mobile privy makes its appearance; pulled through the streets and heralded by a crier, it seeks to supply the lamentable needs of the city. Alas, I have excited your curiosity in vain, for all my efforts have not as yet unearthed the details of its meteoric career. But of decency as understood in the island of Madeira I find this account by the Rev. John Ovington, writing of his *Voyage to Surat in the year 1689.* When the Company breaks up (he says) the Porches and Entries of the Houses, and particularly the private place behind the door, are allowed for the convenience of Urine; because that action in the streets is reputed Indecent and liable to the Censure of Drunkenness.

And so to Bed with Sam'l Pepys and Others.—As to our own country, Pepys has recorded the perils of the passer-by in the London streets of an evening; filth was precipitated from upper windows into the narrow alleys, and one might be counted fortunate who had only the stench to endure. (Was this, perchance, the true origin of male gallantry, that still chooses the outside of the pavement?) Here was a fine target for the satirist, and John Gay describes it for us in his *Trivia,* presenting to us the dirt, mire, mud and slime of the City, augmented by those slops that descended from the overhanging casements, telling us of

> *. . . Cloacina, goddess of the tide*
> *Whose sable streams beneath the city glide.*

And Mr. Alfred Russel Wallace reminds me in his work, *The Wonderful Century,* of those lines of Swift:

> *Sweepings from butchers' stalls, dung, guts and blood,*
> *Drown'd puppies, stinking sprats, all drench'd in mud,*
> *Dead cats and turnip-tops come tumbling down the flood.*

From such filth, says Mr. Wallace, only the larger streets were ever cleaned, the houses also having, for the most part, cesspools close behind or underneath them. But there are pictures by Hogarth that will shew most of these things, offering evidence even more grim than you will find in the third satire of Juvenal, describing the streets of Rome in the early days of its decline.

State of the Privies and Observations of Boswell and Johnson.—An anonymous scribbler of the period, who wrote certain *Meditations upon An House of Office,* gives us (together with a terrible description of a jakes) certain observations regarding Scotland which at first I hardly credited. For first he tells of a privy where he saw, among other objects, the leg of a child, which put him in mind of fornication, mother of the greater sin of murder. For this reason, says he: *I could not but admire the wise Institution of the Scotch Nation,* which will not suffer any such destructive Chasms (he means Jakes) within the limits of their Kingdom. But chancing myself upon the edition of Boswell's *Journal of a Tour to the Hebrides,* first published from the original MS. in 1936, by the labours of Frederick Pottle and Charles Bennett, I found some corroboration for these remarks. Boswell describes the streets of Edinburgh as perilous and odoriferous, and the throwing of foul water from the windows had but recently been forbidden. But what is of greater interest is his surprise upon finding an ingenious privy at Brochel Castle. *I did not imagine* (he says) *the invention had been introduced into Scotland till in very modern days.* The contrivance he describes would by us be considered simple enough, being merely a hole set over an abyss, but Boswell claims that such conveniences were still rare among the Scots, who (as Dr. Johnson expressed it) *took very good care of one end of a man, but not of the other.*

Boswell rightly concluded from his observations at Raasay (where the owner of Brochel Castle had no privy of his own) that an ancient art had fallen into disuse; for which cause he upbraided his host as being less civilised than his ancestors. In a lost passage of the journal Boswell appears to have found a good *Little House,* as he calls it, at Talisker; for when he found that Coll, like Raasay, had an old jakes in the castle but none in the modern house, he took the matter so hard that the Doctor told him he had the *Domus Taliskeriana* much at heart. And on another occasion, when Johnson read through the journal, he informed Boswell that one of his faults was *expatiating too much on the luxury of the little-house at Talisker*. But this fault, says the observant sycophant, *he mentioned as if he liked it.* Yet modesty seems to have induced him to destroy the passage.

Well, notwithstanding the preoccupations of Boswell, I would say that in these times any nation would have fared better to follow the custom of the Tartars; and for a further study of how our ancestors dealt with such things I refer you to that account by the Very Rev. Dean Swift of *The Lady's Dressing Room,* and an obscure reply entitled *The Gentleman's Study.*

Surely it was from these times that a curious precedent survives whereby it is still permissible for the driver of a hired vehicle to water his wheel in case of necessity, without being considered to have *committed a nuisance,* as our strange phrase has it. This, I suppose, having once been universal custom, represents not a privilege acquired but a form of license preserved.

A Poet praises the unregenerate Ajax.—And now let us consider the once-bright streams that flow southward into mighty Thames, become the open sewers of the growing city, until, one by one, they are of necessity covered over. At Holywell, Clerkenwell and Aldgate Pump a man may drink of the fever and be thankful that he does not drink of the plague. As to washing or bathing themselves, Londoners knew little of such things until late in the last century. And their dying was as filthy and congested as their living; for in the crowded cemeteries the dead lay so near to the surface that they infected the air of the churchyard, so that those who sought ministrations for their souls exposed their bodies to new perils. But who cares? And has not even Herrick written an ode to his *Closet-Gods,* deities (as I suppose) of no metamorphosed Ajax (for the new model is still neglected), but the old, unseemly *gong,* the midden-privy of which so much, alas, must be written in this truthful tale?

When London was rebuilt after the Great Fire, an Act was passed in Parliament making provisions as to the height of houses, the breadth of streets, the construction of sewers and the prohibition of noisome trades. And doubtless a little was effected by such means, though more, it is believed, by the great heat of the fire which destroyed all sources of infection and cleansed the long-festering sores of corruption. But had Sir Christopher Wren been permitted to undertake the remodelling of the City with a free hand, the tale had been a different one indeed, for he prepared a great plan which had without doubt been put into execution but for the opposition of many private interests. John Evelyn also planned for the rebuilding of the city, and both plans were made with some thought to the health of the people. What Wren was permitted to accomplish did much to improve the metropolis, but we may be sure those who prevented a greater achievement regretted that they could not create again their *infinity of ancestral frowsiness and infection*.

In the year 1720 a certain Dr. Richard Mead published a *Short Discourse concerning Pestilential Contagion* in which he not only advocated a better and more humane system of isolating infected persons than that hitherto in use, but spoke plain language upon the necessity of houses and streets being kept clean. For as nastiness, he said, is a great source of infection, so cleanliness is the greatest preservative. And in the year 1752 there was published a book by Sir John Pringle, then Physician-General to the British Forces, who (under the title of *Observations on the Diseases of the Army in Camp and Garrison*) exposed the dangers arising from filth and foul air in the propagation of many diseases. Yet so little progress was made that a hundred years later we read of soldiers living in barracks condemned as unfit for habitation ten years past, of latrines in a state of indescribable filth, and of a death rate in the army very much higher than that of the civil population, due to the diseases from which the soldiers suffered even more than civilians.

Of sluttish Customs among the Fops and their notorious Ignorance.—The eighteenth century concealed with perfume and powder the fact that it was filthy and stank, and its predecessor was no sweeter. For as Herrick says to the lady:

> *From Powders and Perfumes keep free;*
> *Then shall we know how sweet you be.*

In the very dining-rooms where fops paraded their lace and their powdered *perruques,* there were built cupboards with shelves to contain chamber-pots; so that, having besotted themselves with liquor, these dandies might relieve themselves the more readily. Little indeed did such nastiness disturb their minds, for their filthiness was but the reflection of unimaginable ignorance. Did not the constable of Great Staughton, in the county of Huntingdon, record this item in his accounts for the year 1710?— *Paid, Thomas Hawkins, for whipping 2 persons that had small-pox 8d*. Disease being held to be a moral delinquency, to be punished by the lash, dirtiness went unsuspected.

Of the Exhibits in the Parkes Museum, with a Warning to those who would view them.—Here, in a mansion planned for the Earl of Leicester at Norfolk, the architect (who designed it in the year 1734) has arranged a sociable retreat for two, in a corner of the hall, without a window, so that it ventilates into the house. The metamorphosed Ajax is still neglected, though I am told that Horace Walpole makes some mention of such an apparatus in 1760. Not until the year 1775 is the first valve water-closet patented, the proud invention of Alexander Cumming, to be followed three years later by the patent of Joseph Bramah. An example of the first *pan* closet, produced in 1790, may be seen with its heirs and successors at the Parkes Museum, where I recently viewed these exhibits; and in the light of my own unfortunate experience I wrote some lines as a warning to future visitors to the Royal Sanitary Institute, which lines may very properly be

brought to the reader's attention at this point in case he
should be of a mind to follow in my footsteps:

> *All unashamed, on either hand,*
> *The by-gone water closets stand;*
> *Oh, bitter cliché! I've a notion*
> *One could be thirsty on the ocean.*

A Stuart Throne at Windsor.—Repair, then, to this
mausoleum of empty thrones if you would know the details of technique and construction, for here I have no
place for such a collection. The early models were, for the
most part, so constructed as to be easily fouled, and such
few of them as were ever made can have brought but little
improvement to the conditions of health where they were
used. But once more we must pause to do honour to a
royal example, presenting for your admiration the figure
of Queen Anne sitting at Windsor upon *a seat of Easement of Marble, with sluices of water to wash all down.*
Alas for England, we who have suffered so much at the
hands of our kings could not learn the salutary lesson that
two queens would have taught us.

What, then, of the physicians? Were there none to rank
with those of Salerno and give us counsel against the infections arising from a jakes? Rather they seem to have
progressed backwards, but let us examine for a while their
methods of diagnosis and cure, to see what hope there is
here for improvement. For these are to be the new priests,
carrying in their bags as many bodily remedies for a credulous public as the fat Pardoners once had of salves for their
souls. We will therefore turn highwaymen, to hold up
these pedlars and rifle their packs.

Sir Thomas More jests with Death and the Doctors.—
I remember first a seemly story, which Sir John shall tell,
as he will do so better than ever I could, concerning Sir
Thomas More; from which you may learn that a man may

be merry and still be canonised. For before his execution Sir Thomas—or Saint Thomas, if you had rather—being told that he must prepare to die, for he could not live, called for his urinal, and having made water in it *he cast it and viewed it* (*as physicians do*) a pretty while; at last he swore soberly that he saw nothing in that man's water, but that he might live, if it pleased the King. A pretty saying, adds Sir John, both to note his own innocency and move the Prince to mercy.

Judgement by Urine condemned as fraudulent.—But Sir Thomas Browne in his *Pseudodoxia Epidemica* passes censure upon Judgement by Urine and speaks of this practice in these words. Physicians, he says (many at least that make profession thereof), besides divers less discoverable ways of fraud, have made them believe there is the book of fate or the power of Aaron's breastplate in Urines. And therefore hereunto they have recourse as unto the Oracle of life, the great determinator of Virginity, Conception, Fertility and the Inscrutable infirmities of the whole Body. For as though there were a seminality in Urine, or that, like the Seed, it carried with it the *Idea* of every part, they foolishly conceive we visibly behold therein the Anatomy of every particle, and can thereby indigitate their Diseases; and, running into any demands, expect from us a sudden resolution in things, whereon the Devil of *Delphos* would demur; and we know hath taken respite of some days to answer easier questions.

If such was the ignorance and the pretentiousness of physicians in this country, as judged by one of their number distinguished for his sincerity, our *amour propre* demands to know more of the conditions upon the Continent, and here shall we behold such an abundance of brutish customs as should restore us in our self-esteem, though one honourable exception shall first be mentioned, Sanctorius Sanctorius, who taught at the University of

Padua in the time of the great Galileo. This philosopher appears to have spent much of his time in a *weighing chair,* and in the year 1614 published the results of his experiments and meditations under the title *De Statica Medicina,* of which the following shall serve as examples of his acumen: *Insensible Perspiration alone discharges much more than all the servile Evacuations together.* And again he says: If the Body increases beyond its usual weight, without eating or drinking more than customary, there must either be a Retention of some of the Sensible Excrement (for so he terms those losses of which we are conscious) or an Obstruction of the perspirable Matter. But the experimental methods of Sanctorius were no more common on the Continent of Europe than they were in this island; as we will briefly shew from some examples of ignorance and superstition, resulting in the most filthy treatment of those who came under the care of physicians.

Unsavoury Habits of the French.—First, then, I commend to your attention *Social France in the XVII Century,* where Mlle Cécile Hugon will tell you something of French hospitals. Happy was the subject of Henry IV who, being sick, found the Hôtel-Dieu too full for his admission and died in the streets! For those, says our author, who had the even greater misfortune of gaining admission were sometimes placed in a bed with six other persons, all dying of different diseases. Indeed, an eye-witness even declared that at Rouen he had seen eight or ten persons in one bed, and often one living person in the midst of seven or eight who were dead. The incomes of such hospitals were augmented by selling the clothes of the dead to the poor of the city, by which means the demand for hospitals was assured at the same time as the supply; and if this be the way in which France dealt with disease, we may more readily imagine the careless habits of the healthy. (Moreover, if I remember aright, Victor

Hugo has something to say in *Les Misérables* on the subject of the Paris drains; and to this day I can never smell drains without having a nostalgia for Paris, where this smell mingles with that of French tobacco and garlic to make the essential odour of the city.) But Germany fared no better than France, as we may observe in the treatment there of that same mighty pestilence which reached London about this time, not in its first, but certainly in its most memorable visitation.

Agreeable News of Moscow.—It is astonishing to learn from the *Cambridge Modern History* that in the year 1706 Peter the Great appointed *Sanitary Inspectors* in Moscow, *one for every ten houses,* and that in the same year the first modern hospital was built by the River Yanza, with a medical training school. This is strange news indeed, for I know of only two opinions regarding Russia: the present Russian and Communist opinion that civilisation began in the year 1917, and the opinion of most Englishmen and Americans, that Russians were blackguards until the year 1941, when they changed their morals, manners and habits in a single night, like Paul on the road to Damascus, becoming reconciled to the persecuted apostles of Threadneedle Street. Well, it seems we were all wrong, and the Russians had a few virtues before Mr. Pollitt found that they had changed their spots or My Lord Beaverbrook woke up to discover they had changed their skins.

A dissertation on the Use of Vapour Baths.—That intrepid traveller Dr. Clarke tells in his book of *Travels in Russia, Tartary and Turkey,* which was published in this country in the year 1810, of the baths which he found in Russia. These baths he described as being usually filled with vermin, and he observed that nothing could be more filthy and disgusting than one of these places. Nevertheless he remarks of their neglect in England at that time that eminent physicians had endeavoured to draw the attention of the English Government to the importance of public baths, and of countenancing their use by every aid of example and encouragement. For, says he, while we wonder at their prevalence among all the eastern and northern nations, may we not lament that they are so little used in our own country? We might, perhaps, find reason to allow that erysipelas, surfeit, rheumatism, colds and a hundred other evils, particularly all sorts of cutaneous and nervous disorders, might be alleviated, if not prevented, by a proper attention to bathing. He claims that the inhabitants of countries in which the bath is constantly used anxiously seek it in full confidence of getting rid of all such complaints, and that they are rarely disappointed.

I may add (continues Dr. Clarke) my testimony to others. I hardly know any act of benevolence more essential to the comfort of the community than that of establishing, by public benefaction, the use of baths for the poor in all our cities and manufacturing towns. The lives of many might be saved by them. In England they are considered only as articles of luxury; yet throughout the vast empire of Russia, through all Finland, Lapland, Sweden and Norway, there is no cottage so poor, no hut so destitute, but it possesses its vapour bath, in which all its inhabitants, every Saturday at least, and every day in case of sickness, experience comfort and salubrity. Dr. Clarke then recalls that Lady Mary Wortley Montagu, in spite of all the prejudices which prevailed in England against inoculation, introduced it from Turkey; and he suggests that if another person of equal influence would endeavour to establish throughout Great Britain the use of warm and vapour baths, the inconveniences of our climate would be done away.

Perhaps, the learned doctor concludes, at some future period they may become general; and statues may perpetuate the memory of the patriot, the statesman or the sovereign to whom society will be indebted for their institution.

But he adds that when we are told that the illustrious Bacon lamented in vain the disuse of baths among the Europeans, we have little reason to indulge the expectation. In this matter Dr. Clarke did not consider the Russians to be Europeans, for, says he, the universal custom of the bath may be mentioned as an example of the resemblance between Muscovites and more oriental people.

Discovery that the Irish were once accustomed to bathe. —Of the jakes in use among these Muscovites Dr. Clarke says nothing, though I fear they were no better than those we shall describe later, the post-revolutionary privies of present-day Russia. But as to these vapour baths and their use by the Russian peasants, I have read that in the Crimean War British soldiers were known to open the raiment of their fallen foes and admire the whiteness of their skins. Also we know that in the country of Finland it was, and still is, the habit of the people to follow a vapour bath with a bath in the snow, by which they shew their understanding of important principles. And of the Irish we learn that the bath was in use among them until the nineteenth century at least as a therapeutic measure, for the *Encyclopedia of Religion and Ethics,* in an article on *Disease and Medicine* among the Celts, speaks of the use of the *Sweat House* by the Irish as a cure for the rheumatism. These *sweat*-houses (they say) were commonly shaped in the manner of bee-hives, covered with clay and having a low entrance. They were heated by the burning of turfs, like a brick oven; and the patient, having been cooked for a sufficient time, would on his emergence cool his body and seal the pores of his skin by plunging in a pool or stream.

Gibbon appeared to ascribe the Decline and Fall of Rome to the Decadence of her Emperors in that they frequented Baths.—The observations of Dr. Clarke and of other authors shew that the upper ranks of society among the English were not unaware of the value attached by others to the use of the bath, and this was particularly the case among scholars in an age when the classics and classical history received so much more attention than they do today. But what says Gibbon, who refers with sufficient frequency to the baths in use among the Ancient Romans? You will observe that he can scarcely mention them without appearing to read the Decline and Fall in every bather. Follow but his pages faithfully, and you will find his mind has divided the Emperors into two categories: those who bathed habitually to the detriment of the Empire, and those Good Emperors of whom he does not recall that they ever washed themselves in any particular. Truly, Seneca had here a worthy disciple.

The English learn Cleanliness from the Hindus.—Baths were indeed in those days of such a rarity and almost a scandal that when the Lord Mayor of London, as late as the year 1812, asked for a shower bath, he was refused by the Common Council upon the excuse that previous Lord Mayors had done without. Public bathing was known, however, as we may learn from an illustration to *Tittle-Tattle,* a seventeenth-century pamphlet, shewing that such establishments existed in the time of James I (who set an ill example in all such matters). But in general bathing was believed to be a cause of numerous ailments, such as rheumatism; and those who began to bathe themselves daily were threatened with the most fatal results. The Duke of Wellington, having learnt from the Hindus (like others who had been to India) the habit of daily bathing, was considered in this respect a fanatic; and it was long before successive generations of civil and military officers who had acquired in India the practice of bodily cleanliness established it as a custom among the upper classes of English society. As yet they deserved the title of *The Great Unwashed* which their descendants were to confer in ridicule upon the poor; and deserved it better than those for whom the

name was invented, because they were *de facto* both great
and dirty. The habit of the bath, when it eventually began
to spread among our islanders, supposed for the most part
the use of cold water for a display of courage, rather than of
hot water for the purpose of hygiene, the use of hot water
being generally regarded as effeminate in an early Victorian bath.

*The Thames as a Cesspool and Source of London's
Water.*—We need mention but briefly the public works
which improved sanitary conditions toward the end of the
eighteenth century, when a beginning was made with
better paving in the streets, by their widening and the improvement of sewers, by an improved supply of water, the
rebuilding of ancient houses and the increase of light and
air. And in the nineteenth century there followed the re-
placement of water mains made of wood by those of iron,
with pipes to bring water into every house newly constructed. Yet, in spite of such improvements, we find that
baths were still so rare that none was to be found in Buckingham Palace at the time of Victoria's accession, whilst
London sewage continued to be gathered into household
cesses or was diverted into the Thames, which became itself a stinking cesspool. And since the City of London still
drew from this cesspool the main supply of its water, we
may leave the reader to his own reflections as to the result.
In Bradford sewers did not exist in the year 1844, while
regulations enforced in Liverpool forbade the communica-
tion of house drains with the sewerage system. In Exeter
whatever filth did not stay to fester in cesspools collected
in the streets, where (in accordance with the custom of
the time) the paving was *pitched* to create a kennel, or
gutter, in the centre. And the refuse that was to be found
there was gathered by contractors, who paid £63 in annual
rent for the soil thus obtained, looking to the business as a
matter only of commerce and never removing any filth

until the quantity was sufficient to remunerate them with profit for the cost of labour employed.

Such was the condition of Exeter in the year 1832, when Asiatic cholera arrived in the city, resulting in a tardy decision to improve the water supply and to lay down thirteen miles of sewers, with other measures of a sanitary character. Of Bristol at this time we read that 1300 out of 3000 houses had still no water; of Leeds, that whole streets floated with sewage.

Of Sanitation in the Political Battlefield.—Radical opinion, even at that very hour of history forcing the Reform Bill through a resentful Upper Chamber, was not neglectful of such social evils. A broadside that bears the imprint of J. W. Peel, Printer, of 9, New Cut, Lambeth, asks peremptorily, Has DEATH (in a rage) been invited by the Commissioners of Common Sewers to take up his abode in Lambeth? Or from what other villainous cause proceeds the frightful Mortality by which we are surrounded?

In this Pest-House of the Metropolis (reads the broadside) and disgrace to the Nation, the main thoroughfares are still without Common Sewers, although the Inhabitants have paid exorbitant Rates from time immemorial!!!

> *Oh, Heaven! that such companions thou'dst unfold.*
> *And put in every honest hand, a whip,*
> *To lash the rascals naked through the world.*

The writer concludes that unless something be speedily done to allay the growing discontent of the people, retributive justice in her salutary vengeance will commence her operations with the *Lamp-Iron* and the *Halter*. This declaration of popular resentment at the neglect of public health is signed *Salus Populi* and bears the heroic date of 1832.

A Country Town decides that Health is not necessary.—

Of the complacency of rural authorities we may take as an example the history of Beaminster, a small town in the county of Dorset. From the *History of Beaminster,* written by one Richard Hine and published in the year 1914, we may learn of various pestilences, such as the Plague in the seventeenth century and in the year 1791, a *Putrid Fever,* of the smallpox and the precaution of inoculation. But in spite of such scourges and the recommendation by the Board of Guardians (*an.* 1854) that a Board of Health should be set up in the parish, we read that a resolution was *carried unanimously* by the Vestry Meeting to this effect, *that there is no necessity for the establishment of a Board of Health in this parish.* And though in the year 1866 such a Board was eventually established, and from the year 1885 attention was paid to remedy a defective water supply, the local Chronicles could still record in the year 1914 that the sanitary condition of the town *has for many years been under consideration* by the authorities, and various schemes for dealing with the sewage and drainage—*which from time immemorial has flowed untreated into the River Brit*—have been suggested. Suggestions they long remained; while the crude sewage flowed on through Bridport to the sea, polluting the stream and wasting the food of the soil; but we are anticipating.

As to the provision made for soldiers, until the year 1827 their sanitary arrangements were so foul that John Fortescue, in his chapter concerning the Army, which will be found in *Early Victorian England* (edited by Mr. G. M. Young), says *it is literally impossible to set down the disgusting details,* and I would not like to be thought less sensitive to decency. Indeed, as late as the Crimean War there was little improvement to boast of. Is it not common knowledge that only the labours of Miss Nightingale and of a Sanitary Commission sent to the scene of war saved a British army that had survived Cossacks and cannons, the venality of army contractors and the unexampled stupidity of its own officers, but nearly became a victim of plain filth?

Some Evidence of Improvement.—Dr. Charles Singer, in his *Short History of Medicine,* nevertheless contends that the standard of health in this country actually improved in the towns during the eighteenth century, and his figures are not easily to be explained except upon this assumption. If that be so, I can only suppose that there must have been more care given to drains, privies and the like than would appear from the records; for with the rise of new industries and the growing congestion of the cities there must otherwise have been the most hideous results. But the rate of death falls after the year 1730 (though London reached its highest figure for the century ten years later) and there are other small signs of sanitary progress.

Observations on Water-closets, Chimneys and Bells.—By the year 1814 the water-closet must at least have been reasonably common, for in this year a certain Mr. John Phair published his *Observations on the Principles and Construction of Water Closets, Chimneys and Bell Hanging.* A strange medley, indeed; but Mr. Phair had discovered that the bell-hanger looked after the perpendicular track of the soil pipe of a water-closet to convey his wires to the under-part of the house. He describes water-closets that must surely have been neat and elegant in appearance, however much they neglected the sordid principles of sanitation. For lack of a proper sewerage system, they commonly disgorged their contents into pits; and of one such this writer tells us, with a privy set over the pit, to be used by the servants of the household. And such was the state of this pit that two workmen (who had opened the flags and sought to examine the shaft with a naked light) were met with an explosion of sewer gas which split a bucket and stunned them both. Indeed, they narrowly escaped death.

Medicine was still neglected at Oxford and Cambridge, described as *the conservatories of the ignorance of the inland peasant;* and it was not from these seats of learning that science was to arise in answer to the challenge of disease, but in the new and growing towns, where the dread of plague and pestilence was best known. Already two ancient cities, Hull, in the darkness of the Middle Ages, and Plymouth (as we have seen), had, it is true, procured themselves supplies of pure water from a distance. But the modern town of Liverpool, a horrible wen newly grown to a population of 50,000 persons, possessed but a few poor wells; and as late as 1844 the Liverpudlians fetched their water in carts to the town, the poor being reduced to beg or steal such water as they used at the risk of savage penalties. Small wonder, then, that the state of this place and of other towns in Lancashire became such a scandal to their inhabitants that from Liverpool and Manchester there began the movement for Sanitary Reform; and the *Manchester Board of Health,* as a private association termed itself, became the forerunner of national improvement.

Efficacy of Cholera as a Sanitary Inspector.—Mr. Gilbert Slater (from whose work on *The Growth of Modern England* I gleaned some of my knowledge) remarks that such pioneers as manned the Manchester Board of Health were not numerous, and that even where they were active their efforts were not equal to the struggle; for industries soon began to grow like mushrooms and industrial towns like toadstools. Typhus thrived in their contaminated water and the condition of the people was but little improved in matters of sewage, drainage and the removal of refuse from the courts, where commonly it was left to stink. Indeed it was not until we were smitten by the cholera (a dreaded plague, observes Mr. Slater, but a most helpful and valuable *sanitary inspector*) that public attention was forced to the true cause of such scourges. This plague was visited upon us in the years 1831 and 1832, and among the results may be counted the *General Report on the Sanitary Condition of the Labouring Classes of Great Britain,* by Edwin Chadwick, in 1842.

An Epitome of the Victorian Age.—Here, then, we will pause, having now taken leave of powder and perfume, and standing upon the very threshold of *Reform*. Before us (like some widening road that gathers the straggling lanes of the countryside together, and sweeps their traffic into its growing caravan, hurrying towards the city) the Great Age of Victoria leads on to unseen doom. And, like prophets wise after the event, here we will apostrophise the rising class that shall rule this land, telling them of baths and closets about to appear in the drab houses that are now to be built. You, the future men and women of an era that will dazzle itself with its own splendour, conscious of greatness, like your Elizabethan ancestors, soberly self-satisfied where they were most bibulously boisterous, yet not without some of their charm; you who will first hear that *cleanliness is next to godliness;* you who will carry Respectability to the cannibal, sending your missionaries forth as prophets of decency and salesmen of Lancashire cotton; you who will breed slums and socialists, new diseases and modern medicine, whose plumbing will rival that of Rome no less than your rapacity; what do you know of the nemesis awaiting your descendants, when the science you will bequeath to them has grown to giant stature, and the dark, secret god of force and fraud by whose power you lived has begotten his bastards?

Their Epitaph shall be that they attended to Plumbing.
—They cannot hear us; not because they are dead, but because we are not born. They know nothing of the Ter-

ror by Night and the Thing that is being born in the womb of civilisation. They are proud, and for one thing at least we will share their pride; *they learnt, however slowly, that true greatness does not disdain unsavoury detail.* For all their crimes and all their blunders, the greedy policies for which we pay in blood today, let us then praise them for this; *they attended to plumbing.* It is the kindliest epitaph on the Victorians and without loss to truth. But before we proceed further with the burial service they shall live again for us in our next chapter.

CAPUT VII

Of the Struggle for Cleanliness and the Conversion of the Aristocracy

Reprehensible Behaviour of Lord Byron.—My Lord Byron, as I have read, was barred from Long's Hotel in Bond Street as a result of a very regrettable incident which would no doubt be thought more to his shame now than it was in his own time. My authority is that young man whose knowledge of London's *necessaria* flows so instructively through the pages of *For Your Convenience,* a work to which I hope to refer again in good time. His explanation, as he phrases it, is that *on a cold wet night Lord Byron deemed the hall to be a less inclement place than an uncovered yard.* That this would not have been considered culpable in many other places or in earlier times my authority considers to be well established in the writings of Ned Ward, Dean Swift, Smollett and Gay. But the ban of the hotel must surely be accepted as evidence of *progress;* and as this chapter is largely concerned with the progressive abolition of such Byronic behaviour, I begin thus upon a note of hope.

New Water-closets at Windsor.—Once more a British queen sets an example neglected by so many of our kings. In the reign of Victoria bathrooms are installed at Buckingham Palace. As to privies, I have no notion of the fate that befell the flushed closet of Queen Anne at Windsor, but Albert the Good persuaded his wife and sovereign (to whom retrograde Hanoverians had bequeathed nothing better than *commodes*) to allow the introduction of the most modern type of water-closet then known, with a system of drainage, into Windsor Castle. For which alone Albert surely deserved his title, since the persuasion was no easy matter, Victoria being convinced that in such a system the inside of the pipes must become foul.

In the previous century it was necessary for Bishop Butler to defend the institution of hospitals against those godly persons who believed that the sick should suffer the Will of God in patience. We· shall expect opposition now to plumbing, and (as you shall see) it was not lacking; but the plumbing will proceed throughout the Victorian era in spite of every conspiracy to prevent it.

Let the name of Edwin Chadwick now be remembered, a most worthy gentleman and (in his own Victorian fashion) an apostolic successor of Sir John, carrying into the realm of politics and the administrative battlefield the brave escutcheon of Ajax. This was the man who had such faith in sanitation that he believed the medical profession not likely to last; and of him it was said by Sir William Collins that he looked to a day when doctors would be unable to live, yet perhaps unable to die.

Divers Commissions on Filth.—Yet another of these Great Victorians was Dr. Southwood Smith who, in the first years of the queen's reign, busied himself in collecting information regarding the sanitary conditions of the metropolis. His findings were published in a report, supplementary to that of the Poor Law Enquiry Commission (on which he served), shewing the filthy, close and crowded state of houses in the quarters of the poor. The better to arouse the consciences of officials and medical practitioners, Dr. Smith informed them of the poisonous conditions which he found, from the total want of drainage and the masses of putrefying matter of all sorts which were allowed to remain and accumulate indefinitely, and such (he said) are these conditions that during the last year, in several parishes, both relieving officers and medical men lost their lives.

It was this report which, in great measure, inspired that of Edwin Chadwick, to which we have made reference in the previous chapter. Chadwick was a man so essentially reasonable (they are to be found in every age) that his conceptions, accepted as self-evident in a later generation, ensured him the reputation of a *fanatic* in his own. He was born into an age when corruption was considered so normal that it is perhaps relevant to recall an anecdote with which Sir William Collins illustrates this notorious fact, in a brief monograph on *The Life and Doctrine of Sir Edwin Chadwick*. A fellow minister having told Lord Melbourne that he had to choose between two candidates for a valuable office, admitted that one of the two was a relative of his own and that, *ceteris paribus,* he proposed to give the post to his relative. So should I, replied His Lordship, and damn *ceteris paribus.*

Edwin Chadwick and his Sanitary Idea—He offends The Times *and Big Business.*—To such an attitude Chadwick opposed the principle of competitive examination, always the terror of a venal and incompetent aristocracy, fighting all his life against the system of political patronage that clogged the machinery of reform. But above all other things he fought for what he termed *The Sanitary Idea,* the consciousness among the public and among officials and administrators of the need for cleanliness and for devising the means to achieve it. Among practical achievements he secured the adoption of glazed earthenware drains for domestic and public use, to replace those of stone or brick, and for the manufacture of such drains a factory was established at Lambeth by Henry Doulton in the year 1846. But

Edwin Chadwick, for the sake of hygiene and cleanliness, made more enemies than any man in his time, which is a good measure of a man's worth in a corrupt society; and the more so if we consider that these enemies included *The Times* and Hudson, the first railway magnate. But this man Chadwick, who was taunted with despotism and dictatorial behaviour, understood better than all his enemies the catch phrases which they employed in their attempts to destroy him. *Liberty,* he said, *consists of the power of doing anything that does not hurt another.*

His Opinion of Politicians.—The work of Edwin Chadwick was principally concerned with the life of the poor, his object being to establish sanitary conditions in which, as he believed, disease would become impossible. For he observed that the ordinary epidemics occurred in the greatest proportion in common conditions of foul air, from stagnant putrefaction, from bad house drainage, from sewers of deposit, from excrement-sodden sites, from filthy street surfaces, from impure water and from overcrowding in private houses and in public institutions. And as to our *statesmen,* it was his open opinion that *he knew of no investigation which did not reverse almost every main principle on which parliamentary committees and politicians of high position were prepared to base legislation.*

Sanitation opposed by Commercial Enterprise.—But even the benches of Westminster were rocked a little by the report of Dr. Southwood Smith, and the Commissioners who had reported on the state of London were instructed to extend their researches throughout England and Wales, of which researches Chadwick's report in 1842 was the fruit. What Dr. Smith had said of London, Chadwick shewed to be true of the whole country, and he indicted filth as the murderer of more persons than any war of those times. He exposed also the insufficiency and defects in the water supply, and the great need for drainage.

That little enough was done at first, and that sufficiently slowly, to meet the demands of Chadwick and the Commissioners, scarcely needs to be said. But a further Commission, and this a Royal one, went yet further into the matter and the General Board of Health was born of its travail. With Chadwick on the Board you may be sure it was not lacking in energy; but against it was ranged that *commercial enterprise* (I use the delicate euphemism of Sir John Simon, who must not be confused with a certain Lord now living) which sought to preserve private interests. *Commercial enterprise* included numerous water companies whose supplies to the public the Board condemned as insufficient, impure and intermittent. Lord Ashley, known to history by his later title of Shaftesbury, was on this Board and must be considered among the early Sanitarians, the Sanitary Fathers, and as an embodiment of the return of godliness to cleanliness, for he was an advocate of both.

Which conspires successfully against Chadwick.—Appointed but for five years, a poor probationer, the Board in its zeal for cleanliness landed itself, rather than others, in hot water. To confuse the metaphor, we might add that the Government was but lukewarm in its support. Lord John Russell had become Prime Minister, and appears to have held that all human progress ended in the Reform Act of 1832. Himself the reputed inventor of a mahogany bath (it was seven feet by four, lined with sheet lead, and weighed near a ton—Victorian in every detail), Lord John was, however, no Knight of the Bath, ready to risk a fall for cleanliness' sake. He took the view that Chadwick had not *observed the most conciliatory tone possible* towards what Lord Palmerston described as the fair and legitimate interests of many very intelligent and very active men. Or, in plainer language, that Chadwick had no time for sharks; for which reason he was retired on a pension. The Board itself was with difficulty and a little subterfuge preserved from extinction at the hands of the Parliamentary representatives of *Commercial Enterprise.*

As to technical progress, during the nineteenth century many improved valve closets were devised, notably those of Stevens Hellyer and Henry Doulton, these being followed in the course of evolution by the wash-out, washdown and syphonic types. But use did not keep pace with invention; for just as a new machine of war, once it is invented, will be quickly imitated and copied in great quantities, so a mere device for cleanliness and health is held in contempt among us and the inventor may count upon neglect as the reward of his pains. Then with regard to drains, these long continued to be made of stone or porous brick, while many were open sewers when Chadwick and Smith wrote their reports. Through such sewers the Queen's apartments at Buckingham Palace were ventilated.

Of Victorian Baths.—In the matter of baths there was, for a while, almost as little improvement to speak of. The Victorians commonly used the hip bath (when they used any at all) which was of iron and enamelled. And this they filled with cans of heated water from their basement kitchens; from which I conjecture that (except for those whose wealth could employ servants for the carrying) cleanliness was *next to impossible,* as the saying is. Nevertheless one Victorian inventor made a bath of cast iron with gas burners beneath it, so that one sat in it like a pudding in the pot, in peril of being boiled alive. But if there remained many who lacked the means of cleanliness, they were not utterly forgotten, as witness the considerate provision, by the Duke of Argyll, of posts with nails in them, for the use of private soldiers of the British Army in India. From which it became the custom of these men to say, as they rubbed their infested backs against these posts, *God bless the Duke of Argyll.*

Of Human Inertia.—And so, while scientific knowledge strode forward to an unknown destiny of destructive perfection, social evolution lagged and limped, the poor relation of Victorian Progress. Medicine, it is true, had at last emerged from centuries of superstition, from the doves' dung and powdered shoes of the Babylonians, from the skinned mice of the Egyptian papyri, from the dung beetles of the Byzantines and the horrid remedies in use against the Plague. The *London Pharmacopoeia* no longer prescribed the sexual organs and excreta of animals, human perspiration or the saliva of a fasting man, as Dr. Fielding Garrison tells us concerning the seventeenth-century edition of this work, in his *History of Medicine.* But while medicine now follows the path of scientific experiment and discovery there is no Imhotep, no Moses or Mohamet to write the new Commandments in the language of authority. The Prophet of Israel had his miracles and the Prophet of Islam his sword, but the prophets of scientific revelation have only the sword of reason and the slow miracles that are shewn in graphs and statistics, after years of infinite patience, to justify their inconspicuous labours.

A most fortunate Stink at the Westminster Gas Works.—Consider next the water supply. Though much was done to amend it, Sir John Simon could write in his book *English Sanitary Institutions,* as late as the year 1889, that even the London water supply, after half a century of disgusting disclosures, and after various very terrible disasters, *was not yet secured against gross defilement;* a fact which he said was proved by official reports and was in other ways deplorably notorious. For my part I do not doubt that there would have been little improvement or none at all, had not our legislators suffered upon occasion the consequences of their own criminal apathy. For in the year 1855 Sir Benjamin Hall (immortalised in *Big Ben* among a generation that no longer remembers the origin of this name) found a certain measure designed for the health of the people of London obstructed by the obstinacy of his fellow-members of Parliament. But the condition of the Thames in the summer of that year became so foul that it was impossible to use the committee rooms upon the river side of the House, in consequence of which the opposition was withdrawn and the sanitarians were permitted to have their way, since it was pointed out that only by the necessary powers being granted could the matter be dealt with and these committee rooms rendered habitable once more. O for a magic carpet of infinite dimensions that could transport all the leaking drains and condemned closets from all the slums of the Empire and heap them in Downing Street in such another object lesson to our rulers and governors!

But do not imagine that indifference or stupidity began or ended in these quarters. Proud of his conservatism and even of his dull wits, the Englishman has chosen as his national emblem the gross and repulsive figure of *John Bull,* not uncommonly accompanied by his *Bull-dog,* a scowling, ferocious, snuffling, growling, insensitive and ugly creature, which only a nation devoid of imagination and wit would allow to be the true picture of itself. Let us admit the fact with a proper humility and cease to boast of it as a national accomplishment; *we have the thickest pates in Europe.* And when it was a question of purifying our potable water do you not suppose that our grandfathers argued that it had been good enough for *their* grandfathers? Or that the old woman in the Fens spoke for many besides herself when she asked of the new and pure supply: *Call ye that water?* For she said, *it has neither taste nor smell.*

Lord Shaftesbury describes the Enemies of Sanitation. —The indifference of authority towards the health of the

nation did not fail to arouse the indignation of those who
had appointed themselves keepers of the national conscience in sanitary affairs. In the diary of Lord Shaftesbury
there are many references to the opposition of *the whole
tribe of jobbers who live on the miseries of mankind,* as he
described the opponents of reform. He was sick, he wrote,
to see how little the years of labour had accomplished, and
grieved to learn that *not only nothing is done by the Government, but that the ministers will take good care that
nothing shall be done by anyone else.* And of the intention
to destroy the Board of Health he wrote that its sin was its
unpardonable activity. Also he enumerates the enemies of
the Board: the College of Physicians, because they had
maintained and proved that many a Poor Law medical
officer knew more than all the flash and fashionable doctors of London; the Boards of Guardians, whose selfishness and cruelty had been exposed; the Treasury, whose
subalterns hated Edwin Chadwick; and the Commissioners of Sewers, who hated the Board *with a perfect hatred*
because it had plans which were the contrary to their own.
Cholera alone brought improvement, where reason and
justice had failed; and the appointment of that Dr. Simon
to whom we have already referred (for he was later
knighted) to be medical adviser to the Privy Council, was
the manner in which the Government admitted a tardy
conversion to the principles of public hygiene.

A Defence of Filth because it provided Employment.—
Lest it should be imagined that the arguments with which
(in other matters) we are familiar are in any way new, we
may observe that Edwin Chadwick recorded the views of
certain parish officers opposed to his proposals for improvement in these words. He said that they considered it
*expedient to keep the streets in their present state of filth
in order to keep up the means of employing indigent persons as street sweepers and sweepers of crossings in re-*

moving it. And those who have experienced the cogency of such arguments will best appreciate the opposition to Edwin Chadwick, the neglect and rancour from which he suffered for the great part of his life, also the reason why the honour of knighthood did not overtake him until he was within a year of his death, at the age of ninety.

Conversion of the Quarterly Review.—Dr. Simon, who wore the mantle of Chadwick with a greater public success, reaping where Chadwick had sown, first distinguished himself as Medical Officer of Health for the City; and his *Report on the Sanitary Condition of the City of London* for the years 1848 to 1849 is among the historic documents to be considered in our study. For this report so moved the Olympian editor of the *Quarterly Review* that in September of 1850 its pages were for the most part devoted to matters of health and sanitation, to the denunciation of private·monopolies in the supply of water and·of impurity in that supply, to the dearness of water, the lack of it in the poorer quarters, the combination of private interests against the public. And of the Thames they said in this journal that it was still foul with guano, stable dung, rotten sprats and the discharge of all the London sewers.

New forces of publicity began, indeed, to be enlisted in the cause of cleanliness about this time; and we may trace our slow progress from the growth of a group of writers prepared to break a quill upon the matter. One such, in a later number of the *Quarterly Review,* in these words castigates the corruption of Smithfield. Like another Troy, he says, this citadel of filth has stood a ten years' siege; and its sturdy garrison, led by their chieftains in Common Council, the Hectors and Memnons of intramural muck, so far from thinking of surrender are engaged at this moment in fortifying their defences. But the Defenders of Filth, says this writer, have ruled London long enough.

Great Antiquity and Respectability of Vested Interests in Dirt.—Dr. Stella Churchill, in her account of *Health Services and the Public,* has a whole chapter on the private interests that have throughout our history opposed themselves to public health. For even as early as 1343 there was an attempt on the part of the persons living in the streets which led down to the Thames to close these streets and exact a toll from all who fetched water from the river. But the point needs not to be laboured; for it is surely understood that in this matter as in all things, where a reform is proposed in the public interest, men will divide for the most part into two groups: those who are opposed to the reform because they fear to lose money by it, and those who (like Drake in the matter of the Plymouth Water Supply) support it because they hope to profit thereby. Was not our patron saint, St. George of Cappadocia, a profiteer?

Of Paris under the Second Empire.—It must not be thought that the picture we have provided of English nastiness was less true of the continent of Europe. Indeed there is little doubt that in the past century, because our industries were more advanced, our towns more congested, our need for this cause being the greater, more progress was made in Britain (under the threat of loathsome diseases) than in other countries of Europe. Hence we find that the worst squalor was accompanied by the most vigorous efforts at reform, which, making some slow progress against the phalanx of *vested interest in dirt,* placed England unwillingly in the very van of the sanitary offensive. It is even recorded of Chadwick that, being asked by the lesser Napoleon what he thought of Paris, he replied in these words: Sire, they say that Augustus found Rome a city of brick and left it a city of marble. If your Majesty, finding Paris fair above, will leave it sweet below, you will more than rival the first Emperor of Rome.

But others have it that his reply was more epigrammatic, and that he described Paris under the Second Empire as *fair above, Sire, and foul below*.

The true Story of Minnehaha.—As to Germany, the progress of that country in the present century need not be permitted to conceal the fact that in the last the Germans were as dirty as any, though the story that Goethe bathed but once in twelve months has been discredited. Even in the United States of America, that land of progress and promise, the use of water-closets spread very slowly, for we read that among the first to install such a system was the poet Longfellow, in the year 1840. We may well suppose that some such project was in his mind when he wrote that stirring ballad, *Excelsior,* and certainly some thought of it must have inspired that line in *The Goblet of Life,* where he says

The prayer of Ajax was for light.

Mr. Stanley Walker writes, in his book *Mrs. Astor's Horse,* that the instalment of this water-closet in the house of Henry Wadsworth *gave a tremendous impetus to the new scheme;* but thirty years later, he says, a distinguished American died a victim of a closet that was not properly drained, which was still considered by some the act of *an inscrutable and mysterious Providence.* As to baths, I believe Benjamin Franklin sponsored the tub in America in about 1770, and bathing spread slowly enough.

Discovery that Sanitation pays Dividends.—The labours of such philanthropists as Chadwick were not (as we have already hinted) without support from others whose enlightenment originated in different considerations. Thus Captain Douglas Galton, in a speech from the Chair at a *Conference on Sanitary Subjects* (on the occasion of the International Health Exhibition in June of 1884), made these observations. He said that a house for the farm labourer was as much an appendage of the farm as a stable; that good stables were built for horses, and if the land were to be cultivated in a proper manner good houses ought to be built for labourers, so that they might be healthy and be able to do their work properly. And even in cities, he said, he was not sure that it would not be desirable for manufacturers to build houses for their workmen, as had been done at Mulhouse, and in various parts of the Continent, where the workman was made *almost an integral part of the factory.*

Nematoid Worms in the Lord Mayor's Drinking Water. —Moreover, once the initial stupidity and conservatism of the upper classes had been sufficiently disturbed by disease, a dread arose among them that diseases engendered among their helots might spread to themselves, or as Arnold Sorsby has it in *Medicine and Mankind,* Dives feared for himself rather than felt for Lazarus. Also in such matters as the water supply it became apparent that private interest in the shape of my lord's health could only be pursued through attention to public interest in the proper supervision of a pure supply to the generality. This must have been tolerably plain to that Lord Mayor of whom Mr. Lewis Angel spoke at a *Conference on the Promotion of Social Science* (in London, *an.* 1884). For he said that it was not long since there was found, in the cisterns at the Mansion House, three-quarters of an inch of fungi scrub floating on the surface and three-eighths of an inch of mud at the bottom, while a bottle of water on his lordship's table was found to contain nematoid worms by the hundred. And such things he said also of the Athenaeum Club, enough to put the fear of God even into a bishop.

A Bishop also among the Prophets.—This makes relevant the contribution of religion to the general problem of health at this time. We have referred in previous chapters of this book to an attitude, not unknown in the nineteenth century, which, having interpreted infectious maladies to be the will of God, deemed all efforts to abolish the sources of infection to be a form of impiety. Such an attitude was less common among the clergy than that of indifference, the spiritual leaders of the people waiting (like the Golden Calf) to be dragged forward by their followers. Nevertheless a few honourable names among the religious leaders of the nineteenth century may be mentioned as those of *eminent sanitarians;* and of these the evangelical Earl of Shaftesbury and that lusty Protestant, Charles Kingsley, deserve first consideration. Dr. Blomfield (as Bishop of London), under the inspiration of Chadwick, played a leading part in the House of Lords, where he put on the whole armour of the faith in defence of the principles of bodily health. The Radicals were, upon the whole, supporters of sanitary reform; and from this we may assume a good body of Dissenters to have been in the ranks. But I am as yet uncertain whether to include with these Mr. Spurgeon's housemaid; for she, being converted, and having been pressed to shew with what works she proved her faith, replied that, whereas she had formerly swept all dust under the mats of hearthrugs, she now removed it entirely from the rooms.

Indifference of the Learned.—Support was often least available where most might have been hoped for, among the learned, whose studies, as in the Middle Ages, did little to profit humanity. Of an earlier century there is the familiar story that Samuel Johnson met a lady's accusation (it was true enough) that he *smelt* by observing *You smell, I stink.* The Doctor was concerned with the correct use of language but unmoved by the imputation of bodily dirtiness. In the century of which we now speak the universities of Oxford and Cambridge maintained the same academic detachment and remained mediaeval to the last insanitary detail, Minerva sitting upon a cesspool. And of a famous college at Cambridge it is recorded that the Master exercised his veto to prevent the construction of baths for the students, remarking that *these young men are with us only for eight weeks at a time.*

That the great industrial towns which were forced by the circumstances into the vanguard were not, however, always aware of their responsibilities is shewn in a tale concerning Lord Palmerston and the city of Glasgow, which will be found in *The Preparation of Peace,* by Mr. Laurence Housman.

Some eighty or ninety years ago (writes Mr. Housman) a terrible epidemic visited the city of Glasgow. And the city fathers of Glasgow invited the Prime Minister to ordain, by Order in Council, a day of national humiliation and prayer, so that the plague might be stayed. Lord Palmerston very sensibly replied that if they would practise humility at home *by looking to their drains,* it would be very much better and more effective than imposing humiliation upon others. Of this excellent advice, Mr. Housman says that he has no doubt that a great many pious people were shocked by it; and he considers (this present blood-bath notwithstanding) that we are today a more godly people than *that adulterous mid-Victorian generation which wanted signs and wonders, and the uncovenanted mercies of God, to take the place of sanitation.*

Virtues and Vices of the Victorians.—Well, Mr. Housman calls himself a Victorian and has a better right than I have to be harsh at their expense. But for my part I am inclined to thank them for such sanitation as we have; for if they moved but slowly and were a stiff-necked generation, nevertheless they moved, and whatever water-closets, drains, baths and other civilised amenities of this kind we enjoy today, I suppose we owe them something for these things. And if ever I curse them it will not be for their shortcomings in plumbing but for their most vaunted achievements, for a growing *prosperity* and a deceptive *peace* that had their roots in land-grabbing and money-power, in coveting their neighbour's vineyard and seizing it by ruses worthy of old Ahab. And I will dare to say that if they had plumbed their own souls and the national diplomacy but half as well as they plumbed their cities, we might be in a better case today; but as it took cholera to arouse them to the need for good drainage, so it may be that only war will bring us to our right senses in certain other matters. Where, then, are the Chadwicks and Shaftesburys of today, the prophets of Social Sanitation and Spiritual Regeneration? For if they are lacking, or being present should speak to deaf ears, ours is a worse crime than that of the Victorians, whom God spared as he did the people of Nineveh, whose sons they so nearly resembled.

The Vastness of their Undertaking.—The labour of creating sanitation, when it was undertaken in earnest, proved to be both vast and formidable. It was not enough to build new houses with a proper sanitary complement, and to provide a water supply adequate in quantity and quality, with an effective system of drainage. Old houses needed to be adapted to the same pattern and hidden sources of corruption lurked like evil spirits in the very bowels of the earth. For a speaker at the Conference on the Promotion of Social Science, in 1884, observes that whenever a person bought, or hired, or inherited or altered a house, he should first of all look for forgotten and hidden cesspools. And speaking of his own experience, he said the number of these forgotten cesses was inconceivable, and that the mischief they were doing was immeasurable. Also he said that there were no more treacherous buildings than those of the generation before his own, when mechanical science had attained a high perfection and chemical investigation had not advanced equally.

Dignity of the Victorian Water-closet.—In the Health Exhibition held at that time many models of water-closets were shewn, of which a most notable example was the *Pedestal Vase* of George Jennings. A likeness of this *Pedestal Vase* is to be found among the illustrations to Mr. Lamb's article in the *Architects' Journal* (March 4th, 1937), to which we have already made reference, and it appears as an elegant and decorated fixture. Of its name Mr. Lamb says that at this period *the W.C. was cloaked with a certain amount of dignity,* and he reminds us of the platforms upon which such thrones were not uncommonly mounted, in a carpeted room. Thus the Victorian sense of *dignity* could find its place even in a closet. This *Pedestal Vase* was beautified with the famous *willow pattern* and its cisterns covered in carved woodwork, whilst another product of the firm had a seat of red mahogany, with a silent flush that functioned discreetly from behind the wall.

It was but recently that My Lord Beaverbrook told us of his visit to the Kremlin, where His Lordship and the British Mission, together with Comrade Stalin and others, contributed to the united war effort by enjoying the *biggest slap-up party* (says Lord B.) *at which I have ever assisted.* And having done their best to help the men at the front by drinking some thirty toasts, including one to the Freedom of the Press, they not unnaturally had need of some relief, which they found in a toilet with fittings by Shanks of Barrhead.

The Works of Mr. Shanks discovered in the Kremlin by a British Mission.—Fortunate indeed are those who sit in the seat of the Czars, however uneasily their heads may lie; for the works of Mr. Shanks which were shewn with such pride to the English Comrades are, alas, all too rare in Russia. Here at least, we may hope, they found uncensored paper, and may have reflected that if the newspapers of Britain and Russia carried as little cargo they would not have drunk in vain to their freedom. But it is of Barrhead and Mr. Shanks that I am thinking, of that original Shanks of whom I learn from *Reynolds News* that sixty years ago he called his workmen around him to inspect his latest model. Then, seeing the unexpected volume of water sweep into the pan, this pioneer seized a cap from the head of a 'prentice boy, stuffed it into the lavatory basin, and as the flood engulfed it cried out, *It works! It works!*

The Closet a Symbol of that Democracy for which we are now fighting.—There was the spirit that animated this technical vanguard, the Pilgrim Fathers of the Privy, whose traffic dwarfed the enterprise of the *Mayflower;* for what fame can compete with theirs, who furnished the Vatican and the Kremlin, the Courts and Chancelleries and Senate Houses of the world, with the comforts of civilisation? The politicians pass, the jakes remain, serving the Just and the Unjust with divine impartiality. Do you imagine the works of that Clydeside firm deal less kindly, less equitably with proletarian sewage than they did with the imperial excrement of the Romanoffs? The name of Barrhead may perchance be remembered by posterity as the native town of James Maxton; but it has a far surer title to fame, which is blazoned upon the most intimate furniture of the people in the most democratic of all health resorts. The common need unites us, the universal considerations are present, whether we go slumming with earnest women to write reports on the privies of the poor, or pause, caught by this same necessity, in search of a public convenience, or visit Buckingham Palace to collect ribbons as public benefactors. Did not Mr. Bertram Hellyer write in all reverence that *in 1897 the temporary sanitary arrangements at the Abbey were placed in our hands on the occasion of Queen Victoria's Diamond Jubilee; and again on the occasion of the Coronation of King Edward VII in 1902 we were so honoured?* Not even the *Daily Express* has produced better proof that *we are a Democracy.*

Concerning the Masterpieces of Henry Doulton.—In the *Sanitary Record* for April 15th, 1890, I find many interesting facts relating to contemporary closets. Thus, in a monograph on the works of Messrs. Doulton, under the general heading *Notable Sanitary Engineers,* there is an account of the newest and best arranged closets made by this firm, hight *Combination* and *Simplicitas,* and it may be that Messrs. Doulton will stand me some of their wares for this free advertisement. Of the former model it is said that the front of the basin is lipped to form a urinal and slop-sink when the seat is raised, and that its water area equals in size the hole in the seat, rendering the chance of soiling the basin very remote. This model, we are told, can be flushed by a seat action, or the usual water-waste preventer, with pull handle. It is made in all kinds of ware, and can be highly decorated when required.

As to the *Simplicitas,* we learn that it is somewhat of the same character, and constructed in one piece of stoneware, also glazed ware, or the more ornamental kinds of Queen's ware. This insistence upon *decoration* shews us how the Victorians, in the importance which they attached to elegance, carried their principles to the bitter end; and an illustration shews us a most ornate closet, garnished with a florid conglomeration of Second Empire and South Kensington Acanthus, twined with vine leaves; a model worthy to be placed beside the Albert Memorial as a monument to an illustrious age. It is also pleasing to read that in 1872 Messrs. Doulton began to employ female labour in general decorative work and that in 1882 a presentation was made to Mr. Henry Doulton to commemorate the ten years of female employment.

Among the exhibits of this same enterprising firm, at

the Paris Exhibition in 1878, was the *Lambeth Improved Latrine,* of which I have seen an excellent likeness in their brochure of that date. And below this picture the script reads that the use of latrines has been acknowledged as the best possible system for schools, asylums, workhouses, barracks, factories, and public buildings of all kinds, *where it is neither safe nor desirable to entrust the control of water or discharge apparatus to those using them.*

Elegance of the American Models.—Some such bygone privies are described by Mr. Stanley Walker in *Mrs. Astor's Horse,* from the catalogue of an American company, one of them (says this writer) very ornate, ivory-tinted with gold pencilling and with a choice of either cherry, antique oak, walnut or ash copper-lined cistern with carved panels, and a seat and back panel to match. I could spend long in the description of such luxurious retreats, but time presses. Herr Hitler is still, I am told, behind his time-table (of which every editor in Fleet Street appears to have a copy), but I fear that at any moment his train may be signalled, and I have even known him to arrive when the Prime Minister had solemnly assured me that he had *missed the bus.* So being on the Reception Committee I have no wish to meet him surrounded by Victorian water-closets. Like our generals and statesmen I must put on all speed to catch up with the twentieth century.

Sanitary Reform held by Lecky to be the greatest Achievement of the Victorian Age.—The Public Health Act of 1875 was introduced by the Prime Minister with the historic words: *Sanitas Sanitatum, omnia sanitas,* and by the year 1888 we find such a new concern for these matters that the *Pall Mall Gazette* threatens the era of *Sanitationists,* who will contract to supply so much public health for every thousand of the population at a yearly charge. The hacks of the press might mock, but the *Sani-*

tationists had their way, and are still (we trust) on the march. Of their efforts Lecky wrote in his study of *Democracy and Liberty* that the great work of sanitary reform had been perhaps the *noblest achievement of our age,* and if measured by the suffering it had diminished, had probably done far more for the real happiness of mankind than all the many questions that make and unmake Ministries. And this he said in the year 1896, but eight years after the jibe of the *Pall Mall Gazette.*

But as to how much remained to be accomplished (and yet remains) a man may see for himself in such of our city slums as Herr Hitler has left standing. In the year 1913 there were still 43,000 houses in the town of Birmingham where no water was to be had within the house, and all must be fetched from without, which (and I speak from some experience) is no encouragement to washing and bathing. And in the country such things were, as they still are, even more commonly to be found; while baths, whether in town or country, are even rarer. As is well known, the philanthropists who built houses for the poor, without providing them with baths, did this because (so they said) the poor would use their baths for storing of coal. And as they purposed to deprive them of the means to purchase the coal, they desired to remove the temptations of envy and covetousness that might be inspired by the sight of an empty bath with no coal to fill it. As to the miners, having no lack of coal, they needed baths the more (and that, unbelievably, for the purposes of cleanliness). But no exception being made in their case, they were reduced to a tub in the kitchen. And in the poorer quarters of London officers of the Government have, in private, confirmed the opinion of Lord Horder that the absence of epidemics in the air-raid shelters (in the present war) is due to the fact that *conditions in these places are less evil than those in the houses of the people,* so that *those only survived to fill the shelters whom a life in the slums had already partially immunised to diseases.*

A Solemn Reminder to the Newly Clean—Their past Indifference to bad Drains.—Let those who boast of their cleanliness now reflect upon the history of the more fortunate classes, considering how new and recent a thing is the cleanliness of the rich, and that cleanliness is nurtured by two things, *opportunity* and *habit.* Baths, with a plentiful supply of cold and heated water, well-appointed closets and some measure of leisurely occasion—these constitute opportunity. Opportunity with education creates habit. And if a man reflect upon the ignorance of those who, having the necessary means, first furnished their houses with water-closets, he will see the relevance of education and offer no scorn to those who lack it. For were not the first water-closets (until nearly 1850) placed nakedly in bedrooms and unventilated places, in substitution for *commodes?* If such was the ignorance of the rich, which habit has now taught them to despise and self-esteem to forget, the ignorance of the poor may be as well understood and added to lack of opportunity in explanation of what are termed *slum conditions.* And this is well known, that a hundred years past drains were not considered as pestiferous or as being causes of disease when they stank; for Lady Georgina Peel, who was the daughter of Lord John Russell, says in her *Recollections,* when speaking of the death of her mother from fever, that *in those old careless days no one thought of bad drains.* But bad drains, she recalls, were considered in the manner of a jest, so that, if they smelt, it was held to be a sign of the approach of bad weather, the omen being altogether mistaken.

Concerning Victorian Earth-closets in unventilated Cupboards and other Forms of Nastiness.—Thus the difference between standards of cleanliness among persons of different rank, where it exists, can be attributed to opportunity; and to habit formed by opportunity with knowledge. And those who live in slums are less to be held responsible for this than Queen Victoria, who was found in the year 1844 to be sitting at Windsor Castle over fifty-three overflowing cesspits. This is recorded in the first volume of the account of *Early Victorian England,* edited by Mr. G. M. Young, where the writer mentions that in the early part of the period earth-closets (the invention of a Victorian vicar, as I learn from another source) were to be found in small rooms, in the houses of the wealthy, as follows from the context, or even, he says, *in a large unventilated cupboard adjacent to the dining-room,* billiard-room, gun-room or, as it was called, the hunting parlour. And here, too (he says), *were kept the articles which gentlemen who drank deep and long might be expected to require.* So here is slum life writ large, and modified only by a host of domestic servants, whose unpleasant labours preserved the rich from the effects of their own filthiness.

Let them further remember—these present Pharisees of Cleanliness—all that has been said of the opposition of their class to those reforms which sought to make decency and hygiene possible in the lives of the poor. Let them recall the ferocity with which Chadwick was opposed, the *Private Enterprise Society,* expressly founded to resist the passage of the Bill of 1848, whereby the Board of Health came into being. Let them read *Two Years Ago* and see in the character of Thomas Thurnall, created by Charles Kingsley, the very picture of the sanitary reformer to whom they owe their present health and cleanliness; and let them reflect that such men fought single-handed the hatred, the meanness, the corruption, the insolence and the ridicule of their great-grandfathers. If they are clean today, it is in spite of themselves, and the dirtiness of others is the very measure of their own greed, apathy and moral turpitude; for it is still true (as Chadwick affirmed in the last century) that *by no prudence on their part can the poor avoid the dreadful evils of their surroundings.*

Cleanliness held to be the Secret of Class Distinctions—Cleanliness is the Reward of Idleness and Dirt the Punishment of Labour.—Even the provision of pit-head baths, in the case of the miners, is not commonly, as might be supposed, an act of *charity* or common decency on the part of those who grow wealthy by the labour of the miners, but where such baths are to be found at all they are commonly provided, or largely provided, out of funds raised by the men themselves. Mr. George Orwell, who recalls this fact, with many others relating to the sanitary provision in the life of the working class, observes that the real secret of class distinctions in the West is summed up in four words which were once common enough, though the mention of this secret among other ranks of society has now become *taboo.* These words are, he says, *the lower classes smell.* Had he considered the origin of *Untouchability* among the Hindus, he would not, perhaps, have written these words of the West alone; for it may be observed that the origin of the caste system, like that of class among the Europeans, is to be found in the fact that we ostracise and despise those who do the most necessary and unpleasant tasks with the least opportunity to keep themselves clean; the provisions of sanitation being always found in greatest profusion where they are least needed, in proportion to means. Thus wealth and cleanliness are the marks of idleness, dirt and poverty being the insignia of labour; for which reason many of the early radicals and socialists made it a point of honour never to appear clean or dressed in clean garments, for they mistook the punishment of honest labour to be its natural badge and reward.

Mr. Orwell's remarks will be found in *The Road to*

Wigan Pier, a book which shows its author to be a good observer but an hasty philosopher, as he has often proved elsewhere. He cites *Mr. Somerset Maugham* as being one of the few who in our time has broken the *taboo* upon this subject and declared plainly that *the matutinal tub divides the classes more effectually than birth, wealth or education.* Such, indeed, is the common impression among Mr. Maugham's class, for the enlightenment of which I have made these observations on their own past and on the present condition of those against whom their contempt is directed.

The Author defends his Controversial Treatment of the Subject.—What now, says one, this is plain *propaganda* in a book that should surely be objective and *impartial.* O sacred shibboleth of hypocrites! I can remember but one *impartial* book that I ever saw, dictionaries and encyclopaedias notwithstanding, and that was the telephone directory, never ranked highly among spirited or entertaining literature. Who then demands this *impartiality?* Those who have most to fear from criticism; as I saw today, being November 11th, and celebrated in honour of those who died to end war. And so there began a discussion that I heard, in which one said that flag-days were a form of public blackmail to make a man give unwillingly for fear of appearing mean. Why unwillingly, said another, if the cause is good? Because, says the first, if I would give you a shilling I know a better way than to give twenty shillings to a broker, who will spend nineteen in administrative charges and hand you the odd. If that be so, then, says one that stood by, why do you wear that in your buttonhole? To which he got the reply (that I thought shrewd but somewhat unmannerly) that he wore it as a prophylactic against being solicited by whores.

The Enemy of the People is the damned compact Majority, as Ibsen shews.—Now at this point in comes your peacemaker, your dispenser of bromides for all controversies, and says *surely we must live at peace with the community into which we were born*. Woman, said I (for I could no more hold my peace), I am now writing a book very largely about lavatories, and am this day completing a chapter on the progress made in the past century. Do you know, have you ever read, of the filthiness of this country one hundred years ago? Do you ever ask yourself, as you walk into a clean bathroom or a well-appointed privy, how such things came to exist? I will tell you, then. They exist because Edwin Chadwick, Lord Shaftesbury, Charles Kingsley and a small band of heroes *fought the community* for half a century with all the forces of filthiness marshalled against them in the name of established customs, *pro bono publico*. They fought the *damned compact majority*, as *The Enemy of the People* termed it (and he fought upon the same issue, as I recollect), with no reward but abuse and ridicule.

Yes, read your Ibsen, now I am put in mind of it, for there is the true picture of the thing as it was then and will be for all time, in the character and crusade of Dr. Stockmann; the struggle of one man against the mass, by which alone the mass learns to take one single step forward. You owe your water-closet to Edwin Chadwick and Dr. Cholera, one persuading and reasoning, the other punishing and threatening; and if your descendants ever thank your generation for anything at all, it will be for a few rebels whom you would pacify with platitudes while others would gladly kick them to pieces.

That being, as I firmly believe, the plain truth about history and any progress we have to boast about, the historian is a miserable liar if he writes otherwise. Let us therefore do honour to our true benefactors by acknowledging their struggles, and by clearly seeing (with no nonsense *de mortuis*) the public stupidity and private graft against which they contended. And, having thus ruthlessly surveyed the past, we shall find ourselves in no mood to flatter the present age, which we shall next consider. Are there no political cesspools, no social muck-heaps, no spiritual drains that call for plumbing? If so, my friend, we will not fear to discover them.

CAPUT VIII

Of the Present Age and Ajax Vindicated, with a Digression upon Prisons and Hospitals

OF WHAT NOW shall we sing, who have surveyed the long river of human history, from the crystal springs of antiquity through mediaeval quagmires to the broad plains of the Victorian era? How shall we tell of the very estuary of Progress, where sanitation branches into so many separate channels, with the uncharted ocean of the future before us?

There is now but one God, Ajax, and the Plumber is his Plenipotentiary.—The plumber has now become a national figure, a despot in every home whose aid the frantic householder desperately implores, as men once called upon their gods, with loud entreaties and secret imprecations. Leisurely he surveys our needs, his forgotten tools and his mate a proverb among us. Not even Downing Street, since Mr. Asquith brought in baths for the mighty, escapes his nonchalant jurisdiction. The water-closet has become so common to the lives of urban folk that to many of them life without it is unimaginable, a nightmare horror which they never expect to experience in reality. And yet, even today (as Mr. Anthony Armstrong reminds us in *Cottage Into House*) *the lavender man* is still sent at dead of night, in certain rural districts of this England, to collect his cargo in a cart and bear it away to some mysterious destination, known only to the Rural Council. Or (if

I were minded to discuss in any detail the anomalies of English sanitation) I should like to ask what is the explanation we have to offer to those Continentals and Americans who ask with amazement why we persist in exposing our drain-pipes to the rigours of the English climate, allowing most of our drains from sinks, baths and such places to pass outside our houses, where they inevitably freeze in a hard winter, and attributing to an act of God the calamity which follows from our own obstinate stupidity.

Ars est celare artem, *and only bad Plumbing is ever remembered.*—But I will not weary you with an account of our English sanitation as it is today, except for a few observations on prisons, hospitals, the effects of the war and of *evacuation,* as it is called, for you have but to walk a few yards to see for yourself fair samples of our common domestic provisions. Already the ingenious devices of the past have become museum pieces, exhibited only as curiosities in houses such as that of which Mr. H. D. C. Pepler wrote

> *Where they shewed*
> *A commode*
> *Made by Spode,*
>   *China lace.*

Vast labyrinthine drains and sewers dispose discreetly of our daily problems, and like our own stomachs remind us of their existence only when they are out of order. Such disorders are still far too frequent, though I have never believed the story of that child on a tenement privy, who was said to have been lifted from the seat by the brush of an industrious sweep at work upon a lower floor. Even our trains are equipped for their longer journeys with conveniences for which the traveller by stage-coach must often have sighed vainly; and, indeed, I remember some discussion I had on this matter with an old sorter in the

Post Office, who told me of the perplexities attending the sorting of mail in the earlier days of railways. A sheet of paper, he said, served for one purpose, an open door for the other; and it was well that the door should open towards the rear of the train, or the consequences might be disastrous. (How, I wonder, are these problems solved upon aeroplanes?) And if paper were lacking, he said, some citizen might be the poorer for a lost letter or parcel. Such were the *bad old days,* which we should remember with gratitude towards those whose enterprise has provided us with our present amenities.

Intimations of Immortality.—We will not discuss at this time that further problem (to which, perchance, you have given even less thought) of what is the ultimate fate of sewage. You pull a chain, and for you an episode is ended. It is almost an epitome of our earthly life, which I remember to have seen described in a quatrain that ended—

> *God pulls the plug, and down we go.*

The sceptic sees here nothing but what his eyes have told him: that which was is no more. But as with the spirit, so it is with matter, however humble: both are indestructible. Therefore in a later chapter we may usefully consider— and I promise you it is a lively subject—the Purgatory through which this forgotten matter is to pass, the Heaven or Hell of its final destination; for both, I assure you, are to be found. Scatology and Eschatology have more in common than is commonly known.

The Future Life of Garbage.—Or consider the contents of your dust-bin. Until the Government and your newspaper began to talk of *salvage,* what did you know or care of that vast mass of refuse, removed each week from your back-door to some unknown place? For the treatment of *garbage* until very recent years I will do no more at this time than to refer the reader to *Metropolitan Man,* a book in which this subject finds its place under the title *Stink and Darkness*. In this chapter Mr. Robert Sinclair described the *merry-go-round* of London's refuse, the garbage of Kensington being sent to Hammersmith, while that of Hammersmith was deposited in Fulham. By such primitive systems we but recently avoided our problems, providing ourselves, in the terms of an inspector of the Ministry of Health, with *extensive fly-feeding belts;* and a *noble monument* of London at Rainham was thus described by Mr. Sinclair, *a midden ninety feet tall, which rises up to welcome to England the passengers on the decks of the great liners passing up the Thames to Tilbury Docks*. Such were the outer defences of the metropolis, infested pyramids of corruption breathing smoke and smell, generating flies and breeding rodents, the licensed storing-houses of infection with which we surrounded ourselves.

In the last ten years much has been done to remedy these evils, but as the methods employed often appear to me wasteful and destructive, I will say no more of them until I come to discuss the disposal of sewage and refuse, a subject vastly more fruitful for the sociologist (and even for the philosopher) than ignorant or over-fastidious minds might assume. But for the present purpose it is sufficient to say that the increased use of Controlled Tipping and of other methods (equally sanitary, though more wasteful) has greatly improved the position in the matter of what is termed *dry refuse*.

On the Merits of Disease Germs—A New Peril for the Modern Troglodyte.—Leaving the disposal of all manner of filth for later consideration, and most other present facts to your own powers of observation, I will therefore hasten forward to a brief consideration of certain results of the present war which may not be so widely known as their importance indubitably merits. There was, as I recollect, much talk at one time of the possibilities of *bacteriological warfare,* an ingenious method of killing which is still to be considered not unlikely, worthy as it is of the inventive genius which has devised so many means of slaughter; so that the list provided by Gulliver (in his description of the habits of Yahoos) seems today feeble in comparison. Moreover, this conception of *bacteriological warfare* was known at least in the time of Charlemagne, if not earlier, and is therefore a very venerable and respectable way of destroying persons who have the bad taste to be born in another country. But I refer to this question only to remark the curious fact that, although (as yet) no deliberate efforts appear to have been made by the present belligerents to spread disease among their enemies, there are at least two cases upon record when measures were taken in this country which might well have had the same effect, that is to say, the wholesale spreading of infection among the population. For I was recently present when a doctor of great experience in all matters affecting public health informed an audience that upon two occasions, when other water had been unobtainable to extinguish the fires caused by the incendiaries dropped upon our towns, *sewage water had been used.* And of this the doctor observed with good reason that he marvelled at the absence of any epidemics following such procedure.

Of the Sanitation provided by the paternal State for its Guests.—Hygiene and sanitation among prisoners, since these are the guests of the State, is in some respects a valuable guide to prevalent ideas of health and cleanliness as expressed in official procedure. I will not detail at length the loathsome conditions which existed among the prisoners in the eighteenth century and the greater part of the nineteenth, though I propose to discuss briefly their condition in the twentieth. Those who reflect upon the admitted improvement affected since the time of Howard can best surmise the condition of the prisons before his time if they are still what I shall shew them to be.

Among the first official recognitions of a need for improvement and an intention—largely unfulfilled—to remedy existing evils, there will be found an Act of 1774. By this Act it became obligatory that prisons should be whitewashed yearly, that they should be regularly washed and properly ventilated, that the sick should be accommodated in separate apartments, that hot and cold baths should be provided and that prisoners should be kept above ground if it could conveniently be managed. In view of the uncommon character of bathing at that time, one may reasonably doubt whether great attention was paid to this injunction; but *whitewash* has never been spared at any time since.

The Filthiness of an English Prison.—Of our English prisons today I will say that only those who have known the stench in the sanitary annexe, where vessels are emptied in the morning, will understand the repugnance with which I recall this matter. For I once elected to spend seven days in a jail rather than to pay a fine of seven shillings and sixpence, and of all the things I discovered at this time this alone surprised me; for I have long been wise enough to expect all in power or with authority to be harsh and tyrannical, but had imagined filth to be contrary to any official sense of order and decency. Nevertheless in prison I found stinking privies opening upon halls little ventilated, where men waited their turns with their loathsome burdens and in turn would fill jugs with drinking water or rinse their beastly vessels at the same tap and in the same stench.

Mr. James Phelan in his work entitled *Jail Journey* makes mention of a matter on which I made enquiries and found his statement to be true. He says that a rule of the prisons allows the prisoner at any time of the night to ring his bell, when an officer must unlock his door and suffer him to make his way to the closet, if he has need of it. But he says that this rule is never known to be invoked, because of the fear inspired by the officers of the prisons, who have so many ways to be revenged against those who transgress their own laws (these being more powerful than those written and printed), that a man, when shut for fourteen hours in a cell, will rather foul his own nest by using the vessel provided for urine than hazard the ringing of the bell.

Unsavoury Stories of Prison Laundries.—From the monumental work on *English Prisons Today,* by Hobhouse and Brockway, published in the year 1922, we learn of many other filthy practices ordained by the system then in use in English prisons, of which it may be observed that some have changed. But I commend to the reader their chapter on *Diet and Hygiene,* and especially that section dealing with *Personal Cleanliness,* for an account of the truly horrid and noxious habits until recently cultivated by order in these establishments. Especially he should notice the curious rule that formerly compelled a prisoner to keep his washing-bowl polished, in such a manner that he could best keep the rule (if, indeed, that was not the only way open to him) by abandoning his own ablutions. Also concerning the foulness of prison laundries much is said, which is the more loathly because a prisoner has no clothing of his own, but wears those supplied to him, which may have been worn before him by some filthy person and improperly washed. But I forbear from citing the evidence given in the last two pages of this chapter upon *Diet and Hygiene,* hoping that the charges made there are no longer true, though nothing (after what I have myself seen and smelt) would cause me surprise. Those who have a stomach for such sordid realities as wit cannot lighten, to make them less emetic than they are, may read this culminating horror for themselves.

Ingenious Forms of Torture employed in the Glasshouse.—This shall suffice for our civil prisons, though I leave the subject with regret, but I am approaching another hobby-horse upon which I propose very shortly to take a gallop, as you shall see in good time. By all rights there should follow here some account of the *Glasshouse,* where an ingenious mode of punishment often practised upon refractory soldiers is *to prevent them from using the latrines,* thus forcing a number of men to use an open communal pail in an unventilated barrack room. In one of these institutions certain indoor closets were recently kept unused, in a state of immaculate cleanliness, for inspection by the Medical Officer, whilst the men were fortunate to secure a bare five or ten minutes each day (and that at no time of their own choosing) when 250 men were permitted to make use of four outdoor latrines of incredible filthiness. For this they waited in a queue and often had to *share a seat.* But as these matters are, I trust, to be the subject of an enquiry, I will say no more, in the belief that the full facts will prove infinitely worse than such cautious statements as I have made, shewing the opportunities for washing and bathing, as well as those for answering the calls of nature, to be abominable and barbarous.

The Horrors of Hospital Life.—Lastly (before I pass from the question of sanitation today in Britain to consider briefly some prominent features of sanitation in other countries) I have something to say of hospitals, of which I write again for these two reasons; because they should be models of hygienic method, and because I have some special concern with them, having passed all too many months in hospital beds. What memories I have of one hospital, where the stench from the urinal bottles was a matter of common comment among the patients! How, we would ask, could these loathsome articles, thickly coated with crystals, be of value in the use to which they were so frequently put, that of *collecting specimens?* Or those unpleasant cloths—a concession to a mistaken sense of decency at the cost of hygiene—in which a bottle would be handed to a patient, cloths that too often were wet from the clumsy handling of an overfilled bottle—shall I ever forget those damp and reeking covers which had to be unfolded before the bottle was to be found? In this hospital these same cloths were also used for that most unpleasant of all hospital contrivances—*the bed-pan;* and I have seen them with revolting relics of this use left upon them.

The Paradox of our Hospitals as the Epitome of Human Wisdom and Futility.—Here indeed are foul details, more of the kind that we should expect to read of in the Middle Ages than in an account of our own time and of these centres of healing. How does it come about that in these places, equipped with all that is most ingenious, elaborate and costly to heal the sick, with the service of our finest physicians and surgeons, such things are possible? It is one of the enigmas of our time that is to be seen in all we undertake; for in these same hospitals you will find the greatest skill in the use of drugs combined with a diet that defies every law of dietetics, a diet based very largely upon white bread, peeled potatoes and polished rice—solid starch deprived of vitamins, and in such quantities that a person lying in bed can only be rid of it by the constant use of violent purges. Is not this a true cross-section of the universal insanity which cultivates science principally for mutual destruction and educates young men with care and great cost for the same purpose?

If your wisdom can explain that, then you can understand what I never could; as, for example, that a surgeon's instruments are carefully sterilised and the most scrupulous care is taken in the operating theatre; but the patient may be offered for his ablutions a bowl of water coated with black grease and shavings from previous use, as I have often found such bowls to be. Or he may discover, when taking what is called a *blanket bath,* that a disagreeable odour which disturbs him comes from the blankets, communally used for this purpose and clotted with the suds of countless predecessors. But I have said enough, for while there are hospitals to which my words have not application (and I pray there be many), those whom the cap fits may wear it. Let their former *patients* remember that they are also *citizens* and speak as plainly as I have, in the public interest; then we shall not be long in amending matters.

An Apology and an Exhortation.—With this I will take leave of English sanitation in the present age, having said far more than ever I intended of its defects, and notably of prisons and hospitals; but having passed some time in both, and found nothing else so objectionable in either as these things I have confided to you, I was constrained to shew how evil and unnecessary are such insanitary ways which, I am convinced, are no more conducive to reforming the criminal than to healing the sick. To you therefore, with your pleasant bathroom, your sweet and decent privy; to you, the fortunate heir of a century of sanitary progress, whom I have nothing to tell of the amenities you enjoy, I commend the cause of the afflicted, whether their misfortune be disease, crime or merely poverty.

Here indeed, in an age that is justly proud of its sanitarian achievements, is scope for the reformer and the humanitarian, aye, and for the inventor too, who will devise some contrivance to rid our hospitals for ever of bed-pans. Thousands of patients will bless his name, their eyes moist with the tears of sincerest gratitude, and great Sir John himself will keep him a place among the Immortals.

CAPUT IX

Concerning the Nastiness of Natives and the Filthiness of Foreigners

Definition of a Native per genus et differentiam.—As to my title, I suppose some pedantic person might assume that I denote by the term *foreigners* those who live outside this island and that by *natives* I mean those who live in my native land. Therefore let it be clearly understood that I use these terms not as a mere philologist but as an Englishman, who divides all who are not English into two categories; those with white skins, called foreigners, and those with dark skins, called *natives*. Did I not read in that most erudite article by Mr. Lamb, in the *Architects' Journal,* of the *Eastern pedestal closet,* described by that writer (with an excellent illustration) as *really the most rational of all,* that this most excellent of contrivances was *only suitable for native races?* Manifestly, then, we cannot be natives, since we are not sufficiently rational to use a closet where, as Mr. Lamb explains, *it is necessary to adopt a squatting position for use.* This will provide us with a second or supplementary definition of *native:* one who is sufficiently rational to squat, which is the correct scientific position; but this we will discuss at greater length in a later chapter.

My purpose, then, is to discuss the present ways of those *lesser breeds without the law,* as Mr. Kipling called them, and to consider whether there is any particular climate, race, civilisation or political system more conducive than another to the practice of hygiene; for which purpose we will first concern ourselves with *natives* and later with *foreigners*.

A Digression into the Politics of Sanitation in India.— And now let those who fear to investigate the sewers of politics, the bad drains of our social consciences, prepare to take a jump, while those with stronger moral stomachs accompany me into a field where the problem of sanitation is more than usually linked to that of *haute politique*. In the vast sub-continent of India we will forget for a while the individual closet, the private privy, and consider collectively the question of *dirt versus hygiene* as a political problem demanding a political remedy. Such matters, more especially where they relate to the affairs of the British Empire, are proper subjects for our consideration before we turn to the vast problems of the future; for which reason I propose to take a glance first at India, next at some other portions of the Empire and afterwards at some outstanding countries where a variety of political régimes may be simultaneously observed in operation, to see if in any of these the seeds of future progress are to be found.

Personal Cleanliness a fundamental Doctrine of the great Indian Religions.—Of the insanitary conditions noticed so often by travellers in India, and so often made the subject of official reports, there are a few things to be said that should give material for thought to those who are capable of the process. We shall consider in a later chapter the injunctions of the two great religions of India, that of the Hindus and that of Islam, in respect to personal cleanliness. If the reader will therefore *in tempus* accept my solemn word and assurance that he shall have proof enough of this in another place, we may begin with the assumption that the Moslem religion (and even more so that of the Hindus) enjoins the most meticulous rules of personal hygiene. How does it therefore come about that such filthiness can exist where the traditional culture is founded upon an exacting and fastidious standard of purity?

Why, you say, there is nothing remarkable in such a proposition, for the whole of Christian civilisation is based *de facto* upon the systematic breach of the Ten Commandments and the ethics of the Galilean. Did we build an empire by turning the other cheek? Do not the Kings of the Gentiles still exercise lordship over them, and are they not called Benefactors? Are the disciples of Christ known today because they love one another? Do not the Pharisees still devour widows' houses? Did our settlers in Kenya possess themselves of African land by too nicely observing the Eighth Commandment? And can we defend this Empire in war by a rigid adherence to the Sixth? Are fortunes made by those who fare without scrip, sword or wallet, having given all their goods to the poor and even their surplus coats to him that hath none? Is My Lord the Archbishop a pattern of Christian humility and Holy Poverty? Or can nations that sound their own praises with fife and drum *walk humbly before God* when they are drunk with their own pomp and circumstance? Why, you would think, if you did not know better, that you had come among idolaters to see the worship lavished upon a swastika or a Union Jack, to say nothing of Mammon's graven image on the filthy lucre of Caesar.

The Explanation of Inconsistency.—Well, I knew one honest staff-sergeant who but recently turned Mohammedan because he thought it better to follow openly the Prophet who carried the Sword of Islam than to make a pretence of loyalty to the Prince of Peace. But such consistency, though rare enough among Western peoples, trained as they are in intellectual jugglery, the forgery and counterfeiting of emotions, and especially expert in the Sin Against the Holy Ghost (by which they can always persuade themselves that black is white and white, black), is more common among the simple illiterates of the East. Uncivilised barbarians, they are inclined to practise their beliefs as well as they can; and we shall not find so simple an explanation of any difference between their theories and their behaviour.

A partial explanation is, however, provided by Dr. G. T. Wrench in his little book, *The Restoration of the Peasantries*. Examining the functions fulfilled in former days by the Indian village (once an almost autonomous republic under its *panchayat,* or Council of Five), Dr. Wrench gives us this interesting extract from the work of Mr. John Matthai on *Village Government in British India*. Speaking of the scavengers, Mr. Matthai says:

An Account of the Indian Scavengers.—This class of village servants have furnished the material in most provinces for the useful body of rural policemen. Their duties are multifarious, of which menial sanitary service forms not the least important part. They sweep the lanes and remove impurities, keep the village meeting-house clean, patrol the village at night, act as messengers to the headman, serve as referees on matters affecting the village boundaries, guard the crops, assist in agricultural operations, attend on Government officials who visit the village, and carry palanquins and torches at festivals. *As a rule they are menials of the lowest caste, and take up their residence on the outskirts of the village.*

They are stigmatised as Untouchable.—Here, then, is a sanitary, police and general service which should have functioned well enough; but there are two excellent reasons for its failure, for one of which the people of India are to blame, while the other can be traced to their rulers. As to the first, the social status allowed to these useful

members of Indian society has never been one to encourage in them a pride in their own occupation. Admitted by all to be useful and necessary, theirs has been
held to be a degraded employment, as Mr. Matthai makes
very clear; and the word *Untouchable* by which Hindus
stigmatised those who performed these services has rightly
become a reproach to Hinduism. (Beware, reader, too
ready an approval of this statement. For I will remind you
that there are men who fetch your coal out of the pit at the
risk of their health and their lives. Are you prepared to see
that they are decently rewarded for their labours, or ready
to afford them social equality? If not, my friend, *ferme ta
gueule*.)

On this point, and on the endeavours that have been,
and are being, made to eliminate *Untouchability* in India
(the work of Indian patriots with no help and some
hindrance on the part of the British Government), I will
briefly refer the reader to my own work, *The White
Sahibs in India,* where the matter is discussed at some
length in the tenth chapter. The seventh chapter of the
same book gives some account of the second reason why,
to an ever-increasing extent, the ancient village system of
India fails to function adequately.

*Indian Sanitation declined with the indigenous System
of Self-government in the Villages.*—This second reason
may be summarised in the simple fact, demonstrated by
myself and by others with ample reference to British authorities of different generations, that *British rule has
destroyed the ancient system of village self-government.*
What else would you expect? A despotic central administration, conducted by foreigners in a foreign interest, has
never been compatible with local autonomy. It is true that
previous rulers of India permitted this anomaly to exist,
which is the very measure of their inefficiency; for each in
turn was the victim of internal revolution or conquest and

subjugation by a stronger rival; until a British trading concern (applying to government the accumulated wisdom of the counting-house) founded a régime of such detailed and diabolical despotism that it became secure against every peril. Not until the genius of Signor Mussolini and Herr Hitler discovered and organised an even more precise and devilish machine of tyranny had these drivers of the imperial Juggernaut any reason to fear a fall. They suppressed a system which threatened their own absolutism as much by the spirit of independence which it cultivated as it did by the organisation through which it operated—the village in council, deciding for itself all questions of education, sanitation and public works, the incidence of taxation among its members, the administration of justice, the relief of famine, and all the proper functions of a government.

A necessary Digression to anticipate a foolish, but common, Objection to this Thesis.—And do not say (before I begin to swing this argument, like a bludgeon, at the problem of Indian sanitation) that we have of late begun to reverse the Juggernaut, making a start (contrary to my thesis) with *local autonomy.* For this *local autonomy* of the Indian provinces is a sleight-of-hand trick, a pretty deception that has confused no-one but ourselves, being so arranged as to give some show of authority to those most likely to play our own game; I mean, the propertied classes of India. But of real power even these gentlemen have none whatever, their functions being so hedged around with safeguards, powers of veto, arbitrary executive authority and other devices with which the British have taken care to arm themselves. Or, in plain words, a hand-picked bunch of the more pliable Indians may do as they please so long as it pleases Whitehall; that is to say, Whitehall *de jure* and Threadneedle Street *de facto.* However, lest you should complain of so long a digression

upon my favourite hobby-horse, I will once more insert a
free advertisement for *The White Sahibs,* referring you
principally to chapters ten and fifteen.

*Condition of Indian Towns worse than that of the Vil-
lages.*—Before we leave India there are certain observations to be made regarding the condition of the towns,
those growing monstrosities of mongrel breed where
Western methods of production are applied in an Indian
climate, with Indian labour, very Western dividends being
extracted by the payment of truly Oriental rates of wages.
To these towns the peasants come, faced with starvation
in their own villages (from causes which I long to detail
here, but you know now where to find them discussed). It
is the opinion of Dr. Wrench that the breaking-down of
the old village system has also contributed to this exodus
from the villages, because, he says, any village lad of enterprise, instead of putting his energies to the improvement
of village life, tends to escape to the place which power
patronises: the town. Thus, while the decay of village institutions brings with it a decline of village sanitation, it
helps to drive the most vigorous types to the towns, where
no native institutions exist or have ever existed, haphazard
growths, the product of an alien genius, the great wens
where Western industrialism has begotten its deformed
offspring upon the victim of imperial rape. And here we
shall expect to find sanitary conditions even more de-
plorable than the worst that are to be seen in the villages;
which indeed is the case, as anyone may verify by studying
the *Whitley Report,* the product of a Royal Commission
on Labour in India. But lest you should imagine that we
English have done nothing whatsoever to bring Western
sanitation to India, let me recall some comments in an
illuminating paper entitled *Some Experiences of a Sanitary Engineer in India.* The author shews that the Indian
taxpayer (the dirty peasant) paid £67,500 for sanitary fit-

tings in the Viceroy's house at New Delhi. Twenty-three thousand of this was spent on hot water and central heating, and there were more than a hundred wash-basins and water-closets installed, in addition to over sixty bathrooms. Here at least we did our duty.

Unexplored Avenues for the future Historian.—I wish that I had time and leisure to dissertate at equal length upon every part of our far-flung Empire; to trace the problems, social and political, that may be symbolised and embodied in its various sanitary systems, from certain closets at Malta, made like church pews, with overhanging crosses (as I have heard), to the New Zealand *night carts,* source of so many unsavoury stories, or those of Rangoon. What strange customs we might consider, what paradoxical conceptions of the clean and unclean! In Burma (to cite but one example), where the bath is considered part of the ordinary ritual of the day and bodily cleanliness a matter of religious duty, the people know no greater delicacy than a large coprophagous worm which thrives in their middens; and this worm they eat fried, which must seem greatly repugnant to a European taste, though there are many fish that we eat which are by no means cleaner in their food, and some which are considered to be at their best where most sewage is to be found in the water. Indeed, the manuring of fish-ponds is a most ancient practice, pursued today with great success in many parts of the European continent, of which we will say more in another chapter.

The Great Powers of Europe condemned as Builders of Colonial Slums.—But I will have done with the Empire and take my illustration from another source, lest it should be said that I am *the friend of every country but my own.* For to speak truth, there is not a Great Power in Europe which has not taken a share in the oppression and robbery, the urbanisation and degradation of primitive peoples, making slums where there were once forests and prairies, and all the while boasting of its health services and civilising mission. As to the United States of America, its cities are monuments in the cemetery of the finest and perhaps the cleanest race that has ever lived; so here shall be our example.

Of the Indians in the Americas we read that they were considered to be, for the most part, a healthy people until the coming of the Europeans among them. For the *Encyclopaedia of Religion and Ethics* informs us, under the title *Disease and Medicine,* that such was their condition at the time of the Columbian discovery, and that notwithstanding the effects of their wars with the evils attendant to them, these Indians were holding their own in point of numbers, or, as some authorities believe, were even increasing in population, especially in some parts of the continent. In evidence of this they cite Dr. Hrdlička, who was of the opinion that the Indians were spared at the least some of the epidemics and diseases of the Old World, such as smallpox and rachitis; whilst other scourges, such as tuberculosis, syphilis, typhus, cholera, scarlet fever and cancer were rare, if occurring at all. But since the Europeans appeared in the Americas we learn that these diseases have spread and mortality greatly increased, on account of changes in the habits of the people through the advent of civilisation.

Of Cleanliness among the American Indians in former Times.—Concerning the cause of the good health among these people in former times the *Encyclopaedia* further informs us that the idea that cleanliness is next to godliness was widespread among many American Indian peoples. And in proof of this there is mention of their frequent bathing and other cleansing procedures, the very common use of the sweat-house, the washing of the sexual parts and the attention to the body during menstruation and after *coitus*. And a writer of the last century says of them that men make themselves agreeable to the deity by cleanliness; therefore they must bathe and wash their whole bodies before praying. This general practice of cleanliness is said to have been found in the greatest degree among the ancient Mexicans; but the use of the bath, according to our *Encyclopaedia of Religion and Ethics,* was widespread in all parts of primitive America (with some tribes daily) as a hygienic or medical procedure. Especially was the sweat-house or steam-bath common, both among the uncivilised tribes and among the Aztecs, who built themselves sumptuous structures for this purpose. And this system they followed for reasons of religion, for the cure of diseases and for the love of cleanliness in their persons, as divers authorities testify.

Their Burying of Excrement.—From the same sources we learn that these Indians, or certain of their tribes which are enumerated, are still careful in their manner of answering the necessities of nature. For they retire to a distance from their villages, and having made themselves holes in the ground, fill these afterwards in the manner of cats, so that all excrement is buried in the earth, as it should be. And this is said of the Caribs and Arawaks, also the Caraya Indians of Brazil. Such customs are also still found among many Indians of North America; but for the most part these *noble savages,* dying upon the altar of Civilisation, have lost their own virtues without acquiring such poor substitutes as we might have provided for them.

In all matters of public hygiene, the provision of artificial devices should, of necessity, be proportionate to the extent to which society is urbanised, the practices which are healthy and reasonable in a nomadic or pastoral people being altogether disgusting, if not impossible, among those who live in great towns and cities. Therefore in considering what is termed *sanitary progress* it is not enough, indeed it is utterly false, to measure merely the extension in drainage, the advance in the use of water-closets or in the provision of tap-water; for these can only be considered in relation to their adequacy, and where in one place none of these things might be necessary, they might, in another, be altogether insufficient.

The Sanitary Code of the Nomad and his Contempt for the Townsman.—The men of the desert have, for the most part, neither the means nor the occasion to furnish themselves with sanitary equipment. Thus, in the two volumes of the work by Sir Aurel Stein on *Ruins of Desert Cathay,* there will be found no mention of such matters. Neverthe less the people of the desert are rarely without some code of conduct, as may be seen in the case of Islam, which may be as elaborately devised for *al fresco* performances as for those performed within walls; and how greatly the nomadic peoples despise townsmen in this respect we have already seen.

Justification of this Contempt.—But if we regard our vaunted civilisation in Europe, how can we say that the contempt of the nomad is unjustified, or that either our equipment or the *sanitary sense* of the people is equal to the problems with which we have burdened ourselves by our way of living? How many a French closet have I known with no ventilation other than the door, or a window opening into an interior passage! Indeed, apart from their use of the *bidet* (for which I give them every praise, and only regret that it is still a mystery to most English people who discover it), I cannot see that the French have any claim to a *mission civilatrice* in sanitary affairs, being far less hygienic in other matters than most Africans and Orientals. Or what shall we say of those loathsome baskets, so often found in the closets of Spanish hotels, where *used paper* is deposited?

Or, should you travel into Denmark, in search of a

cleanly Nordic race, uncontaminated by Mediterranean sluttishness, you will find still upon the wall of the toilet in your train these familiar words: *Efterlad toilettet i samme stand i hvilken de ønsker at forfinde det,* which surely should not be necessary among any truly civilised people.

But if some Stalinist should tell me that they manage these things better in Russia, I have innumerable assurances to the contrary, of which one was given me by a gentleman who travelled widely in the country, knowing no more of the vernacular than one phrase, which was *Which way is the gentleman's lavatory?* I will refer you, however, to Miss Ethel Mannin's account of her journey *South to Samarkand,* which I quote with all the more assurance because Miss Mannin went to the country a pronounced Russophil and is even today a kindlier critic of the Kremlin than I am.

Of Privies on the Road to Samarkand.—Follow, then, this enterprising traveller to the incredible bathroom at Ordjonikidze, with its hosts of flies and cockroaches, and over the Georgian Military Highway where Miss Mannin and her companion believed (mistakenly) that they discovered *the most unspeakable sanitary arrangements human beings could devise,* which proved to be but the beginning of many such experiences. Observe the description of those latrines at Krasnovodsk, evil-smelling and indescribably filthy, or those at Samarkand on the railway station, at the end of the Golden Road. Or worse, consider the communal earth-closet that served the professors of Samarkand University, a place so foul that the traveller marvelled to find, even among Soviet professors and their families, no *respect for the sanitary decencies.* Or at Tashkent—but we have followed this pilgrimage of privies far enough; and much as I admire the writer, I would have forfeited a thousand pounds sooner than to have accompanied her.

Reflections upon Sanitation and Political Systems.—If Stalinism has failed to bring sanitation to Russia, or even a better conception of cleanliness, Fascism has done as little for other countries. Always a cleanly people (since the era of plumbing began in Europe), the Germans are neither more nor less so under the Third Reich; while the Italians, who formerly ranked among the dirtiest people in Europe, have held the title under *Il Duce*. So, then, we shall find little in present tendencies of politics to raise any hope of great sanitary reforms; and I cannot refrain from concluding that, subject to political conditions of national and cultural independence (which I have shewed to be so necessary in the case of India), political systems have little effect upon this issue. But religion, on the other hand, is of the greatest importance, as we shall see in a later chapter.

This very day on which I am writing, Japan declared war upon Great Britain and America, which serves to remind me that I have as yet said nothing of the Japanese and might well conclude this chapter on natives and foreigners with a few observations relating to the habits of Japan in the matter of hygiene and sanitation.

Promotion of the Japanese from the Status of Natives *to that of* Foreigners—*Of their fastidious Cleanliness.*—The Japanese were at one time *natives,* but are now *foreigners,* in spite of the colour of their skins. This metamorphosis is to be attributed to the progress of Japan within a few generations from a harmless and insular existence to her present power and pretensions, as the rival of European countries in the Western arts of bullying, murdering, looting, swaggering, lying, moralising, faking and cheating, and in all the industrial crafts that are necessary to support such activities, especially the manufacture of lethal weapons. As it is unthinkable that a *native* should own anything so civilised as a battleship, a bomber or a mechanised army, the Japanese are therefore manifestly no longer *natives* but *foreigners,* and it is therefore permissible for me to remark that these Japanese are very *clean* people, without my being in danger of internment under Section 18b, or so I hope.

With regard to these foreigners, then, I learn that in the Russo-Japanese War they caused the men in their armies, before they went into battle, to take a hot bath and put on clean garments. And this they did to lessen the possibility of their wounds being contaminated by the infection of the skin. So that if they are as careful of hygiene in the present war as they were upon that occasion, and in all other things as scientific and deliberate, they are likely to prove formidable adversaries. In a later place I hope to discuss their very sensible method of sewage disposal, also their singular freedom from foolish *taboos* in relation to the body and its functions. But for the moment I will be content to say that in my own experience I have found them among the most fastidious of people, whose corruption by Western materialism I regret as deeply as I deplore the fact that they must now be considered our *enemies;* for I could wish that all my enemies were dirty and that all my friends and allies were clean. But (for the matter of that) I could wish it took less than ten years to discover that an aggressor had been aggressing, or (better still) that the same people who made such discoveries would tell me whether other empires were born under a gooseberry-bush or delivered in the doctor's bag.

I have said enough, as I think, to indicate that cleanliness is not a speciality of the East or the West, of civilisation or simplicity, of this or of that political régime; but that it is something most likely to be found among free peoples, and especially where a fastidious religion regulates the daily conduct of the people. This last point I have yet to demonstrate with examples; but I propose first to consider certain other questions, the relevance and importance of which will be made clear in my next chapter, on *Comfort and Convenience.*

CAPUT X

Concerning Comfort and Convenience

Discomfort and Inconvenience are shewn to be conducive to Uncleanliness.—Questions of *comfort* and *convenience* are as proper to our subject as the more austere problems of hygiene and cleanliness; for it has been observed that where the habits of cleanliness cannot be comfortably and conveniently pursued, they will inevitably deteriorate. Thus a person who bathes himself daily in his own house will be known to abandon his ablutions altogether if he is reduced to the necessity of washing by inches with the aid of a bowl of cold water or a pump in the open air. And of convenience it has been observed that there are vast sanitary deserts in the Metropolis where one may read minatory notices concerning the committing of *nuisances,* without any direction as to where one may go so as to be in order. This profound observation is made in the course of a dialogue supposed to have taken place between two members of a London club, and the record of it will be found in a work to which we have already referred, entitled *For Your Convenience,* of which the author assumes the name *Paul Pry.* In this book are discussed at length and with remarkable knowledge the facilities to be found in town, and even a map is added for the assistance of the reader, whereon the appropriate places are marked.

The same authority remarks, regarding the question of comfort and aesthetic satisfaction, that a plain metal affair will be found in a district of poor shops and houses, with low rates. But brown stone or porcelain, says he, with work done by Doulton or Adamsez or Twyford's, or Davis and Bennett, denotes a well-to-do district. Thus the theories of Karl Marx are embedded in sanitary architecture.

A Hint to Employers of Labour that Seats should be cut square; which is also recommended to the Attention of M. Stakhanov.—But for a dissertation upon this question of comfort, both physical and mental, nothing could surpass the celebrated work of Mr. Charles Sale, entitled *The Specialist*. In this book a maker of privies discusses his art; and though the field in which he *specialised* is limited to the primitive closets in use among American farmers, he says much that is very discerning and apposite to wider problems. Thus he discusses privies in relation to the interest of an employer, and deserves academic distinction as an industrial psychologist (*honoris causa*) for discovering that the effective output of an employed person can be increased by cutting seats square with hard edges; for this expedient was found to reduce the time spent in these places from forty minutes a sitting to four minutes only. Also Mr. Sale shews himself a sound psychologist in his preference for locating constructions near a wood-pile, so that a suitable excuse may be found for those who need it, and the household wood-box be kept filled. And he gives good reasons why doors should open inwards, why they should face the East, why windows should be avoided in these rustic retreats, and why the exteriors should be painted in two colours. All this should be read by the complete student, who will learn from this source of the use of catalogues and the cob-box, of the famous eight-seated construction and the fate of Mr. Clark, who experimented fatally with a privy not of *specialist* design. Posteriority should indeed be grateful for such detailed information.

Of Injustice to Women and Remedies proposed.—The question of convenience raises another problem which lies beyond the scope of *The Specialist* and was omitted in the strictly masculine discourse recorded by *Paul Pry*. But readers of the *New Statesman* will recall a correspondence which took place in that journal in the year 1934 concerning *Injustice to Women*. On this occasion a rampant feminism shewed its resentment at the payment of one penny for the fulfilment of a natural function which is gratis to the other sex, and an outraged letter from Flora Grierson proposed a militant programme worthy of Mrs. Pankhurst. The discrimination, she said, could be easily abolished if we organised an intensive anti-penny campaign by the simple method of *always using the gutter and going to jail if necessary,* for our convictions. But another contributor to this discussion, signing himself *Equality*, reminded the reader that the removal of the urinal fee would give, not equality, but discrimination against men, while removal of all fees he considered Utopian. In short, said he, the practical difficulty is that women have no *locus standi*.

An ingenious Scheme of Time-switches.—To remedy this defect, *Equality* propounded a proposal which he attributed to his wife, that time-switches might provide a solution, the penny being recoverable within a stated time. This proposal, he confessed, would appear impracticable in point of cost; but no other mechanical device, he said, was free from the element of *trust,* an element which did not easily pass a local council in a pure form. Nevertheless he concluded that the *New Statesman* correspondents would do nobly if their indignation led them to bring a higher and rarer quality into modern society with the slogan: *Trust the Women of England*.

Many further letters on this subject were acknowledged by the editor, from which it may be assumed that the sense of injustice aroused by sex discrimination has some interest to the general public, and it is our present intention to re-vivify this interest to the point of *action*. But there has been some progress at least in this matter since the days when the mere proposal to erect such a place for women in Hampstead occasioned so vigorous an opposition that Mr. Bernard Shaw felt the matter called for his personal intervention, and lent his formidable support to the party of progress.

Inadequacy of the Public Provision.—However, the inconvenience of our public provision is no mere question of discrimination against women; for we are all ill-served, though our miseries do not equal those of the eighteenth century, when the author of *The Grand Mystery or Art of Meditating over an House of Office, Restored and Unveiled,* portrayed the terrible difficulties of both male and female persons in London, and outlined a proposal for the erection of 500 public lavatories in the Metropolis; a project which he considered to be a profitable one. But the Great Wen has spread faster than these public services, which are (moreover) for the most part wretched places, few of them able to compete in any way with the lavatories at Friends' House, Euston; which I have always considered to be the model to be emulated, and a sufficient reason for membership of the Society of Friends, if better cause were lacking. And as to the adequacy of the public provision, I remember that a foreign visitor to our Metropolis, being asked his opinion of it, gave this reply: that London is a city where the public-houses in many parts close at eleven o'clock and the public urinals at ten. This is so well known as to escape comment from ourselves; for tyranny is too easily endured from force of habit *until it becomes utterly intolerable.*

Arrogance of the Civic Authorities; their Doom foretold. —Let the London County Council and the several borough councils of the Metropolis remember, therefore, the storming of the Bastille and ponder whether their offence is indeed less than that of the Bourbons. Do not tell me of petty reforms, of half-penny *urinettes* in the East End, as a concession to our wronged wives, or a few new places for *gentlemen;* does not the very word, arrogantly displayed over West End resorts (while those east of the City are for mere *Men*), shew the necessity for extreme measures? Why, had I the making of a revolution, this would be among the first matters I would attend to; and being more humane, less prodigal of human life, than Danton or Robespierre, I would condemn our Cabinet ministers and financiers, the retired colonels of Bournemouth and the fat dowagers of Mayfair and Knightsbridge, to be attendants in these same places, substituting for the slogan *A la lanterne* the *dernier cri* of poetic justice: *Au lavabo!*

Blue Print for a Saturnalian Revolution.—I know little of the private lives of those who tend to our needs in these places, though there is always upon record the saying, *It may be —— to you, but it's my bread and butter*. And I remember also that in the last war, when my late father complained of a shortage of paper, he was threatened by the attendant that if things continued as they were *they might have to close down altogether*. But I suppose these very necessary functionaries to be, for the most part, persons of blameless and impeccable lives; and it seems to me reasonable that those who have spent so much of their time underground should be recompensed with pleasanter work elsewhere, or a comfortable pension, whilst those who have contributed no good (and often much harm) to society should pass the remainder of their lives in humble but useful employment. I have prepared a list for this very purpose, not omitting certain bureaucrats of Transport House and other privateers of working-class extraction, to shew my impartiality; and my only regret when one of my proscribed names has to be deleted by reason of his unfortunate death is that I have lost another candidate for a seat in a House worthy of him.

Proposal for the better Employment of Idle and Pernicious Persons.—Where else (for I confess I warm to this theme) ought we to have accommodated that South Wales magnate, now (alas) in Iscariot's Bosom, the Chairman of the Swansea Harbour Improvement Trust and fifty other companies, who caused his minions to wear the initials of their employers upon their caps? Where more appropriate? Where else that Victorian statesman of whom legend says that his wife explained to the French Ambassador, *Il est à ce moment dans le cabinet, et je pense qu'il y restera longtemps, parcequ'il a pris beaucoup de papier?* Where else should we employ ex-Conscientious Objectors of the last war, now over-age and keen Conscriptionists? Where else would you place those *soi-disant* poets whose writings are indeed best suited to the walls of the home I would provide for them? I remember well how a friend of mine once wrote of them very prettily, concluding with the words:

> On the fringe of the arts they flirt;
> And they think they are putting the P in pep
> When they take the R out of shirt.

What better place is there in which all these gentry could write their reminiscences, whilst sightseers in town could find whatever relief they needed, and at the same time satisfy their curiosity by gazing at ex-celebrities and odd nonentities. Then there are the bishops—but I must return to the general theme of comfort and convenience, my zeal for radical reform having carried me somewhat beyond its scope.

Concerning Paper.—As an example of the proper spirit

I would ask you what solicitude could equal that of the army authorities whose categories include *chambers, rubber, officers, lunatic, for the use of.* Here indeed is attention to need, the adjustment of the article to the requirement. In this spirit we shall not labour in vain; and there is many a man who must have wished before now that the army was as careful in all such matters; for a slippery pole and a long trench is poor comfort and wretched hospitality, with army form blanks chopped up *pour torcher le cul* in a manner the Reverend Rabbles (as Sir John calls him) would have justly scorned. And since we have come to this question again, for I cannot let the matter drop without some effort to clear up all loose ends, there is a very apposite story in Sir John's *Metamorphosis,* shewing that *one cannot be too careful.* He says that a friar dedicated a book to Pius Quintus, of which one writes merrily that his Holiness, finding it was good for nothing else, employed it to a homely occupation, and forsooth the phrase was so rude, the style so rugged and the Latin so barbarous, that therewith *Scortigavit sedem Apostolicam,* he galled the seat Apostolic. And whoever it was that wrote to his enemy, *I have your letter before me and it will soon be behind me,* may have suffered a like fate; from which we should all learn caution. For comfort and convenience I would favour a paper sufficiently thick but sufficiently pliable, glazed upon one side only and bearing, perhaps, some cheerful distich (*Novio* and *Izal* have set the pattern) to elevate the mind rather than to advertise the product or to proclaim each sheet to be the property of the Government or the Corporation of Margate. Or it might be some edifying proverb, such as *A swinging chain means a warm seat.* And, speaking of such matters, what is more depressing than a notice admonishing one to economy with paper, such as I have seen displayed in a certain building, near Chelsea Town Hall?

Perils attending an inadequate Public Provision.—But to return to the public provision of houses of office, which is admitted to be in most places altogether insufficient, Sir John recalls that no less a man than Mark Antony was the victim of a most indecorous accident, which might have been avoided by a more liberal provision, saving this honourable person from the malice of Cicero, who recalled the affair to his discredit in the presence of the entire senate. The necessity of giving a churlish answer to the calls of Nature, even where it does not end in catastrophe, is conducive to the greatest discomfort and (as the ancients well understood) injury to health. For, as *The School of Salerne* has it (Sir John being once more our interpreter):

> *The Salern school doth by these lines impart*
> *Health to the British King, and doth advise*
> *From cares thy head to free, from wrath thy heart;*
> *Drink not much wine, sup light and soon arise.*
> *After thy meat, 'twixt meals keep wake thine eyes,*
> *And when to Nature's needs provoked thou art,*
> *Do not forbear the same in any wise;*
> *So shalt thou live long time with little smart.*

And to this the physicians added this warning also:

> *Quatuor ex vento veniunt in ventre retento,*
> *Spasmus, hydrops, colica, vertigo, quatuor ista:*

which may serve to explain a certain edict contemplated by the Emperor Claudius (according to Suetonius) for which I must leave you to Sir John, since this is beyond my scope, who treat of more substantial matters.

A Maxim attributed to the Duke of Wellington.—Consider, then, how wise was the Iron Duke when, being asked by a merchant (who was all of a dither at meeting the victor of Waterloo) to give him some motto that had served him in his many campaigns, he replied, *Certainly, sir; never lose an opportunity to pump-ship.* I believe it was this practical understanding which enabled the Duke to contend upon equal terms with Buonaparte, who, being a Frenchman, was born with an advantage which Wellington must have acquired by experience: I mean, an appreciation of the fact that an army marches upon its belly, which every commander should make his first consideration, as it were, by double-exit book-keeping. Any débutante will tell you what agony it is to wait, if this advice is forgotten.

Superfluous Luxury in a Jakes is to be condemned.— Next, as to the furnishing of necessary houses, I make no plea for luxury. And indeed, the seat upholstered with blue satin, which was among the amenities of a certain royal yacht, has ever seemed to me a work of supererogation. And I will say the same of that described by Mr. Stanley Walker in *Mrs. Astor's Horse,* where he says that the late Lilyan Tashman had such a seat covered with ermine in her house at Hollywood. Such fancies seem to me repugnant to the practice of hygiene, and deserving such censure as Sir John passed upon the extravagance of his time, which he found contrary to the Statute of Apparel (33 Henry VIII), observing that there was no reason M. Ajax should have a better gown than his mistress. Of such jakes he says that he has seen them in cases of sugared satin and velvet, but for sweetness and cleanliness, he never knew any of them guilty of it. Such forms of luxury are as inapposite as that of which the Liberate Roll tells (36 Henry III), shewing that at Clarendon they caused the History of Antioch to be painted in a privy (or so I am led to understand) and the combat of King Richard to be painted in the same chamber.

And other Extravagances.—Other extravagances are recorded of America by Mr. Stanley Walker (*op. cit.*), such as the saloon in New York, devoted to lovers of horses, where saddles played the part of the chairs or stools, and the doors leading to the toilets were labelled *Colts* and *Fillies*. Or there was that outdoor closet, designed by some fellow at Hollywood, which fell in pieces when the plug was pulled and left the occupant an object of unseemly mirth for his host and other guests. This author speaks also of perforated toilet rolls which played tunes when pulled, of devices to start chimes or release a shower of confetti and other astonishing inventions. And I have heard it said that an engine was contrived in this country whereby a person sitting upon such a seat caused the National Anthem to be played; whereat he was compelled (if a patriotic person) to rise again, being unable in this way to conduct his business peacefully.

Concerning Sociability and Conviviality.—I say, enough of such things, and let us return to simplicities; for the closet has its dignity and its needs are not of this kind. Indeed, I am of one mind with Dr. Johnson. For when Boswell told him of an elegant jakes at the house of the Dutch Ambassador at Paris, which had quilted seats, *Sir,* said he, *that is Dutch; quilted seats retain a bad smell. No, sir, there is nothing so good as the plain board.* But something may be learnt from the ancients and those nearer our own time concerning *sociability;* and on this (when next you are alone in this place) I conjure you to reflect a little. In the first place, as we have already observed in that notable latrine at Timgad, the Romans believed that such places should be elegant and made for conviviality. That this practice was not without its abuses is shewn by the indefatigable Harington out of Martial, who complains of a fellow poet pursuing him with his verses:

> *Currenti legis et legis cacanti,*
> *In Thermas fugio sonas ad aurem.* ,

But without doubt there were compensations; for the French used the same custom if I may credit Sir John, who tells of a great Magnifico of Venice. This gentleman, he says, being ambassador in France, and hearing a noble person was come to speak with him, made him stay till he had untied his points; and when he was new set on his stool, sent for the nobleman to come to him at that time, as a very special favour. This custom Sir John in another place calls *French courtesy.*

Or if you will turn to the *Gull's Hornbook,* that most instructive *vade mecum* for louts and cads which Thomas Dekker wrote about the same time, you will find the following among his admonitions as to *How a Young Gallant should behave himself in an Ordinary:*

You may rise (says he) in dinner-time to ask for a close-stool, protesting to all the gentlemen that it costs you a hundred pound a year in physic, besides the annual pension which your wife allows her doctor; and, if you please, *you may, as your great French lord doth, invite some special friend of yours from the table, to hold discourse with you as you sit in that with-drawing-chamber;* from whence being returned again to the board, you shall sharpen the wits of all the eating gallants about you, and do them pleasure to ask what pamphlets or poems a man might think fittest to wipe his tail with. By such talk, as Dekker shews, a gallant may abuse the work of any man and purchase the terrible name of a severe critic.

Of Sociable Retreats for Two or Three Persons.—But even among the moderns you will find at least one account of conviviality in such places, as I well remember in *All Quiet on the Western Front,* where Erich Maria Remarque described such a scene. Such also, we may believe, was the true purpose of those sociable retreats we find still in our rural parts, thrones erected for a dual monarchy or even a Trinity in the Temple of the Winds. Of their use I can find little record and can only assume that this was at one time considered to be a family matter. But Cardinal

Wolsey, whom I suppose to have been *de jure* no family man, had such a place of retirement to accommodate the needs of three persons, from which I infer that he gave audience there upon occasion, just as Louis XIV did upon his *commode*. In fine, we may say that conviviality has long been practised in these places (which are even today often used as *rendez-vous*), and this might be revived with advantage to all; but there is one thing I observe, which is that whereas men are wont to sing in their baths, whether they bathe alone or in company, singing is not upon record as one of the pastimes or practices associated with Ajax, unless it should be the singing of the *Black Sauntus* by the pious friars of whom Sir John tells us. In another place you will nevertheless find (namely, in his treatise called *An Apology*) that he praises a stately jakes in an oak, overhanging a pond; which (he says) if you bring but an angle-rod and a cross-bow will afford choice of three royal sports.

The Author protests that the Subject of this Chapter is by no means trivial.—But lest anyone should say that I make too much of Ajax, and that this is but a duty to be performed and done with, a thing to be seen to and forgotten, I must next bring witnesses to shew the errors, fallacies, heresies, treasons and deviations from the party line which are evident in such reasoning. Of these witnesses the first must clearly be Comrade Harington himself, who speaks of the sweet sin of lechery to make his argument more forcible. First, then, he says that when the commination is read, *Cursed be he that lieth with his neighbour's wife,* to which the people should say *Amen,* there are some who say nothing and some who say *he hem* (or, as we should say, *ahem*), while some say *amend,* which, says Sir John, were very well said.

Now, sir, you who think I put this in of a purpose, out of the lewdness of my heart, attend to the reasoning by which the learned knight shall justify us both, for thus he proceeds:

Lechery defamed.—I say *this surpassing pleasure,* that is so much in request, and counted such a principal solace, *I have heard confessed* before a most honourable person, *by a man of middle age,* strong constitution and well practised in this occupation, *to have bred no more delectation in him* (after the first heat of his youth was past) *than to go to a good, easy close stool, when he hath had a lust thereto* (for that was his very phrase).

Let no man, therefore, say that we are meanly employed in considering the questions of comfort and convenience in a place whose functions can compete with Aphrodite for a man's favour and wear her down in the long run as the tortoise outran the hare.

If, then, there are persons to whom these functions are as arduous as the return from Avernus, such as those to whom the Emperor Vespasian was likened (when it was said of him that even at his merriest he looked as if he had been upon the stool), there are others who can put a different face on it. For a certain gentleman, whom we may call Mr. W. C., for convenience, being made a prisoner of war and placed on *parole,* was glad to exchange his parole for a dung-cart, in which he escaped. And when he said later that every man finds his level, a wit replied to him that *he found his level on the occasion of his escape.*

Gargantua discovers Anal-Erotism and expounds it lyrically.—That the solitude of the closet had its voluptuary acolytes was well known many centuries before the theory of anal-erotism was developed by Dr. Freud. For what says Gargantua of this matter to his admiring parent? *J'ay, respondit Gargantua, par longue et curieuse expérience, inventé un moyen de me torchere le cul, le plus royal, le plus seigneurial, le plus excellent, le plus expedient que jamais fu veu.* And having thereafter recounted his various and most enterprising experiments he concludes with these words, in the most famous passage of all the works of the Curé of Meudon: *Je dis et maintiens qu'il n'y a tel torche-cul que d'un oizon bien dumeté, pourveu qu'on luy tienne la teste entre les jambes. Et m'en croyez sus mon honneur, car vous sentez au trou du cul une volupté mirifique, tant par la douceur d'ici luy dumet que par la chaleur temperée de l'oizon, laquelle facilement est communiquée au boyan culier et aultres intestins, jusques à venir à la région du cœur et du cerveau.*

Et ne pensez (such is his peroration) *que la béatitude des heroes et semi dieux, qui sont par les champs Elysiens, soient en leur asphodele, ou ambroisie, ou nectar, comme disent ces vieilles icy. Elle est, selon mon opinion, en ce qu'ilz se torchent le cul d'un oison. Et telle est l'opinion de maistre Jean d'Escosse.*

Opinions of M. Gabriel Chevallier.—Whether that learned schoolman would indeed have adhered to such an opinion I have no means to determine, but the fancy is a pretty one though the ideal may prove a wild-goose chase (or a swan song, for those whose geese are swans). And of a similar function, with the pleasure attendant upon it, the author of that notable novel, *Clochemerle,* has recorded therein his opinion that there are two great pleasures to be derived from wine, to drink it without stint and then to seek relief to its utmost possibility, without haste or hurry, in a fresh, well-ventilated place, flushed day and night with a plentiful supply of water. I give my text from the excellent translation of this work by Jocelyn Godefroi. And a curious thing to be found in this book is the story of the inauguration of the urinal in the town of Cloche-merle-en-Beaujolais, which bears a clear resemblance to one which will be found in the first chapter of this work concerning an inauguration in the Vatican. But I have not as yet been able to obtain from Monsieur Gabriel Chevallier any information regarding this legend, which I leave to the anthropologists to discuss, whether it is a sun myth or a fable based upon fact, or what light it may throw upon rival theories concerning the diffusion of culture, or what relation it may be to the story of that unfortunate who said: *Uxorem duxi et ideo non possum venire.*

The Advice of Lord Chesterfield.—Another connoisseur of the closet was the celebrated Lord Chesterfield, as he reveals himself in a letter to his son dated December 11th, 1747 (Old Style). He mentions here a gentleman who profited even from the time which (he says) the calls of nature obliged him to pass in the necessary-house. Here he read the Latin poets in cheap editions, and tearing off what he had read, sent them down as a sacrifice to Cloacina. Lord Chesterfield commends this as an example to be followed; for, says he, it is better than only doing what you cannot help doing at these moments, and it will make any book which you shall read in that manner *very present in your mind*—a very singular system of mnemonics, as a friend of mine observes. His Lordship considered poetry the most appropriate reading for such occasions, omitting only Virgil.

The Pleasure of Reading in these Places is seldom enjoyed by Women—Tenders are invited for an Explanation. —Indeed, there have always been many who have used their closets as libraries, and this is as common among simple folk as it is among the learned, for examples of which the reader may be referred to Charles Sale and *The Specialist*. Or as Burton has it, in his *Anatomy of Melancholy,* not only libraries and shops are full of our putid papers, but every close-stool and jakes: *Scribunt carmina quae legunt cacantes.* But a certain woman, a writer of my acquaintance, being at one time a guest in the house of a very famous author, expressed her astonishment at the manner in which this man had equipped what he modestly termed a *women's cloakroom* in his establishment. For, said she, he provided the water-closet with shelves of books; and it is astonishing that a man with so much knowledge of the world and its ways should not be aware that to read and to meditate in these places is a masculine habit, and not one to which women are addicted. This I am inclined to believe from many experiments in timing the two sexes; but I believe that the explanation and even the fact itself escaped the notice of Dr. Freud and the painstaking researches of Professor Malinowski. As for myself, I could never regard that celebrated statue of Rodin, which is called *le Penseur,* without considering how normal is the mien and posture in a man, but in a woman utterly unimaginable.

Is there not, in the Apocryphal Boswell, an account of that most English of all philosophers that he spent many hours at a time with his dictionary in these places? And that, returning thence on an occasion when he was passing the day with a lady of his acquaintance, he indicated the seat of Ajax (which he had placed under his arm, thinking it was his manuscript) and observed, *Madame, you will perceive what my occupation has been?* But if this story is not true, at least we learn from the original manuscript of Boswell's *Tour to the Hebrides* that the Doctor interested himself in such matters. As for reading, he did not (says Boswell) *insist for that,* though he mentioned a gentleman who had a set of the *Spectator* in that place; but he said *that if ever a man thinks at all it is there.* Johnson himself thought at such times *with great intentness,* but was uncertain whether he could agree with Boswell that a man was always happy there, too. Then has not a London editor boasted that he was the only person to be blown off the privy in a *Blitz* while reading the works of Jane Austen? Surely Herrick too had such habits in mind when he warned the reader of *Hesperides* against the un-

authorised use of his text, invoking a curse against all
transgressors with the words:

> *May every Ill that bites or smarts*
> *Perplex him in his hinder parts.*

Indeed, I recollect privies of a former age shaped with all
the elegance and comfort of a Queen Anne chair, where
manifestly the occupant was intended to find the comfort
necessary to the full enjoyment of good reading.

Of Earth-closets.—Herein, as it seems to me, is one of
the specific defects of the earth-closet, which, because it
must of necessity be kept dry, is unsuited to durable comfort for those who experience difficulty in separating their
functions and therefore a poor place in which to read.

I must also deplore, from every consideration, those
combined bathroom-closets where a man can enjoy neither a leisurely bath nor a book without the possibility of
becoming a bugbear to the diffident or a victim of the im-
patient. How often is the bather disturbed by the timid or
forcible turning of the door-handle by those whose requirements are more urgent than his own, or the reader's
peace destroyed by one who has need of a bath! The lion
will as soon lie down with the lamb as two such persons,
on the average, agree upon the best use to which the place
can be put at any given moment.

Of Posture and Design—Authority of Aristotle and the
Bhagavad-Gita.—In the interests of general health as much
as in that of providing comfortable accommodation for
the reader, I must add here a word concerning the proper
height and shape of closets. We have already observed the
fact that the low-built *rational* closet is considered suitable only for *natives,* since these alone adopt the natural
position required by such conveniences. The ideal closet
is therefore built like the *Health Closet* of Messrs. Doulton, allowing the exercise of the abdominal muscles. It is

very low, sloped sharply downward from the front, and is curved to match average physical proportions; indeed, for those who can afford such luxuries it could be made to measure from a plaster-cast (as I have often advocated in the matter of chairs, which should be bespoke for those individuals who most use them). The squatting position is admirably shewn in an illustration to Mr. F. A. Hornibrook's book, *The Culture of the Abdomen,* where the dangers and disadvantages of the common position adopted in the West are also illustrated and discussed, with quotations from Dr. Leonard Williams on *Middle Age and Old Age* to shew the superiority of the position adopted by the Hindus and many other peoples, which I regard as a relic of a very ancient civilisation where men understood the importance of *posture.* Was not posture the subject of one of the first questions which Arjuna addressed to Krishna in the *Bhagavad-Gita?* Did not even the learned Aristotle make it the ninth of his ten *Categories?* The correct carriage of the spinal column and the proper position of the colon, neglected today by Western science and modern habit, may be considered as basic propositions to the oldest and most highly developed art in the world, that control of the body and the mind which the Hindus call *yoga.* But for our purpose it is sufficient to remark that a little study of *posture,* and especially at such moments as we have in mind, would do much to eliminate haemorrhoids and cure constipation, delivering us from the necessity to resort to purges and patent medicines. Of how many might those words have been written which Dr. Johnson used of the learned Edmond Smith —who, resolving (says the Doctor) to ease himself by evacuation, prescribed for his use a forcible purge, and swallowed his own medicine, which in July 1710 brought him to his grave. He was buried at Hartham. *Sic transit:* an everyday tragedy.

Next, to return to the adequacy or otherwise of the public provision, and the great importance of this question; since we do not all enjoy the privileges and statutory rights of cab-drivers (who may legally perform what it is a *nuisance* for others to commit, subject to various sub-clauses and notwithstanding, etc.), I say this matter is greatly under-rated. For I have heard a gentleman declare that what he most condemned in the city of New York in the 'twenties was the lamentable lack of public conveniences; and a nation can acquire an ill name for so small a thing as this. And rather than see a few very splendid edifices, of imitation marble and alabaster, which seem only to mock themselves of our shabby persons, I would prefer to see the money spent upon cheap and efficient places of great number and frequency in our streets, to serve our needs promptly rather than to crush and dominate our inadequacy with their affluence and magnificence.

A Merry Jest of King Louis the Eleventh.—If I had my way, then, I would give equal care to internal and external comfort, which are indeed inseparable, the care of the *Sewage System of the Human Body* (as Sir Arbuthnot Lane appropriately terms it) being dependent for most of us upon an adequate external provision. How often, for want of the necessary place, or of the necessary courage (if we were truthful), have we found ourselves in the same case as that Cardinal La Balue and the other guests of King Louis the Eleventh, of whom Balzac tells in his *Contes Drolatiques*. We talk of the pains and sighs of lovers, but what are these to the misery of those unhappy men who, having enjoyed to the full the hospitality of the king, were deprived by a diabolical stratagem of the opportunity to relieve themselves? And as the pangs of an unsatisfied passion serve to increase the pleasure of ultimate fulfilment, so we can imagine from our experience

the joy of those guests as they sought relief in the Mall at
Tours, from which time (says Balzac) the citizens of that
town have never failed to imitate them in defiling it, taking their fashion from the Court. In a more civilised age,
when such practices are deprecated, those who value *comfort* will surely arrange things better so that we need not
to choose between misery, with its attendant perils, and
the filthy habits of the French Court, which are now accompanied by the perils of the law. Surely our street air-
raid shelters, however useless for their intended purpose,
could be adapted to that for which their design fits them
more appropriately.

Story of Sister Petronille.—Or (to consider further the
evidence of Honoré de Balzac) we may reflect upon the
history of Sister Petronille, who sought canonisation by
way of constipation, perhaps in imitation of St. Catherine
of Siena; and certainly from the account of this enterprise
it is clear that she deserved to be placed in the Calendar
of Saints, if mortification of the flesh could achieve holiness. If, therefore, the greatest pain and discomfort should
be sought in that direction, enough to earn a halo for the
sufferer, does it not follow by all the postulates, syllogisms, canons and inferences of the Thomists that those
who seek an earthly crown and a worldly happiness should
be provided with a throne for the flesh and the faculty to
use it? For in the same history we are assured that the
angels are unable to be seated, and could not, though God
Himself commanded it, because they have not the where-
withal, that is to say, having no behinds. But we, who are
not angels, have needs which our corporations and county
councils might provide for more liberally, seeing that few
of us aspire to be saints at such a cost. And if a certain
gentleman had devoted half the time that he spent upon
destroying Waterloo Bridge, in meeting the needs within

the metropolis of persons *in extremis,* his request that we should *go to it* would not be so readily answered by the query: *Where is it?*

Of Courtesy to the Stranger.—Then, for the convenience of such as do not speak our language (and find themselves in the predicament of my friend who, on a certain occasion, could not determine for himself whether he was an *homme,* a *dame* or a *lampiste*), where, I say, those international signs known to some are neither understood nor used, not every borough has yet the courageous simplicity of one I know of. For in this borough the privies which were made in their air-raid shelters shewed a sign, which was of a dog and a lamp-post, to make clear the purpose of the place; and by the lamp-post there stood, as the case might warrant, a man or a woman. This, I maintain, is courtesy to the foreigner, as advocated in the principal religions of the world.

An Appeal for Universal Indoor Sanitation.—Or who will read the account given by Mr. Powys in his *Glastonbury Romance* of what things were heard by the Mayor of Glastonbury when Bloody Johnny slept in the haunted chamber at Mark Moor Court, without some disgust at the primitive equipment of houses, even in these days of plumbing? The ghost of King Mark could hardly have intruded with less welcome upon the vigil of the mayor than this enforced privacy with the affairs of others in the room below. Comfort and convenience, therefore, as much as hygiene, suppose a decent and universal system of indoor sanitation, such as this country yet lacks. For, once more it must be said, we aim to accommodate sinners and not to make saints. Read, therefore, if you are minded, yet another story in this *Romance,* of how Holy Sam, having seen the Sangreal itself, proceeded (upheld by the ecstasy of a mystical experience) to administer an enema to an old man in the most primitive surroundings. Ask yourself, then, having followed as best you can the mixed mysticism of the Holy Grail and what follows, whether a decent sinner, deprived of such uplifting reflections, should be asked to do the same; yet any district nurse will tell you it is common enough.

Evidence from the Anatomy of Melancholy.—The odour of sensual sanctity with which Mr. Powys has succeeded in surrounding such matters is to be found in great profusion by those who care to read his autobiography, which I consider to be the most honest revelation of its kind since Rousseau wrote his *Confessions.* Thus he admits that, not having experienced in some two or three years a *natural* action of the bowels, he has come to prefer his enema, and it cannot be denied that this has long been a popular remedy with some, since the most ancient times. Thus Hercules de Saxonia is cited in Burton's *Anatomy* as saying that he had found by experience that many hypochondriacal melancholy men had been cured by the sole use of clysters. And another he quotes, Amatus Lusitanus (*cent.* 4, *curat.* 54), who (he says) prescribed a strange remedy. Put a pair of bellows end into a clyster pipe; and, applying it into the fundament, open the bowels, so draw forth the wind: *natura non admittit vacuum.* Amatus Lusitanus vaunted that he was the inventor of this remedy, and, by means of it, speedily eased a melancholy man; which I can very readily believe.

Indeed, there is much substance for thought in this venerable practice of attacking *a tergo,* which may serve to amplify the problem of anal-erotism and the theories of Dr. Groddeck, when we come to discuss them. For Burton tells us that in the *Medicinal Observations* of Skenkius there is an account of a merchant going to Nordeling Fair, who for the space of ten days never went to stool. At his return *he was grievously melancholy, and would not be persuaded but that all his money was gone.* This gentleman at last yielded to an enema, whereby he recovered his wits. And Montaigne informs us of another merchant upon whom the mere imagination of clysters wrought so strongly that it was sufficient for an apothecary to bring his instrument, and all to be made ready, when *he found and felt the very same effect which they do that have effectually taken them.*

Of a Poisoned Clyster.—This remedy was known, as we have seen, to the Assyrians, and praised by Pliny, though despised by Plotinus; and Bartholomew Trahern in his translation of *The Chirurgery of Joh. de Vigo* said of it in 1543 that a clyster is a noble remedy to drive out superfluities of the guts. Indeed, I know of but one gentleman who was the worse for an enema, and that was Sir Thomas Overbury, of whom I read in Wood's *Athenae Oxoniensis* that (after many attempts to poison him, while he lay prisoner in the Tower, had made him sick without destroying him) *at length by a poisoned clyster given to him under pretence of curing him, he was dispatched.* But upon the weight of historical testimony this is a valuable remedy and no mean matter, so that we may return to Mr. Powys with a more respectful attention after this seeming digression.

Mr. Powys primarily desires (I suppose) that regularity of performance of which Montaigne writes with such feeling when he tells us, in his essay on Experience, that it is a fault that has grown upon him with years not only to use a prescribed hour but to keep to a particular convenient place and a commodious Ajax (the word is used by Florio) *and make it troublesome with long sitting and nice observation.* So also Mr. Powys gives among the reasons which he advances for his curious preference that circumstances have forced him to read *those great old-world books that alone have the strength, the gall, the spirit, the comprehensiveness, the heroic grossness, to go decently with the process of spending a whole hour at stool.* Thus we return to this absorbing and paramount question of the closet as library, and I observe with approval that John Cowper Powys claims to have read *in situ* the *Anatomy of Melancholy, Tristam Shandy,* more than half of *Don Quixote,* all the works of Rabelais and two volumes of Montaigne.

The Phobias of Mr. J. C. Powys as a Microscope held to Human Neurosis.—From the same authority those who are accustomed to make light of such things may learn the extraordinary importance that can be attached to inconvenience, that is to say, to the lack of proper provision in the matter of *conveniences.* For Mr. Powys considered it the worst horror of a life in the army, which he contemplated without ever experiencing it, that he might have difficulty regarding the major and minor calls of nature whilst on the march, and imagined in his nightmares (for such only can they be termed) how he would implore the sergeant for leave to drop out of the ranks. Also he records of his visit to Hamburg that it was remembered by him for one of his most miserable occasions, which was *of wanting desperately to find a close-stool and not finding one.* This experience, he writes, made so deep an impression on him, that he was still wont to *feel the physical sensations by which it was accompanied* when he saw snow on the ground, since there had been snow at that time on the wharves of Hamburg. Here, indeed, raised to an infinite power, is a picture of the human misery caused by inadequate provision for our needs; and it is as reasonable to consider it in that light as it is to regard a bug through a microscope, in order to understand its properties.

Mr. Pry on the Hiding of Public Conveniences.—The observations of the anonymous author of *For Your Convenience* are at this point most apposite. For he shews that whereas our more luxurious jakes were placed in prominent positions with lighted signs (when such things were to be seen), the meaner houses of office, and more especially those green enclosures that serve but one purpose, are hidden away as though (he says) the authorities were bitter and shamefaced or aesthetically revolted by their own creations. Therefore he finds that only the initiated know where to look for such places, and offers the advice that in our provincial towns they may commonly be found near the statue of Queen Victoria or of a local money-grubber. But he commends as superior the habit of the French, who advertise relief to the wayfarer by plastering these structures prominently placed in their thorough-fares, with the unmistakable *cachet* of *Chocolat Menier* or *Amer Picon;* to which he should surely have added *Byrrh,* that *vin apéritif* so conducive to the proper functioning of the interior.

Parable in a Chestnut Shell.—What, indeed, decides how numerous these places shall be or where they shall be placed? The author of *For Your Convenience* indulges in fantastical reflections on this subject, which you may seek out for yourself, if you have a mind; but I recall a *chestnut* sufficiently ripe to be new again concerning an alderman of one of our towns in the provinces, who would not give his vote for the building of a urinal. However, upon learning what it was that he had opposed (for he was used to more homely language) he said that if that was what they spoke of he would vote not only for a urinal but for an arsenal also. I have an inclination to believe that this story is true in substance if not in fact, in that the decisions taken are not more lucidly discussed by our corporations, which shew so little understanding of our requirements.

A Suggestion to H.M. Government, worthy of its Intelligence, etc.—I have often, like the same ingenious author of *op. cit.,* wondered (and more especially since these days of darkness) how the stranger to our shores discovers what he is looking for. Is this, in point of fact, the true origin and explanation of the *curfew* regulation for aliens, a humane provision, perchance, to save the foreigner from nocturnal embarrassment and our streets from defilement? But why, if this be the case, have those who removed all signposts and even the place-names below the signs of shops and public-houses, neglected to remove these other signs; for inadequate as they are they might still be of some service to a parachutist, who (as I suppose) has the same needs as other men. Surely such a stratagem would not be unworthy of those who propose to check the impact of a Panzer division with a string of barbed wire. Imagine the confusion of the invaders, if faced with such a predicament, looking doubtfully (as *Paul Pry* has imagined the invaders of peace-time) at a subway or a sentry-box, a taxi-shelter or the hut outside the depot where I am writing; but I will refer you once more to Mr. Pry's masterpiece for a summary of further possibilities.

Then again, I have sometimes reflected upon the confusion of Maori visitors to this country, most admirable people whose peculiarity it is that women stand and men squat, like the ancient Egyptians, but entirely contrary to our practice. Of what use to a Maori male is the Jennings Patent, provided with a target offering the ideal trajectory for a silent performance without wetting one's shoes or creating any splash? But I must curb such speculations because they lead me to a greater and more profound matter, which is nothing less than the origin of divergent practice in the great religions and ancient civilisations of this planet. Let us therefore spend no more time considering such personal problems, but leave our hypothetical Maoris and benighted foreigners to find their own way through the lampless streets. For here a new chapter opens, which is concerned with nothing less than the religious observances of certain peoples with regard to the closet and to matters of cleanliness generally.

This subject I therefore propose to approach with the greatest reverence; and if inadvertently I should say anything amiss I will comfort myself with the reflection of that sanguine Frenchman who observed, *le bon Dieu me pardonnera; c'est son métier.*

CAPUT XI

Concerning Cleanliness and Godliness

Of the Observances of the Ancient Hebrews.—The ancient Hebrews concerned themselves greatly with that which was clean and that which was unclean, and their prophet Moses was meticulous in the details of his commandments to the people. In the twenty-third chapter of the book called *Deuteronomy* he gives his instruction to those who go to war; Thou shalt have a place also (he says) without the camp whither thou shalt go forth abroad. And thou shalt have a paddle upon thy weapon; and it shall be, when thou wilt ease thyself abroad, thou shalt dig therewith, and thou shalt turn back and cover that which cometh from thee. This excellent procedure he advocates because *the Lord thy God walketh in the midst of the camp;* for which reason Moses held that the camp should be worthy of such a visitor, *that he see no unclean thing in thee, and turn away from thee.* And whoever reads the *Talmud* or the *Jewish Encyclopaedia* will find further and more detailed instructions to guide his behaviour in accordance with the maxim, *lavatore est orare.*

The Prophet Mohammed enjoins Cleanliness.—The Mohammedan laws of purification differ but little from those enjoined by the *Talmud,* for the Prophet adopted in this and many other respects the civilisation of the Jews. Islam ordains the washing of the whole body, which is called *Ghusl,* to absolve it from uncleanliness after certain acts, before the True Believer may pray to Allah or touch the sacred leaves of the Koran. The acts which are enumerated as defiling the body and requiring *Ghusl* are *pollutio nocturna, menses, coïtus* and *puerperium*. Moreover, there are many other hygienic measures specified by the law of Islam, as *Wazu,* or the washing of the hands, arms and face before prayer (in such cases as do not require *Ghusl*); *Istinja,* or the abstersion of the private parts; *Miswak,* or the cleansing of the teeth; *Tathir,* or the cleansing of vessels and clothing from impurity. And for those who are in the desert, without water, or for whom there is no water of sufficient purity, as defined by the Islamic law, there is *Tayammum,* or the use of sand or dust in the place of water.

Rules for Behaviour in a Closet.—For the Muslims say that purity is half the faith, and this saying they attribute to their Prophet, so that their theologians divide purification into four categories: of the body, from physical filthiness; of the members, from their offences; of the heart, from evil desires; and of the spirit, from all that is not of Allah. And in every particular they are careful to prescribe the way in which a man shall carry himself that he may attain or preserve purity. Thus they say that a man on entering a closet shall place the left foot before the right, and on leaving he shall place the right before the left. And on his person he shall carry no object upon which the name of God is inscribed, nor shall he, if it be possible, turn either his face or his posterior towards Mecca whilst he is closeted, which shall be with his weight upon the left leg. All this I learn from the *Manuel de Jurisprudence Musalman selon le Rite de Chafi;* which was a learned volume of Muslim law, done into French and published by order of the Government at Batavia *an.* 1882. This law-book further says that if a man relieve himself in the desert, where he can take his choice at will as to his direction, he shall in no wise break this order regarding his posture in relation to Mecca. Many other things it tells us regarding the making of water; that it should be done beyond the public scrutiny, should not be done in a hole or in stagnant water, or while holding converse with another, and other orders for cleanliness and decency. And after defaecation the law ordains cleansing with stones or with water; or, if it be possible with stones first and after with water; also that, if stones be used, there shall be three stones employed or three sides of the same stone, and that the left hand shall be used, as among the Hindus (for the right hand is that with which a man eats); and there are other matters which are mentioned as disputed among jurists, for which reason I cannot with certainty say what is true and what is false, unless I should find that these matters have been determined since the year 1882.

The Reason why God swears by the Fig and the Olive. —That the God of Islam is a god of health appears also in this, that their Prophet in the chapter of *Al Koran* entitled *The Fig* swears by the fig and the olive, and the erudite George Sale in his translation tells us that the Islamic commentators say that God Himself swears by these two fruits; for (he observes) the fig is wholesome and of easy digestion and physically good to carry off phlegm and gravel in the kidneys or bladder, and to remove obstructions of the liver and spleen, and also cures the piles and the gout. The wood of the olive tree, he says, is good for cleansing the teeth, preventing their growing rotten, and giving a good odour to the mouth; for which reason the prophets, and Mohammed in particular, made use of no other toothpick.

Of the use of sand in default of water Mr. Sale remarks that this expedient was borrowed from the Jews or perhaps from the Persian Magi, who both prescribe the same method in case of necessity. For the Magi, he observes, were almost as scrupulous as the Jews themselves in their lustrations. This writer also expressed his opinion that the pagan Arabs used such practices of cleanliness long before the time of Mohammed, as most nations did (says he) and still do in the East, *where the warmth of the climate requires a greater nicety and degree of cleanliness than these colder parts*—thus does he excuse the slovenly habits and filthiness of his contemporaries in these islands. But Mohammed made no such excuses or exceptions, saying plainly that *the practice of religion is founded on cleanliness*. Such was long the custom among these Infidels, as Busbequius tells us of the Turks in his time: *Nec alvum excernunt, quin aquam secum portent, qua partes obscoenas lavent,* they do not defaecate without taking with them water to wash their privy parts.

Of the Jinn or Genii.—The Jinn or Genii, no less than Allah and his Prophet, concerned themselves with baths and latrines, for these are enumerated, in the notes of Edward Lane to his celebrated translation of the *Arabian Nights' Entertainment,* among their places of resort. Therefore an Arab, upon entering such a place, exclaims: *Destoor yá mubárakeen; that is to say, Permission, ye Blessed!* But whether Aladdin was in such a place when he rubbed his lamp I have not yet discovered, though I consider it more reasonable to expect Genii in such quarters than in any other parts of the house, because a man is more prone to see these creatures when he is without other company. The reader of the *Arabian Nights* will also observe the frequent reference to baths, shewing the cleanliness of the Arabs at the time when these tales were invented, which was between the eighth and the tenth centuries.

Alas for the frailties of human flesh. The tamarisks of Turkestan bear witness to the decline of good customs, the inadequacy of the most excellent examples and precepts. Each bush has served as an inadequate shelter for the True Believer; and in default of water he has used powdered brick from the tomb of great Tamerlaine. What fate awaits you, my proud contemporaries, the conquerors of today? Behold, the final desecration of all human monuments is in their unconscious defilement, where London pigeons innocently whiten the heads of mounted generals, and the hind leg of a careless dog is raised against the corner-stone of the plinth.

Contempt of the Hindus for the Body.—Among the Hindus also there are many rules to be observed whereby religion makes provision for hygiene, and these are more rigorous than in any other country, for the Hindus hold the body in great contempt on account of its corruption. In the *Maitrayana* this matter is thus plainly stated: in this evil-smelling, unsubstantial body (so reads the text) shuffled together out of bones, skin, sinews, marrow, flesh, seed, blood, mucus, tears, eye-gum, dung, urine, gall and phlegm, how can we enjoy pleasure? This body, originating from copulation, grown in the pit and issuing forth through the passages of the excretions, is a collection of bones daubed over with flesh. And thereafter is repeated the list of its horrid ingredients.

There will be found by the curious reader in the *International Journal of Psycho-Analysis* for the year 1921 (vol. 2, part 3–4) a learned discourse by one Berkeley-Hill on *The Anal-Erotic Factor in the Religion, Philosophy and Character of the Hindus*. The writer of this discourse cites the *Maitrayana* and provides a long account of the *Rules to be Observed by Brahmins when Answering the Calls of Nature*. With regard to these rules, I must myself observe that I never knew a Brahmin, or had reason to believe that a Brahmin existed, who minutely followed their instructions. But as they provide a picture, however distorted, of the meticulous detail with which religion concerns itself in India to regulate such matters, I will give in summary the principal provisions.

Hygienic Rules for Defaecation.—First the Brahmin, provided with a brass vessel, betakes himself to the appropriate spot, which must be at least a bowshot from his house. This place must on no account be the enclosure of a temple, the edge of a river, pond or well, a public road or place; and other exceptions are made for which less reasonable explanation could be offered. The Brahmin shall not himself wear a new garment or one newly washed; he hangs his triple cord over his left ear, covers his head with his loin-cloth and stoops as low as he may.

As the Moslem may not look at this time towards Mecca, so the Hindu must avoid turning his eyes towards the sun or the moon, the stars, fire, another Brahmin, a temple, an image or a sacred tree. But the Hindu law does not concern itself with the direction of his posterior, as is the case with the law of Islam. The Brahmin must be silent at this time, must have nothing in his mouth and hold nothing on his head; what he has to do he must do quickly, rising without delay and on no account committing the offence of Lot's wife.

The Filthiness of using Paper.—Next he must wash his feet and his hands at this spot with the water from his vessel, and afterwards he will go to the stream and cleanse himself on the bank with earth and water. Three times he cleans himself with earth and water, using his left hand, as do the Moslems, for a man eats with his right hand, and Mr. Berkeley-Hill says very correctly that *it would be thought unpardonably filthy to use the right hand*. It is always, he says, the left hand that is used when anything dirty has to be done, such as blowing the nose or cleaning the eyes and the ears, the left hand being commonly used to touch all parts of the body below the navel, and the right hand (except it should be for these less honourable purposes) for all parts that are above the navel. And this custom of washing after answering a call of nature is strictly observed, says Mr. Berkeley-Hill (whose testimony in this matter I can abundantly confirm), by all castes. Also he says that the habit of using *paper* is looked upon by all Hindus, without exception, as an utter abomination, and that they never speak of it without horror, as I can confirm once more. And some there are, he says, who even refuse to believe such a habit exists and think it must be some libel invented out of hatred for Europeans. Moreover, this writer records that the sight of a foreigner blowing his nose into a handkerchief and putting this into his pocket is enough to make a Hindu *feel the need to vomit*.

Other Hygienic Observances of the Hindus.—But we must return to our Brahmin, who has now cleansed himself three times with earth and water, and afterwards washes his hands five times in the same manner, beginning with the left. Then must he wash his private parts with water and potter's earth, and so also each foot five times, beginning with the right, and afterwards each of these parts of the body must be washed with water only. Next must he wash his face and rinse his mouth eight times; for it is necessary (observes Mr. Berkeley-Hill) to rinse the mouth after every action calculated to cause defilement, four times after micturition, eight times after defaecation, twelve times after taking food and sixteen times after sexual intercourse. This is not all, but the greater part of the ceremony as this writer has described it; and he records also the rules for the cleaning of the teeth with twigs of trees and with water. But in this matter, as with the other, I never knew such rules to be followed in all their particulars, observing only that the teeth were cleansed in the morning and at night, also after food; and I have myself used the twigs which Hindus use and found them to be of an astringent quality, imparting a fresh and bitter taste, very excellent also for cleaning all cavities, and more hygienic, as I should imagine, than the toothbrush, because the implement used is clean and new on every occasion.

Mr. Berkeley-Hill mentions also the daily bath, which is best taken in a river or (as he calls it) in a sacred stream; but in India all streams are holy because running water cleanses; and this we now know to be the case, for so great is the oxidisation in running water that the greatest sources of pollution are in time destroyed. But if there is no such stream nearby, the Hindu washes by throwing water over himself, so that he ends with clean water; for he despises those who sit among the floating scum and filth of their own bodies in baths; and if he has money to build himself a bathroom it will be a shower-bath. There are many such things of which Mr. Berkeley-Hill makes no mention, such as the daily changing of garments among all who can afford to do so; and it is the opinion of Mahatma Gandhi that all should wear white, for coloured cloth he holds to be deceptive, concealing its own foulness, as the outer garments of Europeans commonly do. And the vessels used for eating and drinking are scoured with earth before they are rinsed in running water. But a Hindu, drinking water, will not touch the vessel with his lips, for he pours the water down his throat, throwing back his head as though he would fill a cup from a jug. Thus many persons may drink from the same vessel without defiling it; and among the poorest and most ignorant classes this custom obtains as well as it does among those who might be thought more fastidious.

As to their closets, they despise our custom of sitting upon a common seat, but make these places in a manner familiar to those who have visited the standing privies to be found in France. In this too they shew themselves more sensible than ourselves to considerations of hygiene, as also to the best posture for the purpose, which we have already discussed. And here I must mention that in the province of Bengal these privies are infested by evil spirits whom the people call *patni,* these spirits appearing as females with club feet and black hair of great length, with which they will sometimes strangle the solitary pilgrim who seeks these places at night. But whether these *patni* are the same as those *genii* of the closet, of whom we have already spoken, and were brought to India with the Moslem faith, I am at a loss to say.

A Digression on the Supernatural.—Indeed, if I may digress for a while from this Hindu theme, I have reason to believe that the supernatural terrors accompanying the natural functions are of great age. For Hesiod, in the first book of his *Works and Days,* has something to say on this matter, which is thus rendered in an eighteenth-century translation by Thomas Cooke:

> *When you would have your urine pass away,*
> *Stand not upright before the eye of day;*
> *And scatter not your water as you go*
> *Nor let it, when you're naked, from you flow:*
> *In either case 'tis an unseemly sight:*
> *The gods observe alike by day and night:*
> *The man whom we devout and wise may call*
> *Sits in that act, or streams against a wall.*

You might almost have thought Hesiod to have been an Hindu, he is so nice upon the point and as superstitious as St. Paul found the men of Athens to be when he came that way. And Pliny in his *Naturalis Historia* (xxviii. 19), tells us that magicians in his time (following Pythagoras) warned men against uncovering themselves to urinate when exposed to the rays of the sun or the moon, also against letting any shadow be touched by their water. Moreover, he quotes Osthanes as maintaining that there was a prophylactic value in allowing some urine to fall upon the foot in the morning. But this is a very mild piece of nastiness among many foul remedies and prophylactics that old Pliny advocated, very noisome and excrementitious, such as suppositories made from swallows' dung and honey.

Here shameful Matters are freely discussed.—However, to resume: the freedom with which all matters of hygiene are discussed among the Hindus (all things that are regarded among us as shameful being treated by them as matters for public discussion) should be an example to prudes. For on my first meeting with Mahatma Gandhi, being at that time a guest at his *ashram* near Ahmedabad, I had no sooner exchanged with him a few words of greeting than I was asked *how were my bowels*. In this specific question there was far more of true courtesy than may be found in general enquiries as to health; and at all times I found Hindus would ask such questions and offer advice where it was needed.

The Anal-Erotic Complex, according to Mr. Berkeley-Hill.—The reason assigned by Mr. Berkeley-Hill to the habits of the Hindus is what he terms the *anal-erotic complex;* and he writes with such scorn and venom of their customs that it is necessary to examine his reasoning so far as it can be discovered. This writer makes no effort to prove the theory of anal-erotism, because he says that the facts upon which it is based are so widely known as to make it superfluous to do so. Thus he follows in the best tradition of those *psychologists* who find it a more profitable pastime to fit facts into a theory than to establish its validity. The reactions against anal-erotism, he says (accepting *a priori* the assumptions of Ernest Jones), are to be found in the desire to *keep back,* in affection for symbolic objects, in the desire for orderliness, in generosity and extravagance, in the impulse to stain or contaminate, and in industrial and artistic creations. And (since these mutually incompatible tendencies are to be found among all peoples in all parts of the world) there is no difficulty in discovering them among the Hindus, even though facts have sometimes to be somewhat stretched. For Mr. Berkeley-Hill tells us in one place that the Hindus are mean and avaricious, though I never found this to be the case; and in order to establish the fact he is reduced to citing the evidence of a character in a work of fiction by Mr. Kipling, to which he adds that *no one conversant with Hindu character, probably not even a Hindu himself, would hesitate to admit that as a class the Hindus are niggardly and avaricious*. Such appeals *ad hominem* tell us more of Mr. Berkeley-Hill than they do of the Hindus and their anal-erotism. But next, in order to fulfil the scriptures, he must discover generosity and extravagance, the very opposite of avarice; and these characteristics he finds in *stories* shewing the extravagance of Indian princes, nobles and plutocrats, as though such *stories* (true or otherwise) were not told in every country.

Supposed Manifestations of this Complex.—Next this author has observed that the Hindus are fond of children, and in this unique characteristic he discovers their affection for *symbolic objects*. In their litigous habits and philosophic pedantry he finds their *desire for orderliness*. When they sprinkle one another with powder or fluid, as we do with rice or confetti, he finds the *impulse to stain or contaminate;* and when they create objects of art and beauty the impulses of anal-erotism are manifest in *industrial and artistic creations*. These strange phenomena, it is true, he observes in other countries; but where they have become vices among the Hindus, others, and notably the English, have turned them to virtuous account.

Thus, while the anal-erotism of the Hindus is found by Mr. Berkeley-Hill in their incapacity for happiness, irritability, bad temper, hypochondria, miserliness, meanness, pettiness, slow-mindedness, proneness to bore, and in tyrannising, dictating and obstinacy, he observes that the anal-erotism of the English is not so displayed. For he finds them better-tempered than the Hindus, which is astonishing; and he has not observed avarice to be among the impulses of Empire, nor does he see tyranny in our rule, though he can see it well enough in the system of *caste;* and Englishmen, *mirabile dictu,* do not bore him. But he finds them individualistic, determined and persistent (such are the names for *obstinacy* when applied to ourselves), and they love order (not *pedantry,* which is the orderliness of others) and are powerful in organisation. Also they are competent, thorough and generous (but not *extravagant,* like those princes of India or those whose fortunes, he says, *seldom survive the second generation,* among the Hindus), and Englishmen have *the bent towards art and good taste* (not merely creating beautiful things, as the Hindus do) with a *capacity for tenderness,* which is not to be confused with the Hindu love of children.

Worship of Baal-Peor among the English.—And again, he says, the English have learnt to make a fetish of *sanitation.* For he says that an Englishman's bathroom, water-closet and laundry form a triad of reaction-formations of his anal-erotism before which he will, so to speak, *prostrate himself in a rhapsody of adoration.* This seems good to him; but the observances of the *Hindus* in such matters he finds to be only an *apotheosis of ceremonial purification,* combined with *conditions indescribably filthy;* which is the exact manner in which a Hindu regards the habits of bathing in stagnant water, *sitting in one's own dirt,* or the use of paper where water (they say) should be employed; for they will ask with the greatest disgust *Can paper cleanse?* And to this there is no answer.

From this we may learn that this question of sanitation

and hygiene is as much confused as any other with prejudice, so that there is little hope for exact information or balanced judgement even among persons of scientific pretensions. And those who read such writings should beware of what they read. For, like another writer on the depravity of the Hindus, who did much to confuse our minds on these matters, Mr. Berkeley-Hill is not ashamed to cite as one of his principal witnesses the Abbé Dubois. This Dubois was a French missionary who, together with like authorities, greatly influenced the mind of the historian James Mill; and these *authorities* were described by Max Müller as *all of them neither very competent nor very unprejudiced judges.* But the worst fault in a scientific treatise is to find that there is no mention of the fact that this Dubois wrote of India at the beginning of the nineteenth century, when the reader of this book will not need to be reminded that the Englishman knew as little, and indeed much less, of *sanitation.* Many other authors are cited in the same manner; so that (without acknowledgement of the fact) the conditions of England *today* are compared with those of India *in the past,* and our new notions of cleanliness set against Hindu superstitions which are already dead or dying.

For those who would know more of the origin of such prejudices I would modestly refer to the chapter entitled *The Evolution of Anglo-Indian Mythology* in my own work, *The White Sahibs in India.* Such prejudices had already become so strong in the last century that Mr. H. H. Wilson, who edited and extended Mill's *History of India,* found it necessary continually to correct the opinions of James Mill, founded upon evidence to which we have already made reference, and particularly to refute the charge of uncleanliness against the Hindus. For he compared these people to their advantage with those of Southern Europe and he said also that *there are many of their prac-*

tices which might be introduced even into the North with benefit. Whether these practices emanate from anal-erotism or no I leave others to decide, but trust that they will find better authorities for their facts than the Abbé Dubois, Mr. Kipling, Meredith Townsend, William Archer and other defunct and prejudiced persons upon whom Mr. Berkeley-Hill relies for evidence.

The Value of Taboo *when properly exercised.*—In the next chapter we shall consider the value of *taboo* as an incentive to cleanliness; but as it is now customary to decry *taboo,* the reader is invited to prepare his mind suitably by considering first an example of the *taboo* against dirtiness without any sense of *taboo* regarding the body.

Among the Chaldean Christians of Kurdistan there was (as late as the middle of the last century) a combination of cleanly habits with a lack of inhibition as to the body which is rare among Christian peoples. For Sir Austen Layard, in his book on *Nineveh and Its Remains* (published in 1854), tells of the Tiyari women, whose beauty he describes also, how they bathed themselves in a rill, stripping their bodies without restraint. And for the better part of an hour their ablutions continued unnoticed by the men who were present, and as unmindful of their presence (he says) as if they bathed in some secluded spot. But on such an occasion he tells us that a Moslem shewed great indignation, complaining that when he told the women to go to a greater distance they replied that *if he did not wish to see them he might turn his head the other way.* If, said the Moslem, these infidels have no modesty, let them know that we Mussulmans have. Mohammed Pasha, upon whom God has had mercy, declared of the Arabs that the men were without religion, the women without drawers and the horses without bridles; but these unbelievers eat more dirt than all the Arabs, and are verily little better than the beasts of the field. The narrator of this story says that he reasoned with a Chaldean priest on what he terms the impropriety of this public bathing, but the priest, he says, did not appear at all sensible of it, which I record here as a matter of weight. And in the same country this custom is also found among the Yezidis, who do reverence to Satan.

From these various observations I conclude that cleanliness is enjoined by three of the greatest religions in the world, those of the Hindus, of the Jews and of Islam; also that cleanliness is not unknown among primitive Christians; and that the *taboo* against filth, which we shall presently examine, may be separated from that *horror of the body* with which most religions have associated it. Your mincing Puritan of today will never be worthy of his piratical ancestors until he can say with the same outspoken assurance, *Praise God and keep your bowels open*. Here are the first elements of religion and hygiene.

Of Taboos, *Useful and Otherwise*

Divers further Examples of Cleanliness inspired by Religion and Privies treated with Honour.—The toilets of the Egyptians were honourably regarded, like those of the Jews, for we read of one in a royal palace that was called *The House of the Morning,* and of another, in the mansion of a nobleman, called *The Cabinet of the Morning;* and so great was the insistence of religion among these people upon the necessity for cleanliness that they used the same word for washing and for breaking their fast, being unable to think of breakfast without having previously done all that was first necessary. Also (since they washed their hands before every meal, and a man would have his hands washed by his wife before he would so much as knock back a mug of beer) they would say *I will purify myself,* where we should say *I will have some food.*

The disciples of the Buddha have also been notably clean in their habits, though Gautama himself mocked at the ceremonial bathing of the Brahmins, and Sister Punna in *The Psalms of the Sisters* warned them that all their shivering in rivers could not bring them so much virtue as a crocodile could acquire in comfort.

Did not also that great generalissimo who presided over the Greek War Council, uniting their forces in Total War against the Unspeakable Trojan, do well to obey the dictates of religion or superstition, when he ordered a purification of the Achaean camp to rid it of the plague?

Nice Behaviour of the Essenes.—Or if you will consult Hippolytus, Bishop of Portus, on *The Refutation of All Heresies* (a manuscript discovered at Mount Athos in the year 1842), you will find that a person upon becoming a member of the Sect of the Essenes was first presented with a mattock, that most essential tool wherewith holes could be dug in the manner prescribed in Deuteronomy. To which the Bishop adds that they chose a lonely spot to do their business, and covered it in carefully with up-turned soil, that they were careful to explain at such times that they did not necessarily insult the sunbeams, and (above all, as he tells us) *they immediately wash themselves, as though polluted by the excrement.*

The practices of superstition have on many occasions been proved to have a basis in the health and well-being of the community. Thus we noted that among the Indians of America the sweat-house is employed as a cure for disease, which must in many instances be true, though the intention is magical. And for ceremonial purification these same Indians use such sweat-houses, achieving a purification which is of necessity more than ceremonial. Also of the peoples of Africa we read that they have the vapour bath for such purposes, and among the Bathonga it is employed to cure many diseases, especially those where a ritual defilement is to be feared. And among such matters we may speak also of the washing after child-birth, which is as much a matter of religion or superstition as a means of cleanliness, from which we may see once more that the one purpose serves the other; and this custom obtains among the Esquimo women, among the women of Malay and those of Uganda, to speak but of a few.

Astonishing Opinion of a Christian Writer.—To the Christian missionary the *taboo* which the savage attaches to uncleanliness is considered misplaced. Thus Mr. H. A. Junod writes in *The Life of a South African Tribe* that such notions will disappear when the knowledge of science spreads among the natives of whom he speaks. And he says, let the natives understand that *what is taboo is not physical uncleanness but moral evil,* and their strong aversion to the act tabooed may become a powerful moral impulse for good. But I venture to amend this to read that when science spreads among the missionaries they will understand that what is *taboo* is not moral fiction but material evil, health and holiness being of the same essence. The *taboo* may be termed good so long as it is relevant to this purpose; and the irrelevance of Pilate's ablutions cannot obscure the importance of those to which we have alluded.

Of Water and Gods of Water.—That Baal against whose prophets Elijah contended upon Mount Carmel, though he failed at fire-lighting, was in one of his departments a god of running water, to which his failure may be attributed; and without doubt he was powerful within his own confines. For that old captain of Syria knew well enough that water was water, and the streams Abana and Pharpar as good as any in Israel, when it came to washing-day. And the habit of bathing in sacred springs may well do more good than all our physic to the diseased, just as the worship of the Nile shews the good sense of the Egyptians. The Hebrew sect of the Essenes, long before the time of Hippolytus, made much of bathing and ablutions, and practised total immersion many centuries before it had attained its value as baptism for the remission of sins; for their religion taught that the body should be purified, but said nothing of the value of water for the soul.

The doctrines of *taboo* relating to uncleanliness led the Babylonians to many sound deductions. For, having postulated that a diseased person must of necessity have broken the *taboo* of purity, becoming unclean, they concluded that to touch such a person, to eat of his bread or drink of his water, to sleep upon his bed, sit upon his seat or to eat or drink from any vessel which he used, was to break this same *taboo* and to become unclean. In this they shewed themselves wise where all infections and contagions are considered.

Confusion of Holiness with Pollution.—Indeed, the learned Frazer (I speak of Sir James of *The Golden Bough*) remarks in his volume on *Taboo and the Perils of the Soul* that the superstitious fear of the magic that may be wrought on a man through the leavings of his food has had the beneficial effect of inducing many savages to destroy refuse which, if left to rot, might through its corruption have proved a real source of disease and death. From the same authority we learn many examples of the *sacred* being at the same time the *unclean*. For, as Sir James observes, when speaking of primitive persons, the conceptions of holiness and pollution are not yet differentiated in his mind.

Mr. Edwyn Bevan, who cites this last observation of Frazer's in his work on *Hellenism and Christianity,* gives as a curious instance among peoples even of advanced civilisation the phrase used by the rabbis to express the sanctity of the canonical scriptures, that they *defile the hands*. This will be found in his chapter on the subject of *Dirt,* where many important observations are made relating to superstition and cleanliness. It seems, he says, arguable that the feeling of dirt was developed as a protection against noxious germs before the presence of such germs could be detected by bacteriological science; that the notion of uncleanness was at the beginning a crude and superstitious way by which primitive man warded off disease and sepsis. And if so (he says) it might seem that, as superstition gave way to reason, the whole notion of dirt, uncleanness and pollution would disappear from the human mind, having fulfilled its function. And in such a society Mr. Bevan suggests that certain things would be avoided for purely prudential reasons, but without a sense of repugnance.

Disgust of a Munshi *at the beastly Habits of the English.*—To explain the difference between a rational and a superstitious sense of the clean and unclean, this writer tells of an English official in India who formed a friendship with a Mohammedan *munshi*. But the *munshi* was one day greatly distressed to hear confirmation from the Englishman of a story shewing the sordid and beastly habits of the English people—that they put into their mouths the bone of a dog with the bristles of a pig, by which he designated a toothbrush. Nor could the feelings of the *munshi* be in any way changed by the reasoning of the Englishman, the object being what it was; and Mr. Bevan concludes by observing that he would never after that disguise a feeling of restraint and repugnance in his intercourse with the Englishman, *as with a person of unspeakably filthy habits.*

A Paradoxical Conception of Cleanliness.—But we ourselves, says this writer, are little guided by reason in our sense of cleanliness. For, says he, the feeling as to the uncleanliness of excrements goes far beyond any logically drawn conclusion from their dangerousness as breeders of disease. And of the mouth he observes that we regard it as holy, with great jealousy protecting it from contact with pollution, so that no idea provokes such horror as that of putting the *unclean* into our mouths. Yet confusing, like primitive persons, the holy and unclean together, we regard the saliva ejected from the mouth as defiling that on which it falls; so that the secretion from the holy place becomes unclean the moment it leaves that place. And Mr. Bevan suggests that most persons of fastidious habits would prefer to place their hands in water where another person's hands had been washed rather than in water into which they had rinsed their own mouths. With this observation I would incline to agree from experience, and to add that the same principle can be applied *mutatis mutandis* to other parts of the body, in spite of the Latin proverb which records our tolerance for our own excretions; for among persons of education this tolerance is rarely to be observed.

The Desire for Cleanliness is shewn to be more than a Human Inhibition.—To these reflections I would append two more, of my own. In the first place, regarding animals, it is to be observed that cats are fastidious in their ablutions; and in their habit of digging holes and filling these in again (for certain purposes) are exemplary, putting both tramps and trippers to shame alike in cleanliness and modesty. Then it is known that pigs, long the object of many filthy slanders by their oppressors (who abuse the poor swine for conditions imposed upon them), are in reality cleanly creatures. For they take care not to foul the straw where they would lie, but keep their messes to one corner of the sty; and with ease they may be trained to use a channel that can be sluiced from end to end, which method they greatly prefer. Also of bats in the Mendip caves I have heard it said that they hang always over the same spot to do their business, shewing a tidy and cleanly disposition. Thus, though dogs and certain other brutes live lewdly and with great filthiness, it may be shewn that many animals have a desire for cleanliness, also that birds take great precaution not to foul their own nests, removing the droppings of their young, which nature fashions conveniently into capsules (except in the case of swallows, who are taught to excrete over the brim of their nests in early youth, as may be seen by those who pass beneath them). Therefore there may well be some instinctive desire to be clean, implanted by nature in certain animals that have most need of it, such as cats, bats, men and swine. And if this be the case we must not look in our *inhibitions* for the source of the superstitions of cleanliness, for it is not to be supposed that pigs or bats are *inhibited*. On the contrary, we shall expect to explain the superstitions relating to cleanliness by means of the instinct that urges us towards it, and not to explain a desire common to men and many brutes by some plausible story of guilt and sin. *Natura homo mundum et elegans animal est,* said Seneca; and Montaigne, who quotes him to this effect, adds moderately that care and cleanliness are in some sort excusable in our homeliest matters and foulest offices.

The Repugnance to Filth is, in general, greatest among those who are intellectually most advanced.—My second consideration is that the repugnance to dirt and the horror of the unclean shew no sign of abatement among the most civilised, the most advanced or the most intellectual peoples. On the contrary, the highest civilisation among the ancients was marked by an increase in personal fastidiousness, which disappeared with the decline of learning and intellectual development in the Dark Ages. And if today we have advanced in our knowledge of the universe beyond the most hopeful speculations of the ancients, our scientific knowledge has not made us less superstitious with regard to the clean and the unclean; for it may be observed that the most intellectual are, in general, among the most fastidious today, the unclean being found more numerous among the dull-witted, and even more frequently among the *half-witted*. Considering, therefore, the fact that among all fastidious persons cleanliness is admitted to be a necessity that has little to do with a reasoned objection to infection, but arises from an inner desire of an urgent character, divorced from reason, we may conjecture that it remains essentially a *superstition*.

A Digression on Goat's Fruit.—Therefore we have here

an inner necessity which is felt by certain animals and by
the most primitive humans, and yet can retain its hold
over the most advanced and rational beings, in whom it
attains its highest expression. In this respect cleanliness
resembles godliness, save that we have as yet no evidence
that a religious sense is known to cats, pigs, bats, *et cetera.*
Which serves to remind me (should you chance to observe
the relevance of this remark) that a Quaker who was im-
prisoned in York Castle, under the dispensation of Cromwell, wrote to Lieutenant-General Lambert a letter which
he concluded with the following curious expression: he
says that now is the Lord come to make a separation be-
twixt the sheep and the goats, and the sheep (he says)
were never persecutors, therefore they must needs prove
the goats, *their fruits make them manifest.* But why God
has always been supposed to prefer sheep to goats, or
sheep-fruit to goat-fruit, has never been explained. The
suggestion is as insulting to God as it is to man, like the
origin (already referred to) of *cretin,* which derives from
Chrétien, and assumes a glandular imbecile to be a good
Christian because he is too deficient to be anything other
than one; such, indeed, was long held to be the case with
the feeble-minded.

The Taboo *of the* Unmentionable *is distinguished from
the* Taboo *of the Unclean.*—From this digression I return
once more to the subject of *taboo,* which must next be
considered in relation to the *discussion* of our whole field
of research. The *taboo* against dirt and against uncleanly
habits belongs, as we have seen, to all time and to all portions of the globe. But there is a secondary *taboo* that
would appear to be peculiarly Puritan in origin, and for
this reason of a specifically Anglo-Saxon character, a *taboo*
found principally in Britain and in the United States of
America, not against dirt itself or filthy habits but *against
any mention of things relating to excretion.* Thus, the

writing of this book is a breach of this particular *taboo* because society conspires to pretend that the principal objects of discussion do not exist.

This particular *taboo* has, indeed, declined noticeably since Victorian times, when the functions of the closet were considered such a shameful secret that to be seen entering or leaving the smallest room in the house was sufficient to cover with confusion the delinquent caught *in flagrante delicto*. That this fear, however, is still with us is shewn by the advertisements which even in recent years have appeared in American journals, demonstrating the advantage of a *silent flush*. In these advertisements three persons will be shewn in a room, it may be at a card table, the fourth having left their company; and their agonised expressions betray the anguish of embarrassment which they experience as the noise of a plug being pulled trumpets abroad the purpose of their absent companion. And then an advertisement which the Ministry of Health sought to insert but recently in our journals, advising readers to wash their hands after using the privy, was refused and suppressed by the prudery of the press. Here the *taboo* against *dirt* is actively opposed by the *taboo* against the *Unmentionable*.

Before passing on to discuss this lavatory *taboo*, we may note at this point the extensive use of *taboo* in advertising and particularly in relation to suggestions of foulness and personal uncleanliness. For it is *taboo* to be foul and *taboo* to mention this matter, most particularly to the breaker of the *first taboo*. Thus certain advertisements insinuate that the reader has broken *taboo* by having a malodorous breath or an odour of the body; and to this will be added the threat that *their best friends will not tell them* (for to mention this would be to break the *second taboo*). The potency of fear and the capacity of civilised man for the worship of fetishes must therefore be considered among the most lucrative assets of the advertising agent and his clients.

Beim Scheissen mit Gestanken kommen die besten Gedanken.—The *taboo* relating to the use of the closet and all that is connected with it is not to be found in any natural instinct. For the late Dr. Freud in his *Introductory Lectures to Psycho-Analysis* remarks that the faeces produce no disgust in the child until this has been cultivated by his parents or guardians; and the child values them, he says, as part of his body and is unwilling to part with them, using them as the first *present* by which he can mark out those people whom he values especially. Or, as Dr. Groddeck says, they are the child's *fragrant offering to the maternal divinity,* which may serve to explain the worship of Baal-Peor and such-like deities. Thus the child, in his generosity, gives what he values himself and not what he *despises,* and growing older he learns (if we may credit Dr. Haire's *Encyclopaedia of Sexual Knowledge*) that *defecation after retention becomes a source of pleasure;* and many children quickly learn to appreciate this and to provoke it, despite the disapproval of parents. This opinion is widely found among psychologists, who hold that the evacuation of the stomach is not regarded by children with anything in the nature of shame or disgust, but with open pleasure. This fact is exploited with advantage by writers of good advice for the nursery; and those who read the works of Susan Isaacs on *Social Development in Young Children* will discover the enormous importance of The Pot discussed *ad nauseam.* The same is true of such periodicals as *The Nursery World.*

Even in later years, when disgust and shame have been cultivated, there are notable exceptions to these sentiments, which are strongly modified by circumstances. Monsieur René Guyon, writing on *Sex Life and Sex Ethics,* recalls the words of Sacha Guitry: *How intimate we have grown; at the end of a fortnight we performed our little needs in front of one another.* To this Monsieur Guyon adds that these needs suddenly recover the repulsive elements with which education has endowed them, as soon as desire wanes, as a result of habituation or separation; from which he deduced with dubious logic the *need for separate bedrooms* as arising from inability to tolerate the intimacies of a honeymoon when its force is spent.

Confusion of the Two Taboos.—In examining these arguments I find a tendency to confuse the first *taboo* against *dirt* with the second *taboo* which is concerned with *shame* and the pretence that natural functions do not exist. We have already observed that the objections to dirt are more universal and more deeply seated than is commonly recognised, and it should be noticed that these have no necessary connection with the second *taboo*. For no person, however cleanly in his habits, can pretend to himself that he knows no natural necessities; so that in privacy he observes the one *taboo* but is unable to observe the other. And a person of great fastidiousness may be at the same time without inhibition in his discussion of these matters and of all the things with which this work is concerned, as I trust the reader will believe of the present writer, or, indeed, of any Brahmin; for in India the elaborate code that governs personal hygiene in no way limits its most outspoken discussion. On the other hand are those who break the *taboo* against dirt but keep the *taboo* against mentioning things considered to be foul. All things considered, it must be recognised that the judgement of psychologists is proved by experience, that the feeling of shame and the affectations found in connection with defaecation and micturition are artificially engendered and are harmful in their effects.

Proposition of Monsieur Guyon examined.—The confusion of these two forms of *taboo* is illustrated in an example supplied by Monsieur Guyon, though he does not comment upon this confusion, which is the true explanation of his case. For he says that few persons could eat jam from a chamber-pot without nausea, even though the pot were quite new and had that moment come from the factory. But this is an example of the association of ideas, in which an object commonly regarded as both shameful and unclean can only with difficulty be considered *clean* because it is regarded in all circumstances as *shameful,* the two conceptions having become inseparable. Such a case I remember to have read in an old journal of the last century, where a writer described a reception given to European guests by an Indian rajah. The Prince, having provided himself with a liberal supply of ware from English firms, offered to his guests quantities of milk which he caused to be placed upon the table in vessels designed for quite another purpose. And observing that the milk remained untouched he continued to embarrass his guests by asking them to partake of it, saying that he was assured that it was an acceptable drink (for as a strict Moslem he could have no wine nor spirits to offer them), so that the whole company was torn between laughter and embarrassment. Such a situation is recorded in one of the books written by my friend Mr. Verrier Elwin, where he tells how one of these articles became an object of veneration (in a chapel, as far as I recollect), being mistaken by devout aborigines for one of Mr. Elwin's gods.

Pleasures derived from the Breaking of Taboo.—But as in all questions of *taboo* the breaking of the unwritten law provides for some the sole pleasure to be found in life, so we shall find that in this matter of egestion there are those who love beyond all else the pleasure of the *voyeur*. These manifestations, writes Mr. Havelock Ellis, have sometimes attracted the attention of the police, notably in Paris; to which he adds that women whom he knew had discovered

that men were looking at them through the openings in
the roof of the toilets in the Tuileries gardens. It is for this
unhallowed pleasure of breaking *taboo* that generations
of writers and artists have produced upon lavatory walls
since the days of Herculaneum and Pompeii (and no doubt
at Knossos and Mohenjo-Daro, if the whole truth were
known) those curious inscriptions and sketches with which
every age has been familiar. Of such Montaigne writes in
his essay on some verses of Virgil, where he speaks of
those huge draughts or pictures drawn by wanton youth,
from which he says (for such is the falseness of these draw-
ings, arousing a vain hope) *a cruel contempt for our natural store is bred*. Indeed, it was the opinion of that great
philosopher that there was much to commend nudity, in
order to dispel the illusions created by such deceptive art.

Then you will find in the Reading Room of the British
Museum a small pamphlet, under the Press Mark 1080.1.15,
in which some anonymous anthologist collected verses
purporting to have been discovered in these places. Of
this collection, published in the early eighteenth century,
I remember little except that some of the verses were supposed to have been found at St. James's Palace, and eulo-
gised the ferocity of His Majesty's expression when upon
a jakes. Another verse included *writing* among the *four
methods of evacuation;* which shewed such discernment as
Fulbeck displayed in *The Pandects of the Law of Nations,*
when he spoke of purging a black jaundice with a clyster
of ink.

Of such efforts on the part of living poets and artists I
have heard it seriously maintained that they comprise almost the only true folklore of our century and the only
mural sketches that will rank with those of the cave-
dwellers as true pictures of the mind of society in this
epoch. A connoisseur of these *graffiti* is mentioned by Mr.
Gogarty in his book *As I was Going Down Sackville*

Street, a gentleman whom he calls Thwackhurst, who complains that he can find nothing in the Dublin *necessaria* except political remarks. This Mr. Thwackhurst regards as a sign of decline, for (says he) *even at their moments of ease the people are obsessed with politics.* This authority considered that persons would be better employed *thinking of the matter in hand,* and that politics had ruined the finest town in Europe for *graffiti.*

The Scribblings in our Houses of Office are held to reflect the true Spirit of the Age.—I wish indeed that I could re-visit Dublin to see the inscriptions mentioned in Mr. Gogarty's book—that at Trinity College on the subject of Shanks' Patent (beloved of Joseph Stalin) and the one behind the Nelson Column, to compare true and corrupt versions and note with Mr. Thwackhurst the descending level on the walls that marks the spread of popular education. But I fear Mr. Morrison will hardly consider a permit. I can only remark that, as to political writings, I am credibly informed of such inscriptions in the Southern States of America, providing a wall-newspaper (for Poor Whites especially) of some interest to the sociologist. In England, however, this is not the common usage. Stereotyped and crude, our lavatory inscriptions are the measure of our social fixations; and that enterprising anthropologist who is said to be collecting photographs of them in all parts of the world should reveal more of the truth than all the bombastic historians who will so soon be clothing our grotesque society with dignified phrases and political stercorations, representing its present antics as studied movements, to be explained in terms of high principles and rational conduct. Mr. James Joyce, whatever his faults, knew this as well as any man, for which alone his *Ulysses* is commendable, despite its barbarous style. These sketches and inscriptions have seldom been valued at their true worth, nor has anyone explained why they are more to be found in men's places than in those frequented by women, and even the author of *For Your Convenience* gives but a few pages to their consideration; but for me they are as eloquent as the writing upon the wall of the king's palace at Babylon: *mene, mene, tekel, upharsin*. And though I am no Daniel, I read our doom in them; for while lust is shackled in impotent fantasies, hatred and death will ride at liberty.

Concerning curious Customs among the Ancient Romans and Celts.—That the *taboo* upon natural functions and those parts of the body most associated with them, though very old, is neither universal nor characteristic of every age in history, may be readily seen from innumerable examples. Moses, who was not suffered to behold Jehovah face to face, was permitted to look upon his *hinder parts,* which we should consider today an outrage, though it was evidently not so intended. This is astonishing among the Hebrews, but among paynims the shame of the body was little known. Indeed, they carried this shamelessness in some instances to the point of finding among those functions which we most despise the occasion of decorative ingenuity. For I have in mind those high-born Roman ladies of the later days, and the more costly courtesans who imitated them, of whom it is said that they consumed turpentine in order to give an odour of roses to their urine. And this they did for the sake of art, as they understood it, even after it had been discovered that the result was a painful disease of the kidneys from which they would die within five years.

Or (while we speak of such things) consider the ancient Celts, who held that the strength and volume of the bladder were proof of bodily vigour. Was it not for this that the Gaelic hero Finn chose his bride in *The Courting of Emer?* And was it not for this cause that the most unfortunate queen (Maeve, I believe it was) who could make the deepest hole in the snow was murdered by her jealous rivals?

Even today you will find elsewhere such an attitude to our less glorious functions (as we consider them). For a celebrated American journalist, at that time a great Russophil, having described to a friend of mine how Stalin presided for twelve hours over a conference (without having recourse to the works of Mr. Shanks so much admired by My Lord Beaverbrook), ended his eulogy with the words: *My, what a bladder*. So also I have heard that an English official in India, having once deposited in the place designed for his own use the mutings, femishings, droppings, slicings or whatever they are called, of an elephant, was surprised to hear his servant remark with surprise and admiration, *The Sahib is indeed a great man*. For, as we have already observed, in this country of superstitious ritual cleanliness there is little of the *taboo* against a proper and healthy discussion of our needs. I believe that in one of the excellent stories by Mr. Mulk Raj Anand there is an account of the shame falling upon a boy who uses a door-step improperly; but where we should hold the shame to consist principally in the publicity thus given to what we would keep private and secret, the greater shame in Hindu eyes is the defilement of the doorstep.

Churlish Behaviour of the British towards Women.—So far from having a healthy appreciation of such distinctions, our only public recognition of them lies in that unspoken *blackmail on the bladder* (I use the phrase of an embittered woman) whereby we tacitly conspire to tax the superior capacity of women in a manner which we have already discussed, callously charging them at a penny a time where the great Gaels would have honoured the best of them with the hand of a hero in marriage. Where once they competed for glory, we have reduced the formula to *sauve qui peut*. What must have been the courage of that husband whom I knew (and of his wife) when he stood at the door of the gentlemen's toilet in a famous London restaurant, keeping all comers at bay, while his wife made use of it as a *pis-aller* in the crisis occasioned by the temporary closing of the Ladies' Cloakroom?

Of the Absence of Modesty *among the Japanese.*—How much better we should fare if we could live as freely as our enemies, the Japanese; for of these people I have often heard it said that they are almost without inhibitions. One traveller I heard of in the interior of Japan who, coming to a house, was offered a bath, which he gladly accepted. But seeing that his host's family sat around to keep him company, and being unable to speak their language, he indicated as best he could by means of gestures his need for a screen. This they brought, a little thing about two or three feet high, such as they thought necessary, no doubt, to protect him from draughts. And when he shewed by signs that he would have a high screen they removed the small one and brought him another, fully seven feet in height, which was made of glass. Also a young woman with whom I spoke, who had travelled in Japanese ships, spoke of their indifference to *shame* as we understand it; for she had the greatest difficulty in finding privacy for her intimate necessities on account of the casual interest of her shipmates and the lack of proper provision. And this interest I speak of was not that of our *voyeurs* in the Tuileries but the idlest curiosity regarding the ways of another race.

Abortive Efforts of a Japanese Emperor.—Indeed, I understand that an Emperor of Japan at one time, desirous to ape the West in all things, attempted to introduce *modesty* with the rest of the disastrous ideological imports from Europe. To this end he decreed that persons while bathing in the sea should wear some minimum of clothing instead of bathing nude, as they had in the past; which decree the Japanese obeyed very literally, playing naked upon the beach until such time as they were ready to enter the sea, when they covered their shame appropriately. And from this one may see how utterly devoid these people are by nature, culture and tradition of our own most cherished virtues, like that child who was seen by a friend of mine coming up the steps of St. Mark's, in Venice; who, finding herself without a hat, threw her skirts over her head as a perfunctory act of *modesty*. Such a story is also told by Sir John in his *Apology*, shewing how little the virtue of prudery is understood by simple minds.

Consider in contrast the heroic agonies of that Welsh minister in one of Mr. Rhys Davies' excellent stories. (Was it not in some *Blue Moon Booklet?* But no matter. Alas that the Blue Moon publications were blitzed with the emporium of Mr. Charles Lahr in Red Lion Street!) This estimable person, torn between dignity and diarrhoea, presents a formidable picture of the lengths to which one of our island race will go rather than publicly admit his humanity and suffer another person to know that he possesses bowels or a bladder. Or imagine the distress of Whitehall, anxious to confer suitable minor distinctions upon faithful lackeys among the subject races, when they found that the only suitable candidate in Burma was a gentleman who had the name, *Ma Tin Po*. But would they have lost any sleep over this in Tokio?

Stratagem of Two Spinsters.—I have seen the story of *Clochemerle* almost acted in real life in an English coastal borough, where two old maids could for months think and talk of no subject but a urinal behind a restaurant, within their vision, from which they would have it that men emerged (as the saying is) *adjusting their dress*. And in order to effect a prosecution they even engaged a photographer to lie in wait behind their window curtains, so that the evidence of the camera might be produced in court. Their efforts were only interrupted by the war, which cleared the place of visitors; the restaurant was closed, its urinal deserted, and the disappointment of the two spinsters was intense, even bitter.

As one said of old, A suspected book, being brought to the torture, often confesseth all, and more than it knows.— Some persons still find it difficult even to enquire for such places, so often ingeniously hidden in back streets or in the interminable corridors of an old English hotel. We console ourselves, perchance, by the thought that things are changing, that we are less inhibited, less conscious of *shame;* but an earlier age than ours can still teach us more than we know. I call to mind a classic work known as *Buick's British Birds,* where (for some obscure reason) the end of one chapter was decorated with a tail-piece showing a pair of buttocks upon a pole, as in military usage. But in later days this tail-piece was blotted out, and to this day *Buick's British Birds without the bar* is a great rarity. Here is a symbol of our prudery, and of false notions of *obscenity* which still afflict us. But I suppose we have travelled some distance since the Victorian Halcyon, or this present work could hardly be published without some danger to the publisher, as may be seen in the historic indictment of George Bedborough by a Grand Jury, which I offer you for your edification:

CENTRAL CRIMINAL COURT, TO WIT—

The Jurors for our Sovereign Lady the Queen upon their oath present that George Bedborough, being a person of a wicked and depraved mind and disposition, and unlawfully and wickedly devising, contriving and intending to vitiate and corrupt the morals of the liege subjects of our said Lady the Queen, and to raise and create in them lustful desires, and to bring the said liege subjects into a state of wickedness, lewdness and debauchery, on the 27th day of May, in the year of our Lord, one thousand eight hun-

*dred and ninety eight, at a certain shop, to wit, Number 16
John Street, Bedford Row, in the County of London, and
within the jurisdiction of the said Court, unlawfully, wickedly, maliciously, scandalously and wilfully did publish, sell
and utter, and cause and procure to be published, sold and
uttered, a certain lewd, wicked, bawdy, scandalous and obscene libel, in the form of a book entitled* Studies in the
Psychology of Sex: Vol. I, Sexual Inversion, *by Havelock
Ellis, in which said book are contained among other things
divers wicked, lewd, impure, scandalous and obscene libels
and matters, which said book is, pursuant to the provisions
in that behalf of the Law of Libel Amendment Act, 1888,
deposited with this indictment, together with the particulars showing precisely by reference to pages, columns and
lines, in what part of the said book the alleged libel is to be
found, to the manifest corruption of the morals and minds
of the liege subjects of our said Lady the Queen, in contempt of our said Lady the Queen and her laws, in violation
of common decency, morality and good order, and against
the peace of our said Lady the Queen, her Crown and Dignity.*

The Author's Debt to Mr. Havelock Ellis.—What
Majesty is here invoked by the ascendant pornocrats to
protect the people against knowledge and their own hidden cesspools against the sanitary inspector! Will there
not be many today as anxious, in their pose of supermen,
to suppress a book which reminds the reader of our common necessities, seeing that we are all (in Sancho Panza's
words) as God made us, and some of us a great deal
worse? To whom I am minded to reply in the words of
Dr. Johnson (to the lady who complained of the improper
words in his dictionary): *So you have been searching them
out, Madam.* It is not my intention to discuss this question
of *obscenity* in any general way, still less to compare my

own poor work to that of Mr. Havelock Ellis; but I will say this for his requiem, that following in his giant foot-steps (like Master Buttons in the track of King Wenceslaus) I hope with more safety to reach the kitchen door, since he has stormed the front gate.

The pioneers of the kitchen door have, indeed, of recent years suffered more from neglect than from persecution. One excellent book I discovered entitled *Troubles We Don't Talk About,* by a certain Dr. Montague, a book full of wise advice regarding those painful and perilous afflictions of divers kinds which a mistaken modesty so often conceals in silence. But how many of those for whose use it was intended even know of the existence of such a work? The same modesty that conceals the ailment suppresses knowledge of the remedy. Hence the simplicity of my purpose, which is to expose an outrageous conspiracy and shew how interesting, fascinating, varied in its implications and ramifications, how rich in content and worthy of your consideration is this vast subject, excluded from polite conversation by the intolerable tyranny of custom.

But he protests he is no Advocate of what is Indecorous or Offensive in any true Sense—Of the unhallowed Attractions of Nefas.—Let it be clearly understood that I am no advocate of the *indecorous,* which I include with the unclean as *offensive* in the only true sense. In a hospital the bowels are, perforce, rationally discussed, but you will have observed that I consider the bed-pan an offence which human ingenuity should contrive to supersede. And in the State Hospital at Copenhagen I could see no sufficient reason for leaving urine in glass jars by a patient's bedside, as though it were something decorative. Or if we consider a certain famous statue in Brussels, though I would never object to it upon grounds of prudery, it may reasonably be urged that the conception lacks taste and the execution, beauty. Or again there are those picture-postcards, formerly sold in the town of Homburg, a spa near Frankfurt-am-Main, shewing graphically the beneficial effects of the waters. Such artistic efforts may have as little aesthetic value as those urinal murals, or *murinals,* to which we have already referred; but it would surely be better to condemn them for bad taste than to suppress them as obscene. Indeed it is the suppression of all reference to, and all representation of, the natural functions, in the name of decency and morality, which encourages the clandestine production of the worst outrages against art and public morals, because of the unholy attraction of *nefas* upon the human mind. The works of that eminent educationalist, Mr. A. S. Neill, are full of examples shewing the disastrous effects upon the minds of children of such *taboos,* alike in sexual and excretory matters, an abnormal and perverted obsession being created by the attempt to silence a normal and natural interest.

Do not imagine, then, that I am an apostle of what we term indecency or immorality, the founder of a modern Hell-Fire Club, if I propose the abolition of restrictions which are themselves an incitement to pornography, and upheld by the ruling pornocracy perhaps for that reason.

The Sanitarian, like the Church, teaches us to remember that which we foolishly forget.—I recollect that a person upon a certain occasion, having informed a lady that he must see a man about a dog, was asked what sort of a dog; which threw him into such a state of embarrassment that he replied, a dachshund with four puppies. Such are the traps we make for ourselves by our feeble efforts at deception. Or there was that English woman who sought for a certain place in a Paris restaurant, *soi-disant se laver les mains,* and, finding it repeatedly locked, complained to a waiter. How cruelly were her foolish pretences shattered by his intended words of comfort, *Courage, madame, j'entends déjà le craquement de papier!* Very wisely does the Church (like the ancient Egyptians, who sat with skeletons at their feasts) bid us prepare our minds for the thought of death, that we may at an early age be reconciled to that which is ultimately inevitable; how much more so should we overcome our reluctance to speak of that which we fear to discuss more than our own mortality, lest, being unaccustomed to such frankness, we should one day face worse than death in those artificial emergencies which arise purely from our own irrational shame and unnatural modesty?

That the lavatory *taboo* is moribund in America, as in England, would, I imagine, be generally admitted; indeed, any *taboo* must be in process of decline when it can be rationally discussed, as this book and many others bear witness. But I notice in *The Bedside Esquire,* but recently published, an article by Aiken A. Dehan on *Washing the Hands* which shews to what an extent this *taboo* is still to be found in the United States, where I suspect that it has survived somewhat more hardily than in England. (Does any man still *cover his feet?*)

Facile Manners of the French.—Mr. Dehan is concerned with the extraordinary subterfuges and devices necessitated in a society where a man cannot openly express his needs and a thoughtless host or hostess provides no easy *alibi* for his escape. Among the euphemisms that he includes, whereby our simple requirements are sometimes expressed (under a poor pretence of concealment), I observe that he mentions the French expression *changer le poisson d'eau.* But no person who has seen a French urinal, which is commonly little more than an architectural fig leaf, or watched an occupant of such a place raise his hat to a smart woman on the pavement (perhaps exchanging a few words of courtesy), will believe that our neighbours are greatly troubled by such questions. Indeed, one has only to travel the French countryside in a *train omnibus* to see the peasants at every station make a very bold use of the bank at either end of the platform; and I have more than once lighted upon—I cannot say disturbed—a Breton woman similarly employed, and passed by exchanging a casual word of greeting.

A Comparison between Women and Camels.—But while the French shew these signs of progress (or, if you prefer, of decadence), the Americans as a whole appear to lag far behind them; and where their inhibitions are found in company with selfishness or thoughtlessness situations can arise, as Mr. Dehan shews, which contravene all the canons of Comfort and Convenience, the importance of which we have already examined. This writer finds women the worst offenders in hospitality, because (he says) *women seem to be so constituted that they can go for hours without ever thinking of washing their hands.* In this respect he finds women to be made in a contrary fashion to camels, which are able to continue for such long periods without drinking; and manifestly a thoughtless camel could be a most inconsiderate host. But even among men Mr. Dehan finds few hosts who consider adequately the comfort of their guests in a household ruled by *taboo,* having in mind (as he says) that they may have recently taken copious draughts of fluid or large quantities of salt or sugar, *all of which tend to soil the hands.*

Of the *taboos* in this realm of England, respecting the natural functions and notions of cleanliness, Mr. Archibald Lyall has written with discernment in a book entitled *It Isn't Done, the Future of Taboo among the British Islanders.* This writer records the rise of a *taboo* in recent years, since the use of the bath became common among those who are proud to claim descent from the unwashed aristocracy of past centuries; for these same persons, he says, are ashamed to confess that they do not bath once, if not twice, every day. This *taboo,* descending as is customary to the middle orders, creates the greatest inconvenience and mendacity in households unsuited in equipment to universal cleanliness upon such a scale. But such is the power of the popular novel, in which Englishmen are always discovered to be *clean-limbed,* that the greatest hardships will be endured by any person of the upper or middle ranks of English society in order to face up to fiction.

Of Taboo *and Euphemism.*—Concerning the *lavatory taboo,* which Mr. Lyall also records, we may observe that a first instance of this *taboo* is to be found in the word *garderobe,* whereby our mediaeval forefathers denoted, as we do, a privy under the semblance of a *cloak-room.* I have pondered in vain over this same word *cloak-room,* rejecting the temptation to seek a derivation in *cloaca,* making it a *cloaca-room.* Then there is the word *lavatory* itself, which shews how the consistent use of one word to describe a function not intended in its origin has, as it were, debased verbal coinage. Indeed, since a privy was once termed a *lavatory* to avoid mentioning such a place by name, and this has led to the word *lavatory* acquiring a *taboo* of its own, we may reasonably conjecture that the word *bathroom* will in time acquire a considerable *taboo,* since this word has now replaced the word lavatory as a current euphemism. Or, as Mr. Lyall observes, *to wash one's hands* has already gathered a sinister meaning, and this, too (I suggest), may soon become unspeakable.

Dependence of Pornographic and Scatological Humour on the Existence of Taboo.—Mr. Lyall speaks of a friend who conceived the idea of contributing to a well-known series, of which his own book on *taboo* is an honourable example, with a work to be entitled *Cloaca, or The Humours of Sanitation.* And of this proposal Mr. Lyall rightly remarks that it shewed his friend to be as much a victim of *taboo* as those whom he intended to put out of countenance. For, says he, *the fact is that lavatories are not an intrinsically humorous subject.* And the amusement which vain and idle minds derive from them Mr. Lyall attributes entirely to *taboo,* because (he says) no-one would dream of writing a book on the humours of gas-fires or boiler-making. But despite these strictures, which we can endorse with the greatest sincerity, it is the opinion of Mr. Lyall that humour of this sort is among the beneficial results of *taboo,* for without the body *taboo* he believes that many stories from which our Islanders derive much harmless pleasure would not be possible; an opinion seemingly shared by Dr. Johnson.

Mr. Robert Graves is another writer in the same series of speculative works who has discussed the problems of *taboo,* as found in these islands, in relation to the body and its natural functions; and this he does in *Lars Porsena, or The Future of Swearing.* Among the curious products of our civilisation he makes mention of the *Bottom Legend,* whereby the word *bottom* has fallen into disrepute among us. But even more has the word *arse* (as Mr. Lyall observes), though this is as honest a word as can be found in our language, endowed with heroic qualities since that good Knight, Sir Thomas Malory, thought fit to use it in his *Morte d'Arthur.* But in the early eighteenth century this word was already considered to be obscene, and such works as the pseudo-Swiftian *Wonderful Wonder of Wonders* were deliberate affronts to decency, *pour épater les bourgeois.*

Cleanliness attributed to the Devil.—The Dean of St. Patrick's was the true progenitor of prudery and of modern lewdness, thus demonstrating the truth of Mr. Lyall's contention with regard to the supposed humours of sanitation. For being possessed of a great horror of certain natural functions, which he displays in his account of Strephon and Chloe, also in the matter of Celia (to which we have already given attention), he found relief for this horror in bawdy wit. Also he shared a belief, common to many even to this day, that cleanliness belonged to the Devil; for witness his surprise in the lines—

> *O comely church! where females find clean linen*
> *As decent to repent in as to sin in.*

For this same reason there were those who were wont to say that one could tell a virtuous woman by her smell, that is to say, by the odour of sanctity, which was not that of soap. And Dr. Haggard, in his work on *Devils, Drugs and Doctors,* cites a famous surgeon as having observed that in French hospitals clean knees are an index of moral frailty; though why he should have said knees I am at a loss to explain.

Alarming Metaphysics of Mrs. Eddy.—Within recent times we have a notable example in Mary Baker Eddy (the originator of *Christian Science*) of an attempt to dispose of all corruption by ignoring its presence, that is to say, by the accredited method of *taboo,* or keeping evil spirits at a distance by refraining from the mention of them. For having decided that matter was an illusion (which did not prevent her from amassing a very material fortune as a reward in this world for her denial of its existence), the author of *Science and Health* concluded *a fortiori* that dirt, being matter displaced, was the displacement of a fictitious substance, having an entirely fictitious importance. Thus, though she compromised by admitting the necessity of some measure of cleanliness, Mrs. Eddy proclaimed *ex cathedra* that daily bathing of the whole body was a work of supererogation; and of children she said that their daily ablutions were no more natural or necessary than taking a fish out of water every day and covering it with dirt. As to the condition of the stomach, bowels, food and clothing of a child, she held them to be of no serious importance.

Few, however, are prepared to follow *taboo* to such extremes. We try rather to combine good sanitation with a pretended ignorance of its plain purpose, inviting our friends to wash their hands and offering to shew them the *geography of the house,* as though we were instructors in ordnance survey. If we speak at all of our necessities it is in language designed to disguise rather than to make plain our meaning, like that poor soldier who could not say where he was wounded *because he knew no Latin.* The reader of *All Quiet on the Western Front* will remember with feeling, and perhaps with sympathy, how Remarque similarly describes the horrible dilemma of a wounded soldier, unable to explain his simple need to a nurse, his comrade voicing it at last in the irrelevant phrase of the school-room.

Clarity and Emphasis produced by a violent and unexpected Breach of Taboo.—These men of whom Remarque tells had among themselves one simple word to express directly the universal necessity of which, in the company of women, they were so unspeakably ashamed. Such words are known well enough and they alone convey the fulness of our meaning. Thus, when Mr. J. B. S. Haldane, speaking passionately upon a public platform, had failed to stir the imagination of his audience sufficiently by some reference to *excrement,* he paused and said, *I mean* ——, using an Anglo-Saxon word of four letters. This, as may be expected, had the effect intended, which was to arouse his hearers to a proper appreciation of what was being told them; for breach of *taboo* is often the only way to make clear one's meaning and to ensure attention to its importance.

There is, indeed, as we have already observed in the first

chapter of this book, no more sense in most *taboos* than is to be found in the customs of savages who see indecency in their mouths. If the elder Disraeli is to be credited (for my authority in this instance is his *Curiosities of Literature*), the Maldivian islanders in his time would eat always in solitude, retiring for this purpose into the most hidden parts of their houses and covering the windows to avoid being observed by others. So also, he says, the Otaheiteans feed separately from one another. Such practices, like those of the Azanaghi, to which we have previously made reference, were the subject of some observations by Montaigne, who speaks of peoples with such contrary customs in the Turkish Empire, and of other such nations; also of a man known to him who shunned company more in filling than in emptying himself. But if we should compare such customs with our own I know not which are the more foolish. Or as Messrs. Ernst and Seagle expressed the matter, in a book which they addressed *To the Pure: A Study of Obscenity and the Censor,* even today there are tribes which make love in public, but eat in modest loneliness. They treat eating, said these authors, *as we, exclusive of college boys and soldiers, do the excrementitious.*

Plain Jolly Mirth.—Our hardy forefathers, though they made no secret of their meals, often shewed a complete disregard for what our squeamish conventions would call *decency,* finding positive pleasure, and that openly, where we see nothing but shame. Thus you will find in Camden's *Britannia* (I quote from the third English edition of 1753, revised, digested and published by a late Lord Bishop of London), on page 444, an account of a curious custom at Hemingston, in Suffolk, described in the margin as *A Merry Tenure.* This passage reads as here follows:

Hemingston, wherein *Baldwin le Pettour* (observe the name) held lands by Serjeantry (thus an ancient book ex-

presses it) *for which he was obliged every Christmas Day
to perform before our Lord the King of England one Saltus, one Sufflatus and one Bumbulus;* or as it is read in
another place, he held it by *a Saltus, a Sufflus and a Pettus.*
He means, by the only international language since Babel.

Of the Diversity of Customs.—Such (my authority comments) *was the plain jolly mirth of those days,* of which a
further account will be found by the diligent student in
Blount's *Fragmenta Antiquitatis.* For our ancestors (like
the public schools of today, which maintain their tradition) firmly believed in the maxim, *Flatum ne retine; pro-
pellito fortiter hostem.* Such was, indeed, their common
practice. Nay, more:

> *But, if suppressed, it upward flies*
> *And vents itself in Prophesies.*

That is to say, with the advent of puritanism and prudery,
the thing took another turn. Or so Samuel Butler suggested in explanation of Quakerism. And the Blessed St.
Augustine did not disdain to discuss such matters, as the
Seigneur de Montaigne reminds us (when he quotes the
Bishop of Hippo and Joannes Ludovicus Vives to shew
how the exercise of the imagination can control the most
extraordinary functions) in the twentieth chapter of his
first book of essays. Indeed, Montaigne shared the opinion
of the ancients in this respect, that inhibition was fatal to
health, and commended that Roman Emperor of whom
good Sir John also speaks, who ordained the most complete freedom in this matter. And if you will travel further
with this wisest Frenchman who ever lived, he will tell
you of stranger customs to make you doubt the sanctity of
your own. Thus (as the great John Florio construes him)
he speaks of a country where the noblest about the King
stooped to the ground to gather his ordure in some fine
linen cloth. Or (on the other hand) of a French gentle-

man who was ever wont to blow his nose in his hand and asked *what privilege this filthy excrement had, that we should have a dainty linen cloth or handkerchief to receive the same; and, which is worse, so carefully fold it up and keep the same about us.* For, like the Hindus, he considered it should be cast away as we do all other excrements and filth.

If from such reflections we now return to the principal object of our study, we may well ask by what canon of Absolute Values we consider certain functions to be lacking in natural dignity. And I will confidently reply that no function suffers more, if any does, from such a defect than the greatest of all human pleasures; yet there are few who share the horror shewn by (shall we say) Mr. Aldous Huxley for the embrace of love, on the ground (if I understand this great man correctly) that such antics are grotesque. There is therefore as good a reason at least to revere *Our Lady of the Three Necessities* (using the phrase of Ibanez), or shall we say that there is as little objection to so doing, as there is in this matter of the worship offered by many good Christians to the pagan Venus.

Melancholy End of a Prude—Of Ghostly Stools.—I will say, then, beware of the Pauline doctrine; and take heed lest you fall into the same pit as the preacher of Alkmaar of whom we learn from the *Anatomy of Melancholy* that, being surprised unawares by some gentlewomen what time he baled out in a ditch (by reason of a sudden looseness), he was so abashed that he did never after shew his head in public. This grave and learned minister of God, forsaking the pulpit, pined away with Melancholy, and all because he could not keep in mind those wise words of Montaigne, that *both Kings and Philosophers obey nature and go to stool, and so do Ladies.* To which he might have added the Early Fathers of the Church; for in another place he reminds us that Irenaeus met his end in a jakes. Nor can St. Simeon Stylites have been so nice upon the point, for we are told of how he was fed, but left to imagine how he fared in other matters, which must have required a bold front and no nonsense. Nay, even *ghosts* have such needs, if we may credit Mr. W. S. Hammond, of the B.B.C., which has a neo-Papal infallibility in our time. For you will find in *The Most Haunted House in England,* by Mr. Harry Price, a book published in the year 1940, on page 218 (Appendix C), the following observation by Mr. Hammond, relating to his investigation of the Mystery of Borley Rectory: *A rather unpleasant odour* (he says) *was noticed in Room 5, which somewhat suggested the lavatory. The same kind of smell was afterwards noticed in the Blue Room.*

A Critique of Pure Paulinism.—Therefore, maugre St. Paul and all the prudes, we must needs, for our peace of mind, learn from the Elizabethans; and cultivate something of the hardy realism that Mark Twain so admirably caught in that curious masterpiece, *1601, or Conversation at the Social Fireside as it was in the Time of the Tudors,* written to entertain a merry parson with *plain jolly mirth;* for only by so doing shall we learn what they knew, that what comes from the body no more defiles than that which goes into it. Custom has cloaked Dame Nature with a mantle of shame and deceit, but our good sense can yet remove it. While we see in necessity only *the daily indignity* we remain the martyrs of our own conceit; but not so did good Sir John portray the uses of Ajax. There you will find he chooses for the figure to seat upon his invention, shewing forth its points and advantages, a dignitary of the Church; and beneath are the lines:

> *A godly father, sitting on a draught*
> *To do as need and nature hath us taught.*

Now here is sense, and where there is sense we shall not look in vain for dignity. The metamorphosis is extended to the spiritual realm, nature transmutes food into dung, dung into food; Sir John transmutes the closet from a noisome hole to a place of comfort and cleanliness; why, then, should we delay to make of this *daily indignity* an honoured sacrament of reincarnation?

Concerning Psychological Constipation.—This belief in the defilement of the body by that which passes out of it has had the most profound effects upon our health, and must be considered in relation to the psychology of constipation, of which I will say but little, though it merits more. My own experience of constipation from psychological causes is limited to that arising from the horror of hospital bed-pans (no doubt assisted by the nature of hospital diet) of which enough has been said. But Dr. Groddeck states that *there is never a case of constipation which is not mentally determined,* or at least that he would almost go so far as to say so. Such a view appears to me exaggerated, for I would defy the most psychologically emancipated person to cope with an unmixed diet of arrowroot, or the worst psychological victim to resist a sufficient quantity of powerful purges; and I suppose that in degree all food has one effect or the other, with results that we all know from experience. The views of Dr. Groddeck on this subject will be found, stated at some length, in his work *Exploring the Unconscious,* and I have no space here either to state them or to comment upon them at any length; but lest any reader should be inclined to regard such opinions as entirely frivolous, I would remind him of the known fact that intense fear may induce a loosening of the bowels; which occasioned an American visitor to this country to remark *very appropriate* when he discovered a portrait of George Washington in his host's lavatory; since Washington, he said, was the only man who ever had that effect upon the English. However, this story is much older than Washington, and was anticipated by Sir John in his *Apology*. (For myself, I have always decorated these places with the most indecorous photographs that I can discover of our Cabinet ministers, who, though they do not induce fear, seem to liberate other and equally efficacious feelings.)

An Ingenious Privy in Norway.—A gentleman but recently informed me that whilst travelling in Norway he had occasion to pass a night in a *saeta,* where he arrived after dark. And being moved to relieve himself after he had breakfasted, he sought the house of office, where he was about to seat himself when he was astonished to spy daylight through the hole beneath him. Looking downwards, he was horrified to discover that the place overhung a precipice of some 2000 feet, and that he was looking into the distant waters of a *fjord,* where a large ship appeared as a small object framed in the *chaise percée* (like the picture of Queen Victoria which an ignorant artisan framed in like manner, thinking so fine a piece of polished wood could hardly have been intended for so base a use). When I enquired of this person what were his reactions, he replied that his principal desire was to feel his feet upon *terra firma,* and that he therefore withdrew in haste from the place without attempting to transact his affairs. But surely, said I, such places were expressly devised to precipitate business by the emotion of fear, which may well have proved a stronger and cheaper medicine than *Enos,* and account for the excellent health of the Norwegians. To this, however, my friend only replied that he would sooner suffer from habitual costiveness than expose himself daily to such peril and to a matutinal fantasy of breaking timber swaying over such an abyss, however much it might *encourager les autres.*

Of Costiveness and the Sense of Guilt.—Few of the doctors will, I suppose, find themselves in agreement with Dr. Groddeck's views on the small importance of the physical aspects of constipation, for he would have us believe that its ill effects are negligible, apart from those which arise from the same psychological conditions which cause it. But the doctors may well consider whether the feeling of guilt with which a state of constipation is frequently accompanied is truly conducive to its relief; and if they are of the opinion that it is not, the many means by which the public is brought into a condition of panic in this matter deserve proper consideration.

For example, by the strenuous endeavours of innumerable advertisers, the terror of constipation has been so played upon that incredible quantities of patent medicines are daily absorbed into systems clogged and glutted with surfeits of unnatural food. The story of some such campaigns is told by Mr. Stanley Walker in *Mrs. Astor's Horse,* a work to which we have already made reference, in which the author describes the methods of *Ex-Lax,* charging the very ether with this terror, by which means some forty million boxes of this product are said to have been sold to the public. The radio programmes of this enterprising company included discourses by *Madame X, the Ex-Lax Reporter,* who detailed the effects of a dose upon solid citizens of America; but there was an end of human endurance, and the Broadcasting Companies eventually discovered that their listeners complained increasingly against unpleasant discussions of bodily symptoms.

Contradictory Conceptions of the Symbolic Character of the Excreta.—Readers of a curious autobiography, published anonymously under the title *Memoirs of Other Fronts,* may remember that there is in that book an instance of psychological constipation, induced on the writer by his possessiveness in relation to his daughter, whom he endeavours without success to retrieve from the control of his wife. But to return now to this matter of defilement, or the Pauline doctrine on dung, the reader will perceive that there are two contradictory conceptions of the symbolic nature of the excreta, both of which may have their dangers. For if it is true that a child will consider his excrement as a thing of *value,* to be given with generosity or retained with avarice, more sophisticated persons habitually regard such matter as the symbol of *defilement,* following the Pauline cult; and by a false conception of purity may retain in themselves that with which they scruple to pollute the outside world.

Examples of deliberate Excremental Defilement.—I have not seen in the works of the psychologists any reference to such a possibility, but I suggest that it is at least as probable as any other theory so far advanced. Those who have followed Mr. Phelan's *Jail Journey* will recollect that astonishing example of prison folklore, the ballad which is quoted in his chapter *Chez Balmy.* Now it is clear that what the Balmy concealed upon his person in order that the *Bitches Bastard* (that is to say, the prison officer) should find it, under the mistaken impression that he had caught a prisoner in possession of smuggled tobacco, was not intended as a *love gift* to the warder. Nor can that child, of whom I heard that he habitually and persistently made use of the waste-paper basket, have intended a token of affection. Also I remember that on the railway running from Eire into Ulster, through Portadown, in County Armagh (a town of Orangemen and Black Protestants), there was found inscribed in a toilet, beneath the customary request not to use the closet while the train was standing at a station, the words *except at Portadown;* and I cannot concede that this was intended as a compliment to the town or its people. Or when that old reprobate in Zola's *La Terre,* who bore the inappropriate name of his Saviour, finding himself not invited to a wedding, threw dung at the wedding party, I should not say his intention was kindly. Indeed, even among animals the idea of defilement by dung is known; for the wolverine, a ferocious and ill-mannered beast, defiles with its own excrement all food which it cannot eat, in order to prevent any other animal from benefiting from its leavings.

Agreeable· Teachings of Yoga *respecting the Control of the Bowels.*—There appears, then, to be sufficient reason to suppose that, since the state of mind and the obscure operations of our unconscious selves effect the action of the bowels, we are as likely to be influenced by a desire to defile or not to defile as by any other consideration; and I cannot but conclude that our condition would be more healthy, and the operation of our personal sewage systems more normal and regular, if these controlling powers now exercised by the unconscious mind could be exerted consciously, as is the case with the Indian *Yogis*. These persons are able to control such matters just as they can control the muscles of the heart and the lungs; and of their extraordinary facility in this matter I need cite but one instance, which is that when they desire to cleanse themselves by means of an enema, they have no occasion to employ the usual apparatus, being able to draw water into their intestines by deliberate suction.

The Author is himself restricted by the Taboos *of Others.*—Much further detail on the general subject of constipation may be found in Dr. Hurst's work on that subject (with some historical illustrations), but I am concerned here only with the effect of pernicious superstitions upon bodily sanitation, and have said enough to make this matter tolerably clear. In this, however, I write with a certain disadvantage, which is that the *taboos* relating to the discussion of the body and its functions are still so strong that it is impossible to write of many things as plainly as one would wish to do. The formula of Uncle Toby may still be applied to many homely and sensible words: Make this dash, says he, 'tis an Aposiopesis; take the dash away and write Backside, 'tis bawdy; scratch Backside out and put Covered Way in, 'tis a metaphor. Are not the very names of patent valve closets shrouded in such obscurantism? Why should one be called *Vespa* (a truncated Gallicism to which we have already referred) and another be known as *Arno,* by association with a sister stream of Northern Italy? And on the other hand you have the vast vocabulary of *latrina lingua* (I thank Sir John for the phrase) by which a hundred pseudonyms, some polished and some crude, some evasive and some offensive, are employed to designate the closet, the *unmentionable* parts of the body and their functions. But behind all this evasion or aggressive breach of *taboo* is the common disgust, contempt and horror with which we are taught to regard our most normal functions and our most natural needs.

Indeed, rather than accept that theory concerning the Fall of Man to which I shall presently make reference, I am strongly inclined to the view that the fruit on the tree of knowledge was a fig (for the fruit is not named and tradition alone records that it was an apple, whereas the fig leaf was clearly to be found in Eden); from which I conclude that the beneficial effects of this fruit were discovered by our forefathers, who appear to have appreciated it. And it is not until the time of St. Paul, with his insistence upon the identification of the things of this world with *stercora,* that is to say, dung, that I find any attempted justification of our present attitude to this question. And were I not unwilling to enter into theological controversy there are questions I should like to ask concerning the digestion of broiled fish.

Opinions of Mr. Eric Gill.—How evil may be the effects of such contempt and horror for our own bodies is shewn by many, but notably I would mention the *Autobiography* of Mr. Eric Gill, in whom England lost a great artist, the

Church a great Catholic and the world a great revolutionary. Mr. Gill does not take the common view, that we make shame of excretion because of the sexual nature or proximity of the parts concerned; but rather, on the contrary, he finds it a disastrous discovery in the experience of the young person that the organs of sex should turn out to be the very organs of drainage which he has been so sedulously taught to despise—or, at most (he says) to admire only as one may admire the ingenuity of any piece of sanitary engineering. And he observes that the diaper or napkin is our first article of apparel, clothes being devised not primarily for dignity and adornment, but *to provide the first privy*. Who, then, will express surprise if shame and lewdness are the companions of sex, when Aphrodite is discovered rising from no dragon-green or wine-dark seas, but, as it were, from human cesspools long dishonoured by secrecy and silence, a deity of hidden fears and privy counsels?

The Secret of Dean Swift's Aversions and the true Analysis of Aldous.—Here is the secret of Swift's aversion, torn between an idealised lust and the omnipresence of excremental mortality. Here is the true curse of *Ulysses,* whose author was rightly described by Mr. Jack Lindsay as a *tormented puritan who stands on every point in a diametrically opposed attitude to Rabelais.* Here is the weakness of Mr. Aldous Huxley, if a cowardly Paris may venture a shaft at the heel of Achilles; for Mr. Huxley is obsessed with sex to shew its ugliness, having a most excremental loathing for what appear to him as the grotesque antics of lovers. Or again, in the *Autobiography* of John Cowper Powys, we have the explicit confession of an idealised love that could not bear contamination by physical realities.

Anatomy of the Misery of John Cowper Powys.—In this book Mr. Powys avows his kindred with Swift through

*the kind of madness revealed in his terrible and revolting
verses;* and of the necessities of nature he says that he *desired to imagine a life entirely free from them and was for
ever trying to think them away.* From what other source
shall we seek the explanation when we find this perverted
genius, upon his own confession, *a perambulating Pilate,*
for ever washing of his hands, afraid to touch a door-
handle, averse to certain fabrics and devoutly wishing that
children were born from trees or from dragon's teeth?
Here, indeed, is real quarry for Mr. Berkeley-Hill! But
Mr. Powys—and I speak of him with unaffected reverence
for a great writer and sincere thinker—only shews us in
exaggerated form the lineaments of a very common neurosis. We may not all refuse to allow masculine guests to
touch a book upon our shelves unless they wash their
hands after visiting the privy. We may wonder (as, indeed, I do) why the touching of books is particularised,
rather than an insistence upon washing, as the Hindus do,
regardless. But (without our knowing it) we may still be
seeing life from a lavatory window and finding in the
throne of Ajax, as Mr. Powys reveals, a subject at once
fascinating and horrifying, the apex of comfort, relief,
well-being, nausea, misanthropy and disgust. All this the
critics will in due course say of your present author.

Martyrdom of a Victorian Spinster.—Consider this parable, supplied to me by an Eminent Victorian from his
recollections of a Victorian boarding-house. He recalls the
morning celebration, an ordeal to spinsters when that
word had some content, and the waiting of one's turn for
the use of the close-stool. How like, he says, was this waiting host to a line of Communicants approaching the altar,
how symbolic the place of their destination in its suggestion of *transubstantiation.* How religious was the mien of
one returning with downcast eyes, to avoid salutation,
having found and sought *absolution.* And yet such was

the horror excited by this solemn and satisfying ceremony that one spinster was recalled by my friend who arranged her intervals so as to make a forced march, as it were, at seven o'clock in the morning, causing her to contract habitual constipation. Here indeed are, in one example, the extremes of valuation in a process which rose almost to a religious mystery and afforded an almost spiritual satisfaction, yet could be feared and avoided like the plague itself.

That this fear is of great antiquity and has its origin in some false conception of human dignity seems to me a likely supposition, though I have little proof of it. But I have heard it said (I know not upon what authority) that one of the Pharaohs was wont to do his business secretly at an early hour of the morning, rising before dawn to seek a privy place in the desert; and this, it is said, he did that he might appear immune from such necessities, as befitting his divinity, which seemed to him altogether alien from the poor claims of nature, just as the Dean in a later age for a time believed his Celia to be immune from such needs.

But how far this is from the truth may be seen in many instances; for Richard Plantagenet who (though called a usurper) was a crowned king of England—and what king is there who does not owe his sceptre to a usurping ancestor?—was supposed to have plotted the murder of his nephews whilst sitting upon a privy, as the matter is recorded in *The History of King Richard the Third,* an unfinished work erroneously attributed to Sir Thomas More and responsible for most of the slanders against good King Richard. (Holinshed copied it almost verbatim, and others have discussed its veracity; but it is a good story, which is my sole excuse for using it.) Here the writer says of King Richard's jakes that this was *a convenient carpet for such a council.* And the Grand Monarque of France, as we have already recorded, was not ashamed to hold audiences seated upon a *commode;* of which affair further apocryphal details will be found in *Clochemerle,* whilst Swift and others have alleged that the fistula from which the *Roi Soleil* suffered altered the course of European history. (May Heaven send a few to the right place in our own time, if that be so.) And you will find in Mr. Huxley's *Grey Eminence* some reference to the sociable uses which the great Cardinal and his circle made of *La Chaise Percée.*

Obscene Blasphemy in a Typographical Error.—Yet this wretched *taboo* has long been known, especially manifest in conjunction with religion and superstition; and as the *Bottom Legend* clearly arises from it I will refer you once more to Isaac Disraeli for an example out of the *Curiosities of Literature.* It appears that Flavigny, being in controversy with Abraham Ecchellensis, applied to him the third and fifth verses of the seventh chapter of St. Matthew. But the printer, having dropped the first letter of the word *oculo,* set the matter out thus: *Quid vides festucam in culo fratris tui?* And for this Flavigny was roundly abused for corrupting the sacred text of the Evangelist, substituting for Holy Writ a word *as impious as obscene.* And was not a whole issue of a famous London newspaper suppressed in the time of Victoria, because the sentence, *the Queen passed over the bridge,* was printed with one letter incorrect?

King Edmund Ironside was attacked a tergo *in a Jakes.* —It is, moreover, possible that even the great Plotinus suffered from some such fear or shame; for Porphyry said of him that he seemed ashamed of being in the body and that he was often distressed by intestinal complaints, but declined clysters, pronouncing the use of such remedies unbecoming in an elderly man. Would that he had been as simple in such matters as Mr. Bernard Shaw, who wrote to Mr. Frank Harris that he was unable to leave the place where he was then lodging because he was full of winds and waters, and unable to venture too far from the appropriate seat (a letter which Harris published in very unmannerly fashion in his book on Mr. Shaw). Had Plotinus known the true humility of Shaw he might have lived to as great an age, though I remember one notable person who sought a jakes to his great undoing. That one was Edmund Ironside, a monarch famed for his great worship in battle, who was believed by some to have been done to death in a privy by the foul treachery of Eadric Streona (*ejus consilio ferreum uncum, ad naturae requisita sedenti, in locis posterioribus adegisse,* as William of Malmesbury has it); a very nasty death, from which one might conclude that Ironside, like the son of Peleus, had a vulnerable spot.

Ajax revealed as a Leveller and Nihilist.—I will presently recall others who fared no better, but it is not my purpose here to fill your heart with terror of these humble places. Rather would I shew how normal and proper a part they fill in our lives. Yet so it has ever been, from the time of Plotinus and even the Pharaohs, we are terrified of our own functions; and it has been said that nothing could cause more dismay in a nunnery than *to find the seat lifted and thrown back.* But (nuns apart) we are all most artificial with regard to those things which are most natural, making the greatest secret of that which every other person knows *a priori* to be as it is. I recall that in our own time a shrewd observer of human frailty, finding himself in the place provided for the convenience of members of Parliament (which was below the hall of their recorded trumpetings), wrote these words:

> *In the House up above, when a motion is read,*
> *The Member stands up and uncovers his head;*
> *In this House down below, when a motion's to pass,*
> *The Member sits down . . .*

But the occasion is privileged and we need not to labour the point. Very rightly does Mr. Mumble observe in *For Your Convenience* that he perceived the poetic justice of accepting man's common structure (and woman's, he might have added) in certain situations, without distinction. These words, which were spoken with reference to the custom of providing certain establishments for *gentlemen* and others for *men,* may as well be applied to all other false distinctions that pride and shame have conspired to create among us with regard to those functions which in very truth level and rase all distinctions whatsoever; more even than the grave (for we are not all buried at Westminster) and certainly more than the Church, where the best pews are reserved for the plutocracy. Some such reflections will be found in an eighteenth-century bumphlet entitled *Meditations upon an House-of-Office,* by Jeffrey Broadbottom, which I remember finding in the British Museum.

But let my mentor and *guru,* the good Sir John of the first *Metamorphosis,* take the floor, for I perceive that he has something to say here, most apposite to the question, since he extols the closet (with a *save reverence* that I will throw in for the Hindus and True Believers) as a place of worship, giving it a new dignity.

Quorum Deus est Venter, eorum templum sit cloaca.— And whereas I named devotion (says Sir John) I would not have you think, how homely soever the place is, that all devotion is excluded from it. For I happening to demand of a dear friend of mine, concerning a great companion of his, whether he were religious or no, and namely if he used to pray, he told me that to his remembrance he never heard him ask anything of God, nor thank God for anything: except it were at a jakes, he heard him say, he thanked God he had had a good stool. Thus you see a good stool might move as great a devotion in some man as a bad sermon; and sure it suits very well that *Quorum Deus est Venter, eorum templum sit cloaca.* He that makes his belly his god, I would have him make a jakes his chapel.

Of Persons who died in Privies.—Now this seems to my mind to make excellent sense, and I wish that all would reflect upon the fact that a man may as well be called to account here as in any other place; which indeed was the case with the wicked Emperor Heliogabalus, upon whose ignoble end M. Théophile Gautier once considered the writing of a tragedy in five acts, as he tells us in the preface to *Mademoiselle de Maupin.* The hero (he says) throws himself into a water-closet (though this is not how I recollect the matter as recounted by Gibbon) and M. Gautier considered this an extremely novel situation, introducing an original form of stage décor. Then there was Arius the arch-heretic, and (according to Montaigne) his Pope, Leo. And some have even claimed that, since Arius was about to be reconciled with an unwilling Church (which had yielded to the *force majeure* of the Emperor Constantine), his death was in fact an act of Providence. This the circumstances even suggested; for Arius being on his way to a reconciliation that was a triumph for his opinions, he was seized with violent pains in the bowels and accordingly retired precipitately *into a common jakes and purged his Inwards* (I use the words which you will find in Patrick Walker's *Life and Prophesies of Alexander Peden*). Here, after further precipitations he as precipitately died, but whether by an act of God or by poison given to him by his Christian brethren (if there is a distinction between the two) I do not know; though Cardinal Newman, as I am told, believed it was a miraculous intervention.

Sir John as a Moralist.—From such events Sir John draws the very excellent moral that even at this homely business we should have godly thoughts rather than (he says) as some have, wanton, or most have, idle. And to make this the clearer Sir John wrote these words, to which I have already made reference, and caused them to be set up in Cloacina's Chapel, as he terms it, at his house:

> *A godly father, sitting on a draught*
> *To do as need and nature hath us taught,*
> *Mumbled (as was his manner) certain prayers,*
> *And unto him the devil straight repairs,*
> *And boldly to revile him he begins,*
> *Alleging that such prayers were deadly sins*
> *And that he shewed he was devoid of grace*
> *To speak to God from so unmeet a place.*
>
> *The reverent man, though at the first dismayed,*
> *Yet strong in faith, to Satan thus he said:*
> *Thou damnèd spirit, wicked, false and lying,*
> *Despairing thine own good, and ours envying*
> *Each take his due, and me thou canst not hurt,*
> *To God my prayer I meant, to thee the dirt.*
> *Pure prayer ascends to Him that high doth sit,*
> *Down falls the filth, for fiends of hell more fit.*

Now of these verses and of the picture that hung with them (which will be found in *The Metamorphosis of Ajax*) Sir John records that a sober gentleman protested to him seriously (as well he might) that they put honest and good thoughts into his head; as I hope will be the case with all who read this book of my own, making them to see that these places are not to be despised, but that they are as honourable in their uses as they are necessary and universal, and fundamentally serious as they are seriously fundamental. And if I am compelled to use terms unpleasing to the ear because of associations equally repugnant to other organs, then let Sir John once more be my apologist; for in these words he excuses both himself and me:

I know (he says) that the wiser sort of men will consider, and I wish that the ignorant sort would learn, how it is not the baseness or homeliness either of words or matters that make them foul and obscenous, but their base minds, filthy conceits or lewd intents that handle them. He that would scorn a physician because, for our infirmities' sake, he refuseth not sometime the noisome view of our loathsomest excrements, were worthy to have no help by Physic.

Sir John lamented the Absence of Christian Teaching on our Privy Conduct.—Sir John observed, before ever I did, the lamentable absence of Christian teaching in that place which has so greatly concerned all other notable religions. And (speaking of those habits among us which so aroused the scorn of the Tartarians, as recorded by Richard Johnson among Hakluyt's *Principal Navigations*) Sir John says that it is common obloquy that the Turks, who still keep the order of Deuteronomy for their ordure, do object to Christians, *that they are poisoned with their own dung;* and this objection, he says, cannot be answered (though he speaks with due reverence to the two most excellent Apostles) with any sentence from the epistles of St. Peter or St. Paul, to satisfy these miscreant wretches.

Need for a Religious Revival.—Indeed, it is not without reason that the author of *Clochemerle* should have represented the great and memorable struggle anent the local urinal as being, in essence, a contest between the anti-clerical forces of sanitation and the clerical party of anti-sanitation. We have provided enough evidence to shew, however, that religion has been used since the earliest days to further cleanliness, and that even Christians, under such pressure as was exerted upon our constitutions in the last century, have been known to gird up their loins in this cause. May we not therefore hope, or (rather) shall we not make it our business to bring it about, that there shall arise in this country a Religious Revival concerned with cleanliness in the widest and deepest sense? Is not soap and water needed everywhere, from Downing Street downwards; or upwards, if you prefer? Is there no flush for Fleet Street, no plug to pull upon the press? But before I say more of this we have a final subject to consider, involving the most profound philosophic speculations, the deepest religious mysticism, if religion can but free itself from an obsession with any world but our own. For my part I will leave those who have a mind for such things to speculate as to what becomes of the spirit when it leaves the body; my own concern is, *What becomes of the matter which also leaves the body?* Such shall be our next quest, and the last on which I will ask you to accompany me.

CAPUT XIII

On the Apotheosis of Dung

A Legend concerning Noah.—The proper use of dung as a fertilizer was understood by the ancients and the practice of manuring fields is of great antiquity. Indeed, I have it from a Holy Friar that Noah was so exercised upon this point that he caused a bulkhead to be constructed in the stern of his vessel in order that the valuable excrement from his very considerable cargo of livestock might not be wasted and thrown into the sea, as is now so common, but gathered up aft of the *Ark* for use when the floods should have subsided. But this great heap of dung (he told me) became so vast that it weighed down the stern below the Plimsoll line, so that the ship's company was compelled to cast all this matter into the ocean in despite of their intentions. From which happening it came about that a continent was born, afterwards discovered by Christopher Columbus; but I have never given a ready ear to such traveller's tales.

Stercutius, the God of Manure, is still worshipped by Christians.—As for the Romans, their god Stercutius was as much concerned with the proper use of dung, in spreading it upon the fields, as *Cloacina* was in preventing its abuses by maintaining cleanliness in the closet; and if you will consult your Sunday astrologer on the potency of Saturn (who I am convinced was none other than this Stercutius) you will find that he was especially concerned with agriculture. He reigns still from Christmas to Twelfth

Night, as I understand, having been adopted by the Christians, who found Stercutius indispensable to their constitutions; and among modern paynims his rights survive in the *bean-feast,* though there will be few to recognise a pagan atavism in the art of overloading the stomach with food.

Writing today at the height of the Christian Saturnalia I am astonished to notice that neither shortage of food nor the wise provisions of Parliament (which has decreed no holidays at this time for anyone other than its own members) has substantially dimmed the glory of this festival, so great is the hold of old Saturn-Stercutius upon us. And lest you should find the weighty evidence in my third chapter insufficient, I have been at pains to provide you with more, as here follows, to shew the true identity of our Christmas festival and its patron saint.

Pliny tripped in his own Mesh.—First, then, as to Stercutius, you will find his name in Smith's *Greek and Roman Biography and Mythology,* where it is given as a *surname of Saturnus,* which is reasonable, since Saturn was *The Sower.* But Mr. Smith tells us that some Romans used Stercutius as a name for Picumnus, the son of Faunus; and I find that Pliny, in his *Naturalis Historia,* seems to have embraced this pernicious heresy, for he says: *Augeas rex in Graecia excogitasse traditur, divulgasse vero Hercules in Italia, quae regi suo Stercuto Fauni Filio ob hoc inventum immortalitatem tribuit.* Now I will ask, if Augeas knew the proper use of dung (and Hercules also, it would seem, learning it from Augeas), why did the one suffer his stalls to be cleaned in so wasteful a fashion or the other consent to do it? To flood them with water and sweep the dung into the sea is worthy of our own intelligence, but not of a pioneer in manuring; therefore the rest of the story is suspect and I do not believe it, the more so because Joannes Ludovicus Vives (as I have already recorded) quotes Pliny in quite another sense, shewing he must have eaten his words. But for the rest I am content to leave the matter to the reader, with a recommendation to consult Macrobius, *Sat.* i, 7, together with Servius Maurus Honoratus, *ad Aen.* ix, 4 and x, 76.

Of the Feast of Fools.—Next, as to the *Saturnalia* (which was a feast of fruitfulness) slaves were served by their masters to commemorate the Golden Age of Saturn, when there had been no social distinctions. This continued in a degenerated form, and (as to its progress) I will refer you first to Brewer's *Dictionary of Phrase and Fable,* where we shall find some observations on the King or Abbot of Misrule, under whose dispensation, until King Henry VIII abolished it, revellers went to church with such a confused noise that no-one could hear his own voice. Such was the festival from Christmas to Twelfth Night which Polydore Vergil said was *derived from the Roman Saturnalia,* and Prynne said much the same in his *Histrio-Mastix,* all of which you will find confirmed by Picart and by the learned encyclopaedists, Diderot and d'Alembert.

And now, lest you should think I have wandered too far, you will further discover in the manner of celebrating these festivals that it was customary to throw excrement about the church as part of the jollities; and Dulaure in *Des Divinités Génératrices* says that revellers would eat from the altar at High Mass *des saucisses et des boudins.* As to the sausages, I have grave doubts, because these were not yet invented in the hey-day of the Feast of Fools; but Mr. John Gregory Bourke, in some curious notes and memoranda on scatalogical matters, made much of the *boudins,* for which Littré gives this curious secondary definition: *Toute chose qui, par la forme, a quelque ressemblance avec le boudin.* But, to put the matter plainly, it is reasonable to suppose that the Saturnalia retained some relics of its pristine glory, as a festival in honour of Ster-

cutius; and though I do not know that the ancient Druids
had any dealings with Stercutius, it is a curious thing that
their contribution to this festival should be the *mistletoe,*
known to us by a name which is surely derived from *mist,*
which in German signifies *dung,* and was believed by our
forefathers to grow where a certain bird had left its excrement upon the branch. This *mistletoe,* with so strange an
aura of dung, fertility and love, served its purpose among
the Norsemen too; for it was sacred to Friga, and only
with a weapon made from it could Baldur the Beautiful
be killed.

Of divers Dung Gods.—Therefore I suppose that this
dung-stick, or whatever it was, dominated the Scandi-
navian and Celtic winter festivities because manure is a very
proper symbol of decay and re-birth; as the Mexicans knew
when they worshipped *Tlaçolteotl,* goddess of dung, whom
they also called *Tlaelquani,* the dung-eater, or *Teteo innan,*
Mother of the Gods, or simply *Toçi,* meaning Grand-
mother; of whom Brasseur de Bourbourg said that she presided *aux amours et aux plaisirs lubriques.* And such another God of Ordure was that Baal-Peor of whom we have
already spoken, whose cult was believed *to secure abundance of crops* (as the *Encyclopaedia Britannica* informs us
in an article upon Moab and the Moabites) with altars
appropriately placed in groves and *under every green tree.*
And then there was *Baalzebub,* God of Flies, whom the
Jews called *Beelzeboul,* God of Dung; all such deities belonged to peoples who knew the value of manure, and saw
in it the fertility of their fields, the promise of the Spring
and a Young Man's Fancy.

In Praise of Saturn.—This Saturn-Stercutius, then, who
in the Golden Age taught agriculture and the arts of peace
to the people of Latium, and especially taught the art of
manuring fields, deserves well of humanity; yet of this general cult of dung I can find little except the brief notes of

Mr. John Gregory Bourke and I have found the *Encyclo-paedia of Religion and Ethics* a poor and broken reed, with only the barest mention of Baal-Peor, who was surely a most significant deity. But the cult lived long and vigorously in such customs as we have mentioned, and much might be found in a study of the custom of electing a Bean King or *Rey de Habas* for Twelfth Night, from which we might even learn why the Egyptians and Pythagoreans so abhorred these same beans. Let us therefore, O· Saturn, renew this ancient cult, thou God of Motion, Governor of Houses and Bodily Stature, before phytamins or even vitamins were made known; hail thou to whom that noted astrologer, William Lilly, ascribes the governance of plumbers, corpse-bearers, scavengers, ditchers and the like, saying that thou, O· Saturn, dost delight in caves, dens, holes, churchyards, sinks, dirty and stinking places, houses of office and such-like resorts. Surely no more is required to shew that thou art indeed *Stercutius,* a dunghill god, a god of the jakes-house (to borrow from Heinrich Bullinger), and thy wild, inverted festival, when slaves ruled their masters, was a most suitable commemoration of thy primaeval purpose. Dust unto dust, we shall all, if we are fortunate, fertilise the fields in the end; and the bones or excrement of a slave shall yield as rich a grain as the most aristocratic remains. Of thee also, then, shall it be said: He hath put down the mighty from their seats and exalted them of low degree. Long may we therefore celebrate the Roman Holiday of Democracy and Dung, whatever Parliament may decree.

Of the Chinese.—We have already related certain matters regarding the Chinese, who are among the oldest agri-culturists to be found in any part of our planet, and of them the celebrated American Professor F. H. King wrote under the title *Farmers of Forty Centuries.* In this great unfinished work the Professor claimed that the Chinese and the Japanese, by using all waste material, such as sewage

and garbage, have proved themselves excellent husband-
men, and in support of this contention he cited the view
of Dr. Arthur Stanley, who was Health Officer at Shang-
hai in the year 1899 and reported as follows: While the
ultra-civilised Western, he said, elaborates destructors for
burning garbage at a financial loss and turns sewage into
the sea, the Chinese uses both for manure. He wastes nothing while the sacred duty of agriculture is uppermost in his
mind. And in reality recent bacterial work has shewn that
faecal matter and house refuse are best destroyed *by returning them to clean soil,* where natural purification takes
place.

Of the Hunza People.—Of this system among the
Chinese Dr. G. T. Wrench writes in *The Wheel of Health*
that it is based upon the principle of the forest and the
prairie, *that everything that comes from the soil, whether
it passes through animals or not, is returned to the soil.*
And those who would know more may read in the work
of Professor King, or more briefly in that of Dr. Wrench,
how this object is achieved in China. But especially I would
commend to every reader this book by Dr. Wrench, because it is cheap, because it was but recently published and
because it is very easily read, setting forth the reasons for
the astonishing health of the *Hunza* people, who inhabit a
fertile valley in Central Asia, where the confines of India,
China, Afghanistan and Russia lie among the greatest
mountains of the world. These people are believed by most
European travellers who have seen them, and notably by
Sir Robert McCarrison (of whom we shall say more hereafter), to be the most perfect now living in physical
prowess and in their resistance to diseases and infections;
and among the reasons for this excellent health which they
enjoy many who have considered it commend above all
other things *their perfect system of agriculture* and their
habit of eating food in its most natural forms.

They dispose of their Dung as do the Chinese and Tibetans.—What says Dr. Wrench, then, of this perfect system of agriculture? He says, among other things, that, as regards the disposal of human excreta, the Hunza here, as in other matters of great importance, follow the same principles as the Tibetans and Chinese. They pass their excreta into hidden privies, as do their Tibetan neighbours in Baltistan. From time to time these privies are opened and the material is added to the compost which they use for the manuring of the soil. And again he says that the Hunza, in their manuring, *use everything that they can return to the soil,* of which he mentions the dung from their cattle, all vegetable refuse, and this human sewage, which is allowed to ferment for six months. By such means they are able to grow crops of great abundance without the use of chemical fertilisers, which are unknown among them, and without exhausting their soil; also, of all that vast and terrible list of plant diseases, listed in the manuals, few are known among these crops, which resist disease by the strength of their natural constitutions, like the men whom they nourish.

How Plants thrive upon Dung, when made into Composts with Vegetable Matter.—This same method of farming having been pursued at Indore by Sir Albert Howard and his chief assistant, Mr. Yeshwant D. Wad, was described by them in a book which they called *The Waste Products of Agriculture.* In this work the authors confirmed the opinions of Professor King, whose book they commended as a textbook for every agricultural college in the world, and described the great success of the ancient methods of Mongolia, applied and tested with scientific precision by themselves. And such was Sir Albert Howard's confidence in the health of his plants and crops, which improved continually under his care, that he offered to import pests from America to do their worst among such

robust enemies; for he said that at Indore he could not recall one case of insect or fungus attack in seven years. Such
resistance to disease was also noted by Sir Albert among
his livestock, fed upon crops *properly manured.*

Indeed, Sir Albert went so far as to say that insects and
fungi are not the real cause of plant diseases, and that they
only attack unsuitable varieties or crops improperly grown.
These pests he regards as censors, pointing out the crops
which are imperfectly nourished. And resistance to disease,
in his opinion, seems to be the natural reward of healthy
and well-nourished protoplasm (which appears to be the
case among men as it is among plants); therefore the first
step (he says) *is to make the soil live by seeing that the
supply of humus is maintained.* As for all this spraying and
sprinkling against pests, he finds it *thoroughly unscientific
and radically unsound.*

Cunning of the Japanese.—Of the agricultural methods
long in practice among the Japanese I find this information
in a lecture on *The Sanitary Condition of Japan* which
was delivered at the Sanitary Institute in March 1890 by
Mr. W. K. Burton, Professor of Sanitary Engineering in
the University of Tokyo. First, he says, in connection with
sewage disposal we are faced with the fact that all the
ordure and the urine have to be collected and carried un-
diluted to the fields. I say *have to* (continues Mr. Burton)
because the disposal of the constituents of sewage just mentioned on the land is so integral a part of the agricultural
system of the country that it would be hopeless to try to
change it even were it desirable, which I do not think it is.

According to this authority sewage was in his time so
highly valued among the Japanese, for the cultivation of
their rice fields, that a country house would be let at a certain figure with the condition that it should be increased
in the event of the absence of the tenant, who was supposed
to make a part of his contribution *in kind.* And the Japanese knew the value of allowing their sewage to ferment,

for a month at the least, which is a vital principle in the dynamics of manure. For this purpose, Mr. Burton tells us, the sewage is first stored in great tanks of stone, which are sunk in the ground by the fields. This custom I understand to be of great antiquity, like that of China.

Industry of Zola's Mère Caca.—That the great value of human sewage was also known to the French peasantry in the past is shewn by Emile Zola in *La Terre,* where he tells of the old woman who was known as *la mère Caca,* because, for want of other manure to nourish her vegetables, she used the household product. These vegetables, we are told, were of the very finest quality; but such was the repugnance incited by the knowledge of their origin, that certain *bourgeois* customers could not stomach them and turned in disgust from the fine carrots and cabbages grown by this most enterprising woman. Such, indeed, has often (for we are anything but *Homo sapiens*) been the fate of fine vegetables grown upon a sewage farm, which will be rejected with nausea by those who would cheerfully consume the products of any other dung but this. And I know of one pioneer, a woman (as they say) of means, who is seeking to experiment in this same direction with her kitchen garden; of which experiment all that I have heard as yet is her complaint that *the maids will not co-operate.* Also it is well known that the excellent products of our sewage works are often despised by farmers in England and Wales, though I have heard it said that in Scotland a past generation within living memory made great use of *night soil* upon their land. Indeed, this was true in the last century of the North of England also, and of Flanders and Switzerland and parts of France around Paris, where they also used a manure made from human urine, which they called *urate.*

The Mexicans sold Dung in their City of Tenochtitlan— Of a curious Habit among Spaniards.—I find, moreover, from Bourke's *Compilation of Notes and Memoranda bearing upon the use of human ordure and human urine in rites of a religious or semi-religious character among various nations* that Bernal Diaz, who accompanied stout Cortés in his Mexican wars, said that at that time human excrements were exposed for sale in canoes in the canals near a market-place of Tenochtitlan. And Mr. Bourke tells us of many uses to which such excrements were put, other than their purpose of manuring the land, as intended by nature. For he speaks of the tanning of leather and how Hans Egede recorded that the Eskimos for this purpose conserved urine in tubs within their igloos, quoting also from Graah's work on *Greenland* in 1837 to shew that the Eskimos used this same substance to shampoo their hair. And according to Diderot and d'Alembert, writing in 1789, in an article on Urine in their encyclopaedia, *Les Espagnols font grand usage de l'urine pour nettoyer les dents.*

But to return to the subject of manuring, an ancient art known to Homer (as you may see in the *Odyssey,* xxiv, 225, though I do not know if the ancient Greeks were as wise as the people of China and used their own products), the water-carriage system of sanitation has greatly added to our problems in spite of the many advantages which we derive from it. This is, I suppose, the fulfilment of the prophecy in Joel iii, 18, *a fountain shall come forth of the house of the Lord and shall water the valley of Shittim.* But the ancient deity of Shittim (who was none other than Baal-Peor, that god of fertility) has had his nose put out of joint in such a way that our soil is visibly declining. For which you may find evidence in almost any work on agriculture, as (for example) in that popular book by Lord Addison on *A Policy for British Agriculture* (pp. 59–60), published as late as 1939.

An extraordinary Proposition to justify the Waste of Sewage.—As to the general disposal of sewage in this country at the present time, much goes into our larger rivers (until recent years untreated in any way), and I have read in the Eleventh Edition of the *Encyclopaedia Britannica* (published in 1910–11) that *nearly every town upon our coast turns its sewage into the sea;* also that it was urged by *competent authorities* that this system was not wasteful, since organic matter forms the food of the lower organisms, which in turn are devoured by fish. And thus, it was said in this compendium of all human wisdom, *If the land is the poorer, the sea is richer.* Here is consolation indeed, as who should say *Though we may starve, the locusts will thrive;* or as Mr. Chamberlain said to the Czechs when he turned all four cheeks to Herr Hitler at Munich, *It is more blessed to give than to receive.* But later editions of the *Encyclopaedia* have omitted this statement.

Wisdom of the Americans.—What, then, when all our riches lie deeper than the Tyrian murex and the land is too poor to bear fruit, are we to live on fish (if we can catch enough of them) for an eternity of Good Fridays? But here is further information upon the same subject, in the 1895 edition of *Chambers' Encyclopaedia,* shewing how long this vast waste has been continuing, as you may read for yourself in the IXth volume, from page 340 onwards (where there is an astonishing account of a sewage system called *pneumatic,* where aerial suction was used in place of water carriage). Here there is no suggestion of alarm at such prodigious waste, but only of consternation at the problem presented by the rapid accumulation of sludge. But if you should think we are now wiser, here is some modern wisdom for you, from the American journal *Life* of May 12th, 1941, where I recently read of the burning of cow-dung in India and was astonished to find this proposition entertained by the writer: *Burning manure is a sensible way of getting rid of it.*

By the Splendour of God, if this be the learning of the

most modern, the most advanced, the most Western of all Western nations, how can any rebuke the folly of the Indian peasant who burns his cow-dung, not because he is ignorant of its value, but because he has no choice; not for lack of knowledge, but for lack of other fuel. For you will find in *The Indian Forester* for April 1930 that my good friend Mr. M. D. Chaturvedi proved this, shewing that the peasant knew well enough that the soil has a better use for dung; but the wretch lacks other fuel, for which he must pay more than his meagre means allow, even though he may live on the border of a forest, so zealously is this *property* guarded from the people. Whether the Scots knew as much in the time of Robert Burns I do not know, but I believe it is true that Bobbie Burns married the champion dung-thrower in his neighbourhood; for that was at one time their custom, to throw the cow-pats at a wall, where they stuck fast and so dried till they were considered fit for the fire. Such, at least, was then the case, whether I am right or not in the matter of Mrs. Burns (and that is at least as true, as credible and stated upon as good authority as anything I have read in today's paper); but this frugal nation must have learnt better in later days, to which fact we have already paid tribute.

Indeed, though, but I begin to think this burning of cow-pats must have been one of the oldest forms of waste, as may be seen in Ezekiel iv, in the twelfth and fifteenth verses. And, according to Bourke, human dung also was commonly burnt by the Syrians and the Arabians, by the Egyptians (who used it to heat their lime-kilns) and by people in the West of England. Of this, he says, more will be found in an article on dung in the encyclopaedia of McClintock and Strong. But that the Jews knew a better use for dung is shewn in the Gospel according to St. Luke (xiii, 8).

Discovery of Auximones *by Professor Bottomley.*—The belief that plants require for their nourishment only inorganic substances, such as water, carbon dioxide and mineral salts, was first shewn to be erroneous by the experiments of an English botanist, Professor Bottomley, who was able to prove that *the addition to the inorganic nutrients of minimal quantities of certain organic substances is absolutely essential if the plants are to grow healthily and normally for any length of time.*

The mixture of organic substances which the Professor discovered to be necessary to plant life contained one which was unknown to him, a substance having the power of maintaining life and stimulating growth in plants. This he termed an *auximone,* and its function in the life of the plant he declared to be similar to that of the *vitamin* in the life of an animal.

Let the reader now employ his imagination. From what source should we expect organic substances in the soil but from the presence of animal and vegetable matter? And what is more consistent with the cycle of nature in all other matters than to suppose that *auximones* in animal manure are as necessary to the plant as the *vitamins* in the plant are necessary to the animal? If this should prove to be the case, then the destruction or waste of sewage not only breaks the cycle of nature in the matter of well-known chemical substances, but it is the progressive destruction of life itself: we are pulling the plug on our own protoplasm.

Awful Extent of the Waste when Dung is destroyed.— When dung is destroyed or flung into the depths of the sea the soil is therefore robbed not only of nitrogen and potash, of phosphoric and silicic acid and magnesia, but of valuable animal hormones and organic substances necessary to the life of plants and therefore to the life of men and animals which, directly or otherwise, feed on these plants. Therefore it is not remarkable that Sir John Russell, in his experiments at Rothamsted, should have discovered farmyard manure to be superior to any combination of chemical fertilisers in its physical and physico-chemical effects upon the soil, producing more steady crops from year to year. And at Coimbatore the experiments of Viswa Nath and Suryanarayana have shewn the remarkable effect of cattle manure on the quantity and quality of seeds; so that more grain is produced in proportion to straw when such manure is used rather than a chemical fertiliser, and the quality of this grain is better for the future production of crops.

The distinguished biochemist, Professor Gilbert Fowler, in a most fascinating work to which we shall refer at greater length in the next chapter, observes of the theory of *auximones* that it is still subject to discussion. Nevertheless he records these experiments at Coimbatore as important and indicates that there are unknown factors which operate in animal manures. For he speaks of an experiment in which grain seeds grown without manure and similar seeds fertilised with an extract of pig manure shewed little if any difference in composition when subjected to chemical analysis. Yet these grains were proved to have different nutritive qualities, as was demonstrated by feeding rats, when the manured grains proved their marked superiority. From this experiment, which was made and recorded in a technical journal by Rowlands and Wilkinson, and from many similar observations, we are surely justified in concluding that dung has certain valuable, if unknown, specific qualities; and we should surely accept at least the cautious deduction of Professor Fowler, that just as animals obtain vitamins from plants, so it appears that the micro-organisms in the soil liberate either when alive or after death some active constituent which is absorbed by the plant and passed on to the seed. In which case we have only to complete the Professor's argument and the cycle of nature by asking, What does the animal pass on to the soil? And to this there can be but one answer.

Learning of the Anthroposophists.—The experiments of

the *Anthroposophists* in this matter should therefore be reviewed without prejudice. Dr. Ehrenfried Pfeiffer, in his work on *Bio-Dynamic Farming and Gardening,* has many references to experiments of which the significance should be more widely known. Thus we are told of white mice fed on minerally fertilised grain, while others were fed upon grain fertilised by *bio-dynamic* methods, that is to say, with specially prepared organic manure, in which cultures are used, as in the preparation of cheese. And not only did the *bio-dynamic* grain produce larger litters, but the death rate in these litters was little more than half that in the litters reared upon grain that had been fertilised with chemical manures.

The Sins of the Fathers are visited upon the Children.— Such comparisons made with fowls shewed that *bio-dynamic* grain produced among them greater vitality and a greater weight of eggs, of which nearly twice as many were hatched as of those produced by hens fed upon minerally fertilised grain. Also these *bio-dynamic* eggs shewed greater resistance to the ravages of age, because (says Dr. Pfeiffer) products of poor quality spoil more quickly, and *possessing less active life forces, they decay more easily.* Thus wheat which is robbed of its dung transmits its weakness to the hen that eats the grain, and the hen in turn passes it on to the egg, which is the poorer for it. And this argument Dr. Pfeiffer follows even further, to shew that the egg will be affected by the food upon which the animals fed from whose dung the wheat was fertilised that fed the hen that laid the egg; so that the circle of destiny is complete and perfect in this as in all things.

By Malnutrition even the Virtue of our Dung declines.— But now consider what spiral of destruction we are descending. Not content with tracing biological history from the manure of the fields to the eggs laid by the hens that ate of the grain, these indefatigable anthroposophists took the dung from the chickens that came of these eggs, those whose sires fed upon grain chemically manured and those whose parents were reared upon grain fertilised by animal manures, *bio-dynamically*. This chicken manure they employed in fertilising two garden beds, with a third as control, which they left unfertilised. In these beds they grew beans and radishes, and what would you expect to find? In the weight of the bean stalks and of the beans, and in the number of beans grown, in the weight of the radish leaves and the number of these leaves, in the length and weight of the radish roots, the manure from the *bio-dynamic* chicken proved its superiority. Hence we may conclude that where plants are deprived of organic manure, not only is their deficiency shared by animals (or men) living upon those plants, and not only is this deficiency discovered in the next generation of the species, but these deficient creatures *actually lose the capacity to produce the best dung themselves, so that disaster becomes cumulative.* And since the very dung itself deteriorates with the deterioration of the species, it follows that the longer we destroy our own sewage and live upon chemically manured plants, or animals fed upon such plants, the less value this same sewage will have, until it becomes too late to turn back. Like our faculties, the excreta decline with disuse; devitalised beings, we yield devitalised dung, which must needs become poorer with each generation, until in the end it will be utterly unusable, and Nature says: *Enough!*

Of Fish Guts.—Was it then so far from the truth that the nobleman in Mr. Huxley's novel, *After Many a Summer,* should have discovered the secret of the longevity of carp *in their guts?* And where else but in our rivers and our seas will you find the cycle of life complete and unbroken, with rich additions from the profligate extravagance of the *Lords of the Earth,* who fling their wealth into the water? Have not the Chinese from ancient times manured their fish-ponds for this very reason? (But never their seas and rivers, a long-term loan upon a meagre security!) Is there not a famous fish-farm at Grafenwohr where fish fed upon sewage bring handsome profits? Are not fish-ponds used in many German towns for the final process of sewage purification? Have you tasted the blue carp of Berlin? Where else but among fish is the longest life to be found, and where will you seek the chemistry of reincarnation save in the faeces? All that I doubt in this story of Mr. Huxley's is that the Earl should have preserved his life by eating the carp guts; rather should he have fertilised his fields with carp guts and eaten the produce, which had been more palatable.

The good Taste of Mice.—I can find, however, no reference to experiments shewing the peculiar properties of fish manure, though I would assume them to be of the highest order. But certain other experiments of which Dr. Pfeiffer makes mention may be considered as further evidence on this subject of the virtues of organic manure. Thus he considers the sensitivity of animals, and particularly of white mice, to the qualities of food, and he tells of an experiment made, in which these creatures were offered two dishes of grain, one minerally fertilised and one *bio-dynamically*. Need I inform the reader, accustomed by now to these inevitable results, that the mice shewed their preference in the most marked manner for the *bio-dynamic* product? This experiment was made with two colonies of mice, one fed for six generations on minerally fertilised grains and one that for six generations had been nourished *bio-dynamically*. With each colony the same result was observed: the mice but tasted the minerally fertilised grain and left it to guzzle the produce of an organic fertiliser.

We will pass over for the moment the remarks which Dr. Pfeiffer makes with regard to the harmful effects of mineral fertilisers through the overbalance of salts, producing plants injurious to the health of the animals that consume them. This might be tolerated; but the progressive devitalisation of the earth and all living creatures that dwell on dry land is *not* to be tolerated, though I should be called a crank and a faddist, or an apostle of dung for saying as much. But here is testimony from another quarter, without the taint of *anthroposophy*. In the Proceedings of the *R. Accademia Nazionale dei Lincei,* Mathematical and Natural-Scientific Division (Vol. XIII, series 6, I: Rome, February 1931), there is an article by G. Tallarico on *The biological value of the products of soil fertilised with animal or with chemical fertiliser*. This writer asserted that he had proved by experiment a more luxuriant growth and a higher yield could be obtained by the use of stable manure than by mineral fertilisation; and he records the result of experiments made in the feeding of turkeys with various diets. From these experiments he was able to shew that turkeys fed upon diets which comprised *stable-manured* grains or green feeds had a greater resistance to the *red crisis* which afflicts these birds than turkeys eating *minerally fertilised* grains or green feeds. Fewer of the birds died, less of them were stunted in growth by the disease, and its duration was less among them when stable manure contributed in this way to their nourishment.

Doctors and dietitians are among those who have testified to the vital properties of organic manure in creating food of the highest quality; but the reader need have no fear of further tedium, for by this time I trust he has already determined to obtain the books to which I have referred and study the question. A few final instances of such tests shall therefore suffice to demonstrate the now widespread recognition of the properties of dung, before we consider our conclusions.

Sir Robert McCarrison, working in collaboration with

Mr. B. Viswa Nath and Mr. M. Suryanarayana, published to the world in the year 1927 certain facts which will be found in the *Memoirs of the Department of Agriculture in India* (IX, No. 4). Having discovered the greater yields to be obtained from organic fertilisers, they experimented in the feeding of pigeons and rats with grains diversely manured, obtaining conclusions similar to those which we have already observed. And in the case of the rats they discovered that these creatures, when fed upon a basic ration to which stable-manured wheat was added, gained more in bodily weight than rats fed upon the same basic ration to which the same weight of *chemically fertilised* wheat was added, *even though this was supplemented with additional vitamins.*

Of the venerable Art of trying to cheat Nature.—Here, then, is the answer to those inventive minds which have ever sought to give us some counterfeit for everything that nature provides, as though our principal object in living was to play the cheat. Would that good Sir John Harington had known all this when he found himself in hot encounter with Hugh Plat, author of the *Jewel House of Art and Nature.* That ingenious inventor, in *Sundry New and Artificial Remedies against Famine,* was, as I believe, among the first Englishmen (I will not tire you with the Ancients) to propose the use of an *artificial manure;* for which the creator of Ajax, who broke some lances upon him with effect, ought rightly to have unhorsed him completely, and would gladly have done so had these facts been known at the time.

But let no reader imagine that we have here nothing but the bald fact stated by Sir Robert McCarrison in a recent lecture, that the same grain, when grown in the same soil and watered in the same way, was of higher nutritive value when the soil had been manured with natural farmyard manure than it was when chemically manured. That (in view of current practice) would be sufficiently alarming of itself. Here, however, is evidence of deficiency diseases in plants, animals and people, caused by our neglect of natural manure. Here is evidence that the effect is cumulative from generation to generation. Our specialists, who (it has been said) *know more and more of less and less,* are victims of what Dr. Wrench has called *Fragmentation;* they see each disease separately and do not see that all disease has its roots in that weakness of constitution which cannot resist infection. The cause of this weakness, as may be seen from the strength of those who do not share it, from their habits of living and feeding, should be sought first *in our food and the manner in which our food is grown.*

We have raped the Virgin Soil of Distant Lands.—Or consider the vast and criminal waste perpetrated daily in the name of civilisation, the prodigality of our way of living. In the plains of the Argentine there grows the food which nourishes innumerable cattle, brought each year to this country. But what becomes of the bones, the skins, the offal, the manure of those beasts and of those who devour them? Does it return to the plains, to complete the cycle of nature? Can chemical fertilisers replace it, either in quantity or quality? Sir John Orr, in his book *Minerals in Pasture,* tells of the Falkland Islands, where (he says) *sheep have been reared and exported for forty years without any return to the soil to replace the minerals removed.* Here, he says, for twenty years it has become harder to rear lambs, while other animals also deteriorate. In Scotland he notes the same process, depleting the hills of minerals; and in Victoria, he says, some 360,000 tons of phosphoric acid were taken from the soil in sixty years through the export of meat, meal and animal products. But this calculation takes no account of those minute organic substances which cannot, like phosphates, be replaced to some extent by artifice.

An Estimate of wasted Sewage.—In India Sir John Orr found the same decline, with 520,000 tons of bones exported in five years and no compensating return to the soil. The evidence presented before the Royal Commission on Agriculture in India shewed, he said, the marked deterioration of the cattle in that country. As to the general loss, Professor King stated it in these words: the people of the United States and of Europe (he said) are pouring into the sea, lakes or rivers and into underground waters from 5,794,300 to 12,000,000 pounds of nitrogen, 1,881,900 to 4,151,000 pounds of potassium and 777,200 to 3,057,600 pounds of phosphorus per million of adult population annually; *and this waste we esteem one of the achievements of our civilisation.* These figures must have increased since the Professor wrote, and they take no account of dry refuse disposal.

For other reasons our system of civilisation is to be condemned, but of these I will only briefly mention two. Firstly, that there is a positive evil in our growing dependence upon chemical fertilisers, as we have already mentioned once, and as may be seen by a study of *excess diseases,* which include those caused by an excess of nitrogen, from the use of certain artificial fertilisers. So that a surplus in the midst of poverty is known even in plant life. But secondly (as you may read at leisure in *The Wheel of Health*), it is beyond serious dispute that the long storage and distant removal of certain foods, notably wheat, can only be effected by processes injurious to these foods, so as to deprive them of invaluable constituents and properties. Thus we have been taught to prefer white bread because only by milling flour in this way can it be transported long distances without danger of decay; but by this very process essential and vital parts of the wheat are destroyed, so that deficiency disease is cultivated by a deficient food. Hence, by the same process, a devitalised food is brought from afar for our consumption and the distant fields in which it is grown are robbed of their fertility by a continual loan upon which neither interest nor capital is paid in the return of human and animal dung or vegetable waste.

A terrible Indictment of Man.—Shall we then marvel at the words of Professor King when he says: *Man is the most extravagant accelerator of waste the world has ever endured?* His withering blight, says this writer, has fallen upon every living thing within his reach, himself not excepted; and his besom of destruction in the uncontrolled hands of a generation has swept into the sea soil-fertility which only centuries of life could accumulate, fertility which is the substratum of all that is living.

Those who will give themselves the pleasure of reading almost any of the books to which I have made reference will discover further evidence of our prodigality, as also of the astonishing results obtained by others who, like Sir Albert Howard, experimented for themselves in methods known and approved by countless generations in China and other parts of Asia. And of these last I will mention especially that good farmer whose experiments in our own country are recorded in George Godwin's book *The Land Our Larder,* published in the year 1939, also the writings of the Earl of Portsmouth and Lady Eve Balfour.

The Dialectics of Dung.—We have already recalled the saying that dirt is matter misplaced, and the case of sewage is a suitable example of the truth of this aphorism. For what is misplaced in the house, and breeds pestilence, is well-placed in the field, where it ceases to be *dirt* and becomes a valuable part of the soil. Therefore, as we proposed to the reader in the introduction to this book, the study of sewage is by nature dialectical, the existence of sewage as dirt being not absolute, but relative to its station; and the method of dialectics has been correctly described as the study of things *in motion*. So whatever truth there may be in the doctrines of metempsychosis, this at least we have established, that there is a true law of reincarnation in what Dr. Wrench calls *The Wheel of Health,* saying also that *Man is a metamorphosis of the re-creating power of the soil*. How rightly, then, have we called this book *The Further Metamorphosis,* that treats of changes more miraculous even than those of which Ariel sang to the disconsolate Ferdinand.

The full Extent of our Loss is Unknown.—*The rainfall to the river, the sewage to the soil:* such was the excellent maxim laid down by the immortal Chadwick. What irony, then, that the system of sanitation which he did so much to further in this country should be used mainly to defeat his far-sighted purpose by a policy of wholesale profligacy. We have yet to discover the full consequences of our folly, for it is not to be imagined that all our loss is included within the scope of present research. Thus Sir Robert McCarrison speaks in his Gabriel Howard Memorial Lecture on *Nutrition and Health,* delivered in 1937, of the food-essentials, *known and unknown, discovered and undiscovered,* we need for normal nutrition; and these, he concludes, *can only be produced on soils which are not impoverished*. For Man, he says, is literally created out of the earth; and if he is to derive all the benefits which the earth is so ready to yield to him he must employ his intelligence, his knowledge and his labour. But in this country, he tells us, impoverishment of the soil goes on apace because we take out of it in the form of crops more than we put into it in the form of animal and other organic manure.

Of the Cheshire Testament.—And now, as our final authority, to put the seal of medical opinion and official approval upon our findings, let us consider the *Medical Testament*. What, you have not heard of it? Now this is as monstrous a thing as I have yet come upon, that you should not have heard of the *Testament* issued *ex cathedra* by the Cheshire Medical and Panel Committee; but I greatly feared it would be so. It is now some twelve years since I heard first of the work carried out in India by McCarrison and his associates, since when I have expected hourly to see such revolutionary discoveries blazoned upon the front page of some newspaper; but instead it has cost me months of searching to discover what little has been written upon this matter. Would you know the reason? Well, you shall have it, though to speak the truth may snuff this poor book like a candle.

And Patent Medicines—A Light that Failed.—Search first your newspaper, daily and weekly, your monthly journals and the whole periodical press, and see whether it be not the case that the greatest and most persistent advertisers are *the vendors of patent medicines*. This pill will cure your rheumatism, this your headaches, and yet another is infallible against the common cold. A fourth, if you will but drug yourself regularly with the panacea, offers you a prophylactic against all three. *Tubo* pills cure tuberculosis; *Canso* cures cancer; *Veno,* some other malady. And the manufacturers of these, as you are doubtless aware, are the gentlemen who pay the Pied Pipers of Fleet Street, for which reason they have called the tune to some purpose. What, in fact, was the fate of that excellent book on patent medicines, giving the precise constituents and true value of each known and much vaunted product? Was it made known to us through our usual *vehicles of information?* God's truth is, that book was blanketed by the heaviest silence that ever fell; and only a fool would have expected it to be otherwise, for the pen may be mightier than the sword, but the scribbler is not greater than his paymaster. So call it gratitude and say *they did not bite the hand that fed them*.

The Organic Gospel proclaimed in Cheshire.—But what has this to do with Cheshire? Be sure, if you have patience and an open mind, I can shew you. Let us then suppose that a County Medical and Panel Committee should conclude, and place it upon record, that the experience of the medical profession in the area for which it was responsible brought it daily to the same conclusion, viz. *that this illness results from a lifetime of wrong nutrition*. Let us further suppose that such a committee, after a full review of the facts, should commend as a condition primary to proper feeding *the better manuring of the home land so as to bring an ample succession of fresh food crops to the tables of our people, the arrest of the present exhaustion of the soil and the restoration and permanent maintenance of its fertility*. Let us finally suppose that this committee endorses the views of Dr. Pfeiffer, Sir Albert Howard and Dr. Wrench with regard to the essential need for *organic manures,* if plants (and therefore men) are not to be the victims of deficiency diseases; and that they hold a public meeting in the principal town, which is addressed by Sir Albert Howard and Sir Robert McCarrison on the subject of Nutrition and the Soil.

Is not this news? Is this a man biting a dog, or is it a dog biting a man? Is this *the mixture as before* or the tocsin of a revolution? Is this, or is it not, a more important and urgent matter (laid before the public in all earnestness by public men) than a pantaloon in a cornet leading a fashionable nonentity to the altar? But did the press jump to its typewriters? Did the wires hum, the placards and headlines shriek at us? Did the newsboys call down the Strand the greatest gospel since the beginning of our era? Yet here it was, for any simpleton to see: *Doctors Advocate Dung; Sewage Must Be Saved; Revolution In Cheshire: Medicos Demand Health For All.*

The Silence of Fleet Street.—For such, indeed, no less, was the message of the *Medical Testament* in the year of our Lord, 1939; and such were the steps taken to make it known. But while there exists in this country and in all parts of the world a vast and powerful trade *which depends utterly upon the existence of a mug public, C_3, ignorant and superstitious,* how will the most credulous person imagine that the press will take the first steps towards enlightenment, when that press is shackled to the pedlars of *Rheumo, Slobbo, Scabo, Gobbo, Blotto, Pimpo* and the rest of the tribe? Where, in a healthy, sane and educated population would they find the *boobs* whom they could scare with imaginary diseases, or the wretches suffering from real ones? In these true masters of human destiny, the prospect of a scheme that could make us a healthy nation within ten years would induce such a headache that they would empty their bottles in vain into their own evil bellies.

Of the true Decline of the West.—Or again, consider the vast interests of those who produce chemical fertilisers, used only for lack of good dung and vegetable waste, by those who are ignorant of their harmful effects. Do you imagine that powerful chemical industries will allow themselves to be replaced without a struggle? Here are the druggists of the soil, offering quick results, dearly bought in the final reckoning; potash, nitro chalk and sulphate of ammonia, used (as all drugs are used) in ever-increasing quantities, until the soil bacteria (by which good *humus* is formed) are destroyed, and with them the earthworms, *the Ploughs of God.* Behold the heritage of the chemical fertiliser, the once-fertile fields of Europe, where for thirty years now, since the first stimulus of these drugs ceased to be effective, the production of crops has declined, while the fields of China continue, even after a decade of war, to nourish her vast population. Did not Professor King claim that in his time there lived upon every square mile of Chinese farmed lands, 1783 persons, while in his own country of America but 61 people were supported by the same area? Aye, they farm there upon the grand scale, getting everything from the soil and giving back little or nothing, feeding the bellies of the great cities, as we have done, that pay in cash and manufactured goods, *as though these could manure the starved lands.* And the same bankruptcy awaits us all when the last *Virgin Soil* reaches the limit of exhaustion and the last mineral deposits have given their final stimulus, *the morphia of science for a dying agriculture.*

A Jeremiad in a Parable.—There is, in the mysterious Service to which I belong, a curious anachronism which is called *Being On the Gate.* This signifies that a person, such as myself at this present moment, shall always sit in a small hut at the entrance of a depot, by day and by night. And so it comes about that I am writing by the light of a Hurricane lamp at four in the morning in a place so completely *blacked out* (with the aid of a former mortuary blanket) that I could not conceivably see the gate, which does not (moreover) exist. Thus an imaginary gate is, in official imagination, surveyed; and though nothing hinders any person, authorised or otherwise, from walking in or out, or from using some other entry or exit, where there is not even an imaginary gate or an imaginary guardian, *officialdom is satisfied.* And you, reader, the brave defender, perchance, of a civilisation which is destroying itself and of a democracy which has never existed, may take this final reflection to bed with you when you close this book: that the fertility of this planet is running out through open sluices, as surely as a clock-spring unwinds itself till the clock stops, if none thinks to wind it. Stand, then, by the open sluices of fertility, or sit with me in the Dark Hut provided by Authority and say to yourself: *I am saving Civilisation from Destruction*. But when you open your stable door in the morning (if there *is* a door) you may discover that your horse, if there *is* a horse, was stolen before ever you mounted guard. For like my own metaphors, our labour and devotion, our principles and policies, end in the same confusion, writing their epitaphs in the macaronics of Babel.

A solemn Warning and a Prophecy.—Here is the final paradox of Ajax for those who can read the microcosmic Zodiac, the constellations of the atoms wherein lie the true horoscope of human destiny. By sanitation we were saved from unknown horrors as our world became industrialised and urbanised; nay, more, for life has lengthened, the old and known diseases have been slowly driven back upon all fronts. But slowly, insidiously, while we have battled with deadly bugs, a new enemy has intrenched himself behind our lines; and in the struggle for health we have become like those wretches who bind themselves to a domestic tyranny in order that the same thing may not be imposed upon them by a foreigner. This new enemy is Sterility: the sterility of our soil and therefore of our crops; of our crops and therefore of men and beasts. In vain we build Maginot Lines of hygiene against the hordes of harmful bacteria: slowly but inevitably Life itself is on the ebb. Mankind is so surely dying that generations to come may like enough grow their first hair grey or white, and every child among them need spectacles from infancy.

Dr. Wrench recalls the warning uttered, many years since, by Professor Shaler of Harvard University, in the *National Geographic Magazine*. If, said the Professor (writing in the year 1896), mankind cannot devise and enforce ways of dealing with the earth which will preserve the source of life, we must look forward to a time—remote it may be, yet clearly discernible—when our kind, having wasted its great inheritance, will fade from the earth because of the ruin it has accomplished. But since Professor Shaler made this prophecy, speaking (like Jeremiah and all prophets of doom) to deaf ears, the waste has not diminished: rather has it vastly increased. Ever-increasing quantities of vegetable matter are made into cloth or paper, the ultimate fate of which is that it is cremated in the name of Refuse Disposal, that is to say (once more) of Sanitation. Yet Sir Albert Howard shewed that all such matter, when composted with sewage, could be used to feed the land from which it came, which otherwise must starve. What are we then doing with these vast *destructors* and *incinerators* but burning up the land on which we live, as surely as the Irish do when they recklessly carve up the rich peat to feed their hearths?

The Scrap-irony of Salvage.—And now, to mock our tragedy of greed and ignorance, a campaign of *salvage* is proclaimed. Salvage for what? Is it intended that anything should be saved in order to conserve the wealth of the world for the use of the people? Had that been so, we should have heard this talk of salvage long before the present war drove us to it. But the word has now also undergone a metamorphosis, emerging as *destruction;* for what else can it be truly named? Hitherto paper was burnt, but now we are to save it for the making of cartridges; and by diligent application to this programme in both Britain and Germany it is optimistically proposed that instead of merely destroying x tons of paper annually we shall destroy the full tonnage of paper plus an incalculable number of human lives.

An historic Example of Megalomania.—Note well, however, the patriotic organ of public opinion which appointed itself the Big Noise of this paper *salvage*. Observe its imperative demands, that we should *forget our past,* give up treasured letters and diaries, books, sheets of music and everything we kept for mere *sentiment.* Are you not, were you not at the time, astonished at such unexampled impudence from the hired hacks of Fleet Street, whose ephemeral scribbling eats up each day acres of good forest land, turned into wood-pulp to make a penny platform for their antics? Did not one of them all ever think, ever consider for a sober moment, whether the suspension of the *Daily Express* for a single week would not save more than all its readers could contribute in the manner suggested? What world is this, where we are asked to send Shakespeare, Chopin and the Old Folks' letters to the slaughterhouse in the name of economy, while Lord Beaverbrook wastes in a day more paper than I could use for all purposes in a lifetime, and encourages me to buy his newsprint at the very moment when I am supposed to be practising economy by a ruthless holocaust of the classics! What name is there for such self-opinion?

But long before Lord Beaverbrook found a vulgar halo as the national Rag-and-Bone Man, a poet and prophet wrote *To Iron-Founders and Others* that they *poisoned England at her roots.* And having described the wilderness of their creation, he said to them:

> *Your worship is your furnaces,*
> *Which, like old idols, lost obscenes,*
> *Have molten bowels; your vision is*
> *Machines for making more machines.*

But when (said Mr. Gordon Bottomley) these slaves of the machine have exhausted the earth, the *priceless slags,* that is to say, the salvage from our wantonness, will be raked over to yield the necessities of a nobler age:

> *Ploughs to make grass in every field,*
> *Chisels, men's hands to magnify.*

Now there is true salvage for you; and if I were discussing old iron I would say more. But as to our chroniclers of cynarctomachy (which Samuel Butler offers as a fine word to describe a fight between dogs and bears) another has written of them very eloquently:

> *Oh, born with ease, how envied and how blest*
> *Your fate today and your tomorrow's rest!*
> *To you all readers turn, and they can look*
> *Pleased on a paper who abhor a book.*
> *Those who ne'er deigned their Bibles to peruse*
> *Would think it hard to be denied their news.*

But this was written before My Lord Beaverbrook, having set up as a Universal Provider in a veritable Woolworths of Journalism, had edited the sayings of Jesus and the prophets in penny instalments, giving us selections from Holy Writ in Gothic type at ten to fifteen words a time for every column of his own OPINIONS.

Beginnings of Wisdom.—But I must return to the destruction of sewage and refuse before some pedantic fellow falls to questioning the incinerator I stick in my face, an ancient pipe which I have christened the *Cloaca Maxima.* A beginning of wisdom may already be seen in such methods as *Controlled Tipping,* in which house refuse is used for its proper purpose, filling up old craters and converting poor land into good soil. This method, I learn, is now upon the increase, and in this country some 5,000,000 tons of dry refuse were thus treated in the year before the present war. The Cornish people have long known this manner of employing garbage, and they are wont to say *No refuse, no broccoli;* but the good manure made by pulverising the products of our dustbins still fails to find general favour with farmers, and a vast quantity of good organic matter is annually consigned to *incinerators* and *destructors.*

On the Apotheosis of Dung 277

Of Progress in India.—Of greater importance is the enterprising experiment made at Leatherhead and at Maidenhead in composting dry refuse with sewage sludge. Such composts of animal and vegetable waste are strongly commended by Sir Albert Howard, and were the basis of his remarkable and successful experiments. That they have been used in some other parts of India was shewn by Mr. F. K. Jackson and Mr. Y. D. Wad in an article which appeared in the *Indian Medical Gazette* of February 1934; and in the same number of that journal there is an account of *Organic Manure from Street Refuse and Night-soil at Mysore City,* by a Sanitary Engineer. This writer, Mr. J. J. Mieldazis, tells us that the manurial value of a mixture of street rubbish and night-soil is recognised to such an extent that in Mysore agriculturists *make periodic trips to the cities for the collection of these ingredients.* Garbage is almost unknown, says this authority; the agriculturist loads his cart with alternate layers of this heterogeneous mass of refuse and night-soil and carts the mixture to his fields, where it is formed into piles and allowed to decompose for some four to six months.

A devilish Paradox for God's Englishmen.—The municipal officers of Mysore assist the farmers in this work to the advantage of both parties, so that the town is kept clean and sweet, while the farmer acquires valuable manure which, *when it is broken down to an odourless humus mass, is used as a fertiliser on the fields.* And yet, when the disposal of refuse or sewage to a better purpose is discussed in our own country, the argument is commonly heard that this valuable matter must be disposed of in some destructive and wasteful manner *because it is not a commercial proposition to remove it* to some place where its true value can be realised. Thus, while the illiterate peasant of Mysore will, at his own cost in time and labour, turn scavenger and remove the filth of the city for his use and advantage, the civilised people of England would rather see their wealth destroyed than be at the cost of removing it to the place where it is needed.

The Problem is, how to have our Dung and yet be rid of it.—The experiments at Leatherhead and Maidenhead are therefore of the greatest value as indicators (we may hope) of greater enlightenment on the part of municipal authorities. Certainly it was not too soon for our municipalities to make a beginning, for this method of composting has not only been used in China for countless generations, and is known today in parts of India, Ceylon, Malay, Kenya, Tanganyika, the West Indies and South America, but it has been the subject of successful experiments by private individuals in Darkest England, as the reader may discover from reading the recent work of Mr. George Godwin, to which we have referred, or the publications of the Anthroposophists. But our urban conditions have encouraged (and, indeed, made indispensable to health) a water-carriage system which has until recently been considered incompatible with the principle of paying our debts to Nature, even where such an honest intention has so much as entered our minds. The system in recent years introduced at Maidenhead and Leatherhead is therefore of supreme importance, because it combines the sanitary principles of Harington and Chadwick with the biological and dietetic principles revealed by Howard, Pfeiffer, McCarrison and so many others. Indeed, it is of such vital importance that we will afford it, together with some account of previous efforts in a similar direction, a chapter to itself, an Odyssey of Progress and (as I hope) a mirror of the future.

CAPUT XIV

Of the Final Metamorphosis and the Hope of Humanity

FROM THE SAD REFLECTIONS of the last chapter, having exposed and laid bare the evils and perils of our present unnatural behaviour, I can now turn without fearing the taunt of blind optimism or lack of realism to the one thread of progress in an unhappy world.

Salvation is not to be expected from Politicians.—Put not your trust in princes, and still less in politicians. Swift's secret code of the people of Tribnia, or Langden, where a close-stool signified a privy council, and a running sore, the administration, still serves to describe them; nor is there a statesman living for whom I would not write such an epitaph as Byron wrote for Castlereagh:

> *Posterity will ne'er survey*
> *A nobler grave than this:*
> *Here lie the bones of Castlereagh.*
> *Stop, traveller . . .*

But I trust we are of one mind.

Two useful Functions for the Press, and some Thoughts on Jobocracy.—The press will be no help to us, as I have already shewn. The Fleet Ditch, oldest of our London sewers, was never fouler than the street that bears its name; one served to dispose of public filth, the other serves to disgorge filth upon the public. Therefore no good is to be hoped for, no devotion to public interest expected, from those whose sole function is to corrupt the public in the interest of its worst enemies. I know of but two useful functions for a newspaper, for both of which it is but poor material, and one of these I learnt on reading that paper will decompose with organic matter in a compost heap, helping to form humus. But putting that aside, the press is otherwise engaged. Good Sir John Harington once wrote (the man was a prophet indeed) of *soldiers who never drew sword out of Fleet Street*. Well, these same warriors have now a war on their hands and need all their ink to squirt at the enemy.

As to local government, it has indeed improved since Chadwick wrote of the *jobocracy of vestrydom*. But do not his harsh censures still apply to many local councillors, when he calls the *vestrymen* of his time persons whose time is worthless, ignorant or wasteful or obscure persons *who have some sinister interests to promote?* Do not slum-owners, as Chadwick said, still get possession of the local boards of sanitary authorities? And are not those words still true, which were most memorably recorded by a Royal Commission on Housing, that many of those whose duty it was to see that a better state of things was effected *were those whose interest it was to keep things as they were?*

But while the main traffic of organised society sweeps forward to destruction, here and there intelligent and public-spirited men are to be found, of the type whose lonely perseverance has so often triumphed, to save this unworthy race from the boomerang circuits of its criminal blunders. Let us, then, repair to the Royal Sanitary Institute; and there, with infinite patience and the kind, most courteous assistance of Mr. Dollymore and his efficient staff, we will unearth the story of these unnoticed efforts. Here we will seek for heroes worthy to rank with Harington and Chadwick, whose efforts will yet succeed against all the massed forces of reaction, however slow the visible progress may appear to be.

Views of Professor Fowler, an Architect of the New Order.—Before all other books, to shew what can be done and what has been achieved, to make scientific knowledge operative in the modern world, I would recommend the great work of Professor Gilbert Fowler entitled *An Introduction to the Biochemistry of Nitrogen Conservation*. The title is alarming, the contents, absorbing. The lay reader needs not to be afraid of the terrifying formulae of Professor Fowler, for the text speaks plainly enough; and if the conservation of nitrogen is the writer's chief concern, you will find that he has much to say upon other matters.

Professor Fowler gives it as his opinion that there are few lines of enquiry to which the chemist can devote himself of more fascinating interest or of greater importance to humanity than the numberless transformations which take place in the journey of nitrogen from the plant through men and animals and back to the soil again. The details of this journey may be left to those who can follow it. We will concern ourselves solely with the more general observations of this writer on his own chosen subject; the utilisation of the waste products of human and animal life for the benefit of agriculture.

Former Pioneers and Prophets.—In the last century there were those who saw and foresaw the perils besetting mankind, especially in centres of what was called *civilisation*. We have already referred to the writings of Professor Shaler in 1896. Two years later Sir William Crookes gave the world a solemn warning of the nitrogen famine to which mankind was hastening. But an even earlier genius had been at work, to whose work we must briefly refer.

This cycle of health and life, and the perils by which we are beset, formed the subject of many profound studies in the last century by that most celebrated chemist, Baron Justus von Liebig, who spent the second half of his life in examining animal and vegetable physiology, from which he drew many conclusions with regard to agriculture. In the year 1840 Liebig published his work on *Die Chimie in ihrer Anwendung auf Agricultur und Physiologie*, shewing how limited in quantity was the supply of minerals in the soil, and measuring the extent to which each crop would exhaust the earth of its supplies of specific substances. But though he was well aware of the ravages caused by foolish systems of sewage disposal, of which we have cited an example in his observations upon the decline of Rome, he sought relief in chemical fertilisers, of which he prepared different types, engaging in personal experiments on the land at Giessen. Thus, while his diagnosis was largely correct, his remedy proved to be fallacious, as more recent research so clearly demonstrates.

As to this question Professor Fowler tells us that in spite of the development of methods of nitrogen-fixation from the air, making nitrogen starvation improbable, our problems are by no means solved, because mineral nitrogen, as manufactured by our vast commercial enterprises *is not fully adequate to meet the needs of plants*. Or, to summarise all that we have endeavoured to demonstrate, he finds that *organic manure is essential*. And in proof of this he cites the work of many authorities already quoted in this book, including the inevitable Sir Robert McCarrison, who shewed in the *Indian Journal of Medical Research* (IV, 14, 1926) that a crop fertilised by cattle manure was *fifteen per cent more nutritious* than one that was artificially manured.

Decline of Western Agriculture.—The reader will find also further confirmation of this truth in a long extract which Professor Fowler has translated from the German of Dr. G. Ruschmann, discussing organic manure in

Biedermann's Central Blatt. Writing in July of 1931, Dr. Ruschmann confirmed much that we have recorded in the previous chapter from the experiments of so many pioneers. However much (he said) mineral manures serve to increase the yield for the moment, so much the less can they safely maintain their position. *This knowledge is spreading both among scientists and practical men,* said the Herr Doktor, for *in spite of constant or increasing use of mineral manures, yields are decreasing.* In the breaking-down of humus he found such fertilisers actually detrimental, for *arable soil is a living thing.* While complaints were rapidly increasing of insufficient or negative results in feeding such soil with mineral fertilisers, Ruschmann turned for hope to *those organic materials which are at present virtually wasted.*

Of the Use made of Liquids and Gases from Sewage.— The problem of sewage utilisation is not, however, purely a matter of solids, for there are valuable effluents from sewage works, containing a very high percentage of nitrogenous matter, and these are commonly turned into the sea or a neighbouring river, even when the solid matter is used in some fashion. Yet such effluents can not only be used to feed fishponds, but to irrigate land or to keep the right humidity in a *compost heap,* which they greatly enrich. And as to irrigation it has been said that the drainage from the city of Cairo is thirty times as valuable for this purpose as the waters of the Nile, even when that mighty river is at the flood and bears much fertilising silt with it. Then in addition to solids and effluents there are gases, which can be collected for purposes of light and heating, as is now the case in Birmingham, and I believe at Essen (where Dr. Imhoff developed his system of *digesting* sludge in tanks) and in other places.

Urea made synthetically, while Urine is carefully wasted. —In the previous chapter we have already noticed the great antiquity of manuring, and particularly of the use of human excreta. The Arabs had a great scientific understanding of this subject, and in the tenth century one of them compiled a textbook upon it, called *Kitab al-Falaha,* telling of the properties of composts, and how these should be made, and of the value of blood as manure, of which this writer said *the best of all is human blood*. The Celts also were learned in such matters. But, in more modern times, the genius of science has been principally occupied in the manufacture of chemical fertilisers, whilst those produced by Nature have been as carefully destroyed, so that we have today the curious phenomenon of urea, synthetically produced in large quantities, and much praised as an artificial fertiliser, while the natural product, of which it is but a poor substitute, is wasted.

The use of *bones* as manure has also been long known, though much neglected until recent times, and I do not doubt that their value contributed to the excellence of the apples I ate as a boy from trees growing in a Quaker cemetery at Bridport. But the advance in the manufacture of chemical fertilisers, with their immediate and highly deceptive results, so confused the minds of many agriculturists that organic manure was for many years greatly neglected; and so great an authority as Georges Ville, the French agricultural chemist, even declared of farmyard manure that it was unnecessary and could be economically replaced by these patent medicines of the soil. Nevertheless Sir E. J. Russell, in his article on *Fertilisers* in the fourteenth edition of the *Encyclopaedia Britannica,* shews how the effects of these chemicals proved only temporary, so that it became known that organic manure was more effective in *permanently maintaining fertility;* to which he adds references to many experiments (similar to those we have mentioned) by which this fact was established, so that practical men came to understand the important effects of farmyard manure on plant growth, which effects are not produced by artificial manures.

The Professor his own Guinea-pig.—It therefore followed that those who were aware of such things looked with dismay at the wastage of human excreta, and Sir John Russell himself speaks in this connection of activated sludge as a promising fertiliser; but of the general system of sewage disposal he remarks that unfortunately no practicable means of realising the value of sewage has yet been devised, though I believe this statement to be no longer true, even if it was so when it was written. Indeed, as we shall see, experiments of many kinds have long been carried out in our own country, achieving this very purpose with varying degrees of success; and these range from the wholesale experiments of municipalities to the private efforts of individuals, such as that celebrated professor of whom I heard recently, who laid out his garden in separate beds, each fertilised by a different member of his family, to observe the variations created by the personal coefficient. The war against waste is therefore seriously beginning, and if that other war serves any purpose worth remembering, I will prophesy that it will be remembered for this fact alone, that it stimulated our desire to conquer material waste.

The Indictment of an evil and adulterating Generation.—Indeed, of all the things that posterity will remember about us, for nothing will it so justly condemn our age as it will for our profligacy. They will say of us in time to come that we wasted human labour in unemployment and human life in war; that we wilfully destroyed food on the preposterous excuse that it was necessary to maintain its price; that is to say, to make it more dear to our own pockets; that we *killed time* because we did not know how to live; that we debilitated our constitutions by destroying vitamins, inventing elaborate methods of ruining

every decent thing that was eatable; and that we destroyed
the soil itself by this same mania for *waste*. But by contrast posterity will surely discover, among those who live
in present obscurity, heroes and pioneers whom it will
measure by standards unknown to us; and it may well be
that some future historian of our time will search the
records of the Royal Sanitary Institute to learn what was
done in this country to combat this suicidal destruction of
human wealth in the sphere which we have chosen to survey. Let us therefore ourselves next examine these records
to see what such an historian will discover to our credit.

Of Bradford and its Revenue from Sewage.—I find in
the *Journal of the Institute of Sewage Purification* (Part
I, July 1933) a paper by Mr. C. C. Beedham, Works Chemist to the Bradford Corporation Sewage Department, from
which I learn that Bradford, since 1912, has not *thrown
away* any of its sewage sludge (the fact is recorded as
worthy of remark) though some has been *burnt on the
boilers*. But for twenty years this progressive town has
sold dry, degreased sludge as fertiliser, with average sales
to the value of £4000 per annum, and I believe they now
use the effluent from their sludge in fishponds. Then in
the same Journal (Part II, 1936) I find some most apposite remarks by Mr. J. A. Coombs in a paper on *Sewage
Disposal Works as Centres of a National Industry of Organic Fertilizer Manufacture*.

*The Demand for Kingston Sludge is greater than the
Supply.*—In the discussion which followed the reading of
this paper by Mr. Coombs, at a meeting of the Metropolitan and Southern Branch of the Institute, the following
facts were mentioned by speakers. Firstly, that the nitrogen cycle had been the subject of observations by Sir
William Crookes in the year 1872, from which we might
long since have hoped for a wider understanding of the
peril in which we stand, but this was not the case. And

secondly, that at Kingston-on-Thames sewage sludge had for forty-eight years been prepared for use as a fertiliser and sold at the cost of production; but *a very large quantity* (observed the Kingston Surveyor) *is going to the Continent*. He had recently turned down enquiries for hundreds of tons *which he would not have been able to execute*.

Consider the implications in all their enormity. The excrement which we despise and wilfully seek to destroy is bought (when we choose to offer it) by our neighbours on the Continent with hard cash; and such is their eagerness to get all they can that our output cannot keep pace with the demand, the Continentals being, as it were, in a scramble to obtain Kingston sewage faster than the citizens of Kingston can produce it. Where will you find such madness outside the pages of Lewis Carroll, when our land starves for the very food we sell to our neighbours, and rather than use it ourselves we will, for the most part, seek the most ingenious means to *dispose* of sludge as though it were a nuisance and an offence.

Of the alarming Future of Foreign Trade in Sewage Sludge.—But if such practices of foreign trade in sewage should increase among the nations the imagination cannot conceive of what may yet become possible. Will there be tariffs against foreign excrement? Will there be Imperial Preference, sponsored by the *Daily Express?* Surely some case could be made for it, combining the ties of race and sentiment, hands across the sea, with a hard-headed estimation of the profits to person or persons unknown. Will sewage be considered among those raw materials for which Have-not Powers go to war with the Haves? Will there be overproduction, and New Deals, with Mr. Roosevelt paying a bonus for the non-production of sewage and scientifically destroying one-half of the year's crop to keep up the price of the rest? I see with the eye of prophecy

the vast hoardings urging us to Buy British Sludge, the
campaign to teach us that British Dung is Best. I hear
aged colonels, as yet unborn, bemoan the ruination of the
country by foreign imports, bringing our sewage works
to a standstill and throwing the entire population out of
employment.

Yet such a fantasy of the future is no more foolish than
the present waste, just as it is no more ludicrous than our
present economics, our present politics and journalism.
In the discussion of Mr. Coombs' paper there arose the
Borough Surveyor of Romford to tell of farms where horse
manure could no longer be obtained from the London
stables, whence formerly the very carts that took crops to
the Metropolis returned with their load of fertility. And I
suppose today a man would scarce dare to approach a
horse on the matter, if he could find one, without a book
of coupons. But while these farmers, as the Surveyor of
Romford tells us, *rely on artificial manures, with conse-
quent soil disorders, such as sourness,* there are throughout the length and breadth of this England great *lagoons*
of sludge (oh, word suggestive of enterprise and adventure!) of which nothing is thought except how to be rid
of the stuff.

Of the Hidden Hand.—Why this continued waste? The
answer is twofold. Firstly because, as I have already said
plainly enough, the *interests* opposed to scientific utilisation of sewage are enormous. Do you suppose those who
own the vast capital invested in companies providing
chemical fertilisers are unaware of the peril in which they
stand? Do you imagine they will allow such compe-
tition *to extinguish their traffic altogether* without re-
sorting to all the means open to them as honest merchants
or manufacturers? Only imagine that you are the posses-
sor of a few hundred thousand shares in a firm manufacturing chemicals, for the slaughter of human beings in

time of war and the corruption of the soil in time of peace, and you will construct your syllogisms from very different premises.

But the second reason has to do with the failure until very recent years to find *a cheap and efficient method* of manufacturing from sewage the best and the most easily portable product. In this the earlier methods which we have discussed were often defective. Either the cost of production was too high or the product was not all that it should be. Or, again, it was not easily removed or could not be readily used. It is to the solution of this problem that we are following this fascinating history.

The Triumph of Sewage is kept a Shameful Secret.—In a discussion of Mr. John W. Finch's paper, on *The Disposal of Air-Dried Sewage Sludge as a Manure,* which took place at a meeting of the North-Eastern Branch of the Institute on March 11th, 1939, I find some most interesting observations relating both to the prejudice against sewage as manure and the commercial interests opposed to its use. Mr. Finch stated in this discussion that such prejudice was common, and could only be overcome by demonstration with samples of the product, and that those who used it *did not broadcast the fact that their produce was grown with sewage sludge.* Thus the public could only be persuaded to purchase a superior commodity by the nature of its superiority being kept secret.

As to publicity in the newspapers, which Mr. Finch considered highly desirable, he said that he had personally written to six large national newspapers to discover their attitude to the use of sewage sludge as manure. In five instances he had received replies, each of about two lines in length, stating that these papers were not interested in sewage sludge; but perhaps the true explanation of their apparent apathy was found in the sixth reply, from an editor who said he knew for a fact that sewage sludge was a GOOD THING, and he had actually used it in his garden, but unfortunately *his paper relied on manufacturers of artificial manure for about sixty per cent of its advertisements*. And this, said Mr. Finch, was the position as applied to all the newspapers and gardening papers in general. Such is the HIDDEN HAND of our enemies.

Dung can only be vindicated by Experience.—Only by patient demonstration can prejudice be defeated, when commercial enterprise feeds that prejudice and stifles every attempt to expose its folly. The allotment societies near Rotherham learnt with surprise that sewage sludge was not the foul and malodorous stuff they had supposed it to be, of such a nature as to be utterly unusable on a garden. They were impressed with what they *saw* (and smelt) in defiance of all they had ever *heard*. The discussion on Mr. Finch's paper does not appear to have included any mention of vitamins and their relation to organic manure, but one speaker referred to rooting hormones such as *skatole* and *indole,* which he said were present in sewage sludge; and this (he said) should be made known to increase the sales of this product. Another speaker recounted the experiences of a market-gardener who used sewage sludge with the most satisfactory results, including the elimination of those diseases to which tomato plants are subject (thus confirming the experiments of Sir Albert Howard); and he spoke of mushrooms thriving upon *composts* made from sludge. Yet another person was reported to have grown the most excellent tomato plants from sludge, without ever having put in any seed, which I can well believe.

Fertilising with Sewage is no longer an Experiment but an Achievement.—Very justly did *The Surveyor* recently criticise the Minister of Agriculture, who months past had refused to take further steps to encourage the use of sewage sludge in farming because further experiments were first supposed to be necessary. Especially when we examine further the success of Leatherhead we shall be forced to agree with the local Borough Surveyor that *we are past the stage of experiments*. The Ministry of Agriculture wants more information and a generation in which to digest it; the Ministry of Health, stepmother of all sewage plants, wants no information at all and takes good care to avoid it. And meantime experiments cease to be experimental. A sewage plant conducted at a profit, with better crops for the farmers and better food for the people, is not an experiment; it is an achievement. How rightly, then, does *The Surveyor* conclude: By all means carry out more experiments, *but meanwhile get the sludge on to the land*.

And now there lies before me, in the library of the Royal Sanitary Institute, where I am writing, the Nine-Year Index of the American *Sewage Works Journal* (Vol. X, 1938) which is a very weighty publication of the Federation of Sewage Works Associations, Lancaster, Pa. My thumb rests upon the word *Fertilizer,* while my eye surveys, with a wilder surmise than that of stout Cortés, a long list of titles. Adaptability of Sewage Sludge as Fertilizer; Economic Preparation and Sale of Digested Sludge as Farm Fertilizer; *Public Health Significance of Sewage Sludge Used as Fertilizer*—that should be of some interest. We shall find Sir Robert McCarrison in this, unless I am mistaken.

Decency *invades Science.*—Here we have it: by a Professor of Bacteriology, F. W. Tanner of Illinois University. He seems to dislike the notion of fertilising with sewage. From the beginning, he says, health officers looked with suspicion on the practice *and rightly so, if for no other reason than decency*. Great God, is this a scientist speaking, or some kind of a puritan who would rather see the human race die of deficiency diseases than endure

the thought of Nature's Transubstantiation? Does he propose to exclude horse-dung and cow-manure on the same
grounds? Are animals not also subject to diseases? Does
not decency apply to their excrement as well as to our
own? But see how he continues: *It is true that in some
Oriental countries human excrement is used as fertilizer,
but such a practice need not be permitted in this country.*
Well I dare say he now wishes the Japanese were not so
healthy on their indecent agriculture. *The primary problem of sewage· disposal is to get rid of waste matter*—No,
I can waste no more of your time or mine on this. Here is
a scientist who thinks Nature is a chocolate machine that
can be cheated of its pennies; he can only bleat about some
remote possibility of infection from vegetables fertilised
by sludge. But as someone else is certain to be speaking of
this sooner or later (it might be some disinterested citizen with a wad of money invested in chemical manures)
we had best answer it briefly.

The Folly of seeking Health in Sterility.—Let this much
be clear then. Firstly, that infection from vegetables grown
from sewage is hypothetical. On the other hand, if we
exclude sewage we should logically exclude all other excrement, and the danger of doing so is no mere hypothesis,
for the path leads direct to perdition by a steep mathematical gradient, as we have abundantly shewn. But
should it *need* to be shewn? How do we expect Nature to
provide for us for ever, if we make no payment or re-
placement? We shall, therefore, if wise, choose hypothetical infection rather than certain and inexorable disaster;
but this still overlooks the most vital of all considerations,
for infection is always with us, and what matters is not
the impossible attempt to sterilise life and exclude all
harmful germs from our universe, but the *building-up of
resistance*. Hence the relevance of Sir Albert Howard's
experiments and his claim that all the plant diseases could

not harm his crops. If we, then, have fortified our constitutions with sound food soundly nourished in well-fertilised soil, what matters an extra microbe or two that the same food might bring to us? For my part I expect to meet innumerable bacteria, whatever I eat or drink, and I only ask for such vigour of body as I shall require to deal appropriately with them.

But I will leave the Americans out of this, except to commend to your attention the Report of the Committee on Sewage Disposal of the American Public Health Association, which the convert and enthusiast will find in Vol. IX of the *Sewage Works Journal;* for there is in that report a summary of American achievements in the utilisation of sludge as fertiliser, which I purpose to spare the present reader. To speak truth I am a little alarmed myself at the length of that list below my thumb, in the index. For once I will be insular, a Little Englander, and say that it matters little to me how much the Americans have done, for our problem is here and now. The method is tried and proved—only the bold application outside present spheres of enterprise is awaited in vain. Come with me, then, to Leatherhead, and I will shew you the New Model for our universe, the cradle of our biological regeneration that is yet to be. Those who desire to know more of America will find evidence enough if they care to look for it, shewing that our Illinois professor is not the last word in American wisdom; indeed, I have reason to believe that in many parts of that great country they are ahead of us in this race for survival, as Milwaukee bears witness, and Paterson (N.J.) where they make humus from house refuse by the Beccari process.

Of Composts from Dung and Refuse.—On our way to Leatherhead we will consider for a while the question of *composts,* for it is with composts that we are now concerned, and Professor Fowler should once more prove an informative companion. These composts, long known in China and certain other parts of the world, are made by a judicious mixture of vegetable and other refuse with human or animal excreta, so that the excreta work as a ferment, breaking up the refuse by the action of bacteria. And when this compost is in the process of fermentation, it can be used as an *activator* for further quantities of refuse, provided that the right moisture be maintained, which can best be achieved by the addition of urine (so frequently wasted, even in the case of beasts) or of the effluent from activated sludge. Both these liquids contain the necessary soluble nitrogen whereby the compost can be enriched.

The Science and Art of their Composition.—It is not our purpose to discuss here the details relating to the making of composts, or the various methods advocated or in use; but it should be noted that much work and thought has been given to this question, in order to achieve the best results. For by an ignorant use of organic manure not only is it possible to waste this valuable commodity but even to do positive harm; as, for example, by making the land sodden or sour, bringing this good material into undeserved discredit, as occurred in early experiments at Croydon and Norwood. But we are here concerned rather with principles than with the details of application, which should be decided by biochemists in conjunction with agriculturists on the one hand and sanitary engineers on the other. Thanks to the work of Richards and Hutchinson at Rothamsted, we now know that the ideal compost contains nitrogen and carbon in a fixed ratio, which must be considered when the raw materials are gathered together, and that the micro-organisms which break down the carbonaceous substances function best in the presence of air. We know that the condition of the compost should be neutral or slightly alkaline, that there is an optimum concentration of the nitrogenous compounds, and a maximum capacity in such substances as straw for absorbing nitrogen. Such are the considerations which we shall very gladly leave to the expert. Our concern is with a principle.

Science returns to the ancient Wisdom of China and Japan.—Here, then, is a system scientifically perfected whereby we can at the same time solve the problem of sewage disposal and that of street and household refuse and all manner of waste materials, combining all the putrescible matter which threatens the health of the people so as to form that which public health has greatest need of: rich humus for food crops and pastures. Science at last (as Professor Fowler reiterates upon many occasions) returns to the ancient wisdom of China and Japan. But in one notable particular we can improve upon these venerable methods, and that is in the use of *activated sludge* rather than crude sewage, for this ideal substance, containing all the organisms to be found in good arable soil (but lacking in dry refuse), has been proved to be the best activator for a compost. Thus Professor Fowler tells us of experiments made with *katchra,* that is to say, rubbish, and fallen leaves, at the Indian Institute of Science; and this mixture, when worked upon by activated sludge and kept moist with *sullage* (which is, in the main, wash water and urine), sets up a ferment of such great power that *when the heap was fully ripe a gunny-bag which was buried in the refuse was completely rotted in about a week*.

Of the Virtues of Activated Sludge in making Composts.—As to this capacity of a good compost to make humus of paper, cardboard, cloth and many other manufactured materials of vegetable or animal origin, astonishing things are told, and Professor Fowler especially recommends the study of H. Rege's *Biochemical Decomposition of Cellulosic Materials,* in the *Annals of Applied Bi-*

ology, Vol. XIV, No. 1, 1929, for a proper understanding of this question, which is manifestly of great importance. For all such purposes activated sludge has been shewn to be the most effective inoculant, breaking down the composition of the dry refuse more rapidly and completely than other inoculants, conserving all available nitrogen and even fixing further supplies from the atmosphere. And though activated sludge is of itself a fertiliser of such value that Professor Fowler considers it best used without the dilution of vegetable matter, it is generally agreed that the difficulties of drying sludge are considerable, so that the method of composting it with dry refuse serves at the same time three additional purposes: the difficulty of drying the sludge is overcome, the problem of dry refuse disposal is solved, and the weight of available humus is greatly increased without a proportionate loss to its quality.

Of the great Heat engendered.—There are many methods of making composts, which every farmer and gardener should study, the most approved methods being known as the *Activated Compost process,* evolved at Bangalore in the Indian Institute of Science, and the *Indore process,* perfected by Howard and Wad. To each process the general considerations already outlined must be applied, and Professor Fowler also mentions the importance of a high initial temperature; for only by great heat can the seeds of weeds and the larvae of insects be destroyed and the whole mass rendered so innocuous that even Professor Tanner of Illinois would search in vain for a solitary microbe of disease. For it was shewn in an experiment by Sir Albert Howard and his colleague that the fermentation in a compost properly made would liberate such intense heat that large quantities of grass seed would be utterly destroyed in such a compost, the ripe manure yielding negative results to germination tests.

The true Measure of the Wealth of Nations.—In a correctly balanced compost we have therefore the solution of our many problems: sanitation, the final disposal of all kinds of filth, the conservation of our mineral wealth and especially of those minute substances which no chemical fertilisers can replace. Nay, more, we have the best means of fixing further supplies of nitrogen from the air, and Professor Haber himself, the inventor of the Haber process of nitrogen fixation by artificial means, is reported to have said that in the future this fixing of nitrogen would not be done through such great industrial plants *but rather through plant and soil bacteria.* Thus the proper use of organic manure, and especially the making of composts, should prove (as Professor Fowler tells us) *a major factor in the world's prosperity.* For this conservation, even of nitrogen alone, he describes as a real measure of the *Wealth of Nations.*

It is for this purpose, then, that I would have you turn your attention to Leatherhead, for at last we have arrived there after so long a journey. Here we shall meet Mr. John L. Davies, a very energetic gentleman from Wales and now Engineer and Surveyor to the Leatherhead Urban District Council. Shall I pause to describe this genial, *dynamic* person as he appeared in the flesh when I came into his office out of the rain, the strangest of strangers, an amateur interested in sewage? Alas, I am so unobservant that I could not tell you the colour of his hair or his eyes, his height or the clothes that he was wearing; and my wife, God bless her, is never tired of telling me that I should never make a novelist. I can only tell you that he wasted no words, came to the point without delay, discussed nothing but the subject I came to discuss with him, treated me with great courtesy, and above all, without any trace of the contempt which professionals so commonly feel for amateurs. In short, he was a model of all

I hoped to find from the letters I had received during our previous correspondence, always courteous, yet never irrelevant, always to the point, yet never formal. And for the rest, by his fruits ye shall know him, and I will quote from his recorded words to be sure of doing him full justice.

The Project of Mr. Davies at Leatherhead.—First, then, let us consider the project as Mr. Davies foresaw and planned it when he read a paper in June 1936 at the Annual Meeting of the Institution of Municipal and County Engineers, held that year at Brighton. I quote from this paper as it later appeared in the *Journal of the Institution of Municipal and County Engineers.*

For some years past, wrote Mr. Davies, considerable difficulty had been experienced in Leatherhead not only in expeditiously drying sludge, but in disposing of it. Under the Local Government Act of 1929 the area of the Urban District was increased from 3508 acres to 11,187 acres, the estimated population being increased to about 254 per cent of the numbers in the old Urban District. The Council, said the Borough Surveyor, was confronted with the problem of disposing of the additional sludge which would accrue, *and which could not be even given away locally.*

At the same time there was a vast increase in the amount of house refuse which would, if disposed of in the usual manner, have necessitated the provision of further sites for tipping or the extra cost of incineration. In such a situation did the Leatherhead Council decide, upon the advice of its Surveyor and Engineer, to adopt a system already in use at Maidenhead, but with this difference: that where the system at Maidenhead was operated by a contractor, the Leatherhead scheme was to be conducted by the Borough itself, a notable improvement.

A Description of the Process.—According to this scheme the dry refuse was first to be separated upon a rotary screen, with meshes for the isolation of ash. After such ash had been separated, making it available for road works and the like, the remainder of the refuse was to pass along a picking belt, where bottles, metals (tins excepted), rags, cardboard and paper sufficiently clean would be extracted for separate use. Next the remainder of the refuse would be pulverised in a crusher, the tins being afterwards removed magnetically; and this order was proposed because it had been found at Maidenhead that the presence of the tins helped in the crushing and *mastication,* as it is termed, of the refuse, whilst the tins themselves, by passing through the crusher before they were separated, became flattened and therefore could be stored in the smallest possible space, without attracting rats or flies.

The crushed organic refuse remaining was to be laid out in beds or bays where it would receive measured quantities of sewage sludge. In his paper Mr. Davies then describes how he will have these beds turned over for aeration within two days and that he anticipates from his mixture the generation of 170° F., thus rendering it innocuous and, after two turns of the mixture, causing the evaporation of all moisture and leaving a dry compost in which *aerobic digestion* takes place. Within fourteen days, he said, fresh sludge could be added and the process repeated to enrich the compost and dispose of further sewage, and as for the value of this process he said that all weed seeds and noxious germ life would be destroyed and a good manure produced which, upon analysis, would contain more nitrogen phosphates, potash and lime than an equal weight of stable manure.

Lack of Interest in the Project among other Engineers. —I hold it greatly to the credit of Mr. Davies that he did not wait until he had operated this scheme for many years before he made these statements, but boldly declared what he intended to do and what results he expected to see, at a stage when most men would have been more cautious. In the discussion that followed this truly historic statement there was little evidence of interest in composts on the part of other engineers, who certainly gave their colleague no encouragement here; though other sections of his paper, of far less revolutionary importance, appear to have met with their approval.

The Heat of the Compost was found to kill Seeds and Pathogenic Bacteria.—Over five years later Mr. Davies wrote a second paper for the *Journal of the Institution of Municipal and County Engineers,* December 9th, 1941. From this it appears that the method of dealing with the dry refuse before composting has been somewhat modified, no doubt by general experience as much as by war conditions. As to the composting itself, all has gone according to plan, and Mr. Davies reports that the heat generated in fermentation has proved sufficient to kill both weed seeds and pathogenic bacteria; so that our American professor should be satisfied upon this point. Even the tomato plants which (says Mr. Davies) are associated with sewage disposal works are here non-existent. Paper remaining in the compost from four to six months was found to be completely broken down, rats and flies were not attracted by it, and no more unpleasant smells were noticed than were usual in other modern methods of sewage disposal; the final result being a fine brown mould that I have seen, smelt and handled without being able to trace any sign of its origin in appearance, scent or texture.

The People of Leatherhead, like those of Kingston, are unable to meet the Demand for their Product.—The achievement of Mr. Davies is above all significant because he has approached his problem with vision, taking care to inform himself of the most recent researches of agriculturists and others into this subject. His article *Compost-Sludge and House Refuse* includes quotations from Sir

Albert Howard and from the work of Mr. F. M. Newell on *Humus and Decay*. It is not, then, merely to an Engineer and Surveyor that we are listening, but to an amateur gardener and a real enthusiast, proud to have put upon the market at ten shillings per ton quantities of *Savital,* the new fertiliser of which the Leatherhead Council was selling locally some 300 tons per annum at the time of writing, in addition to what was sent outside the area. To which Mr. Davies proudly added, when speaking of the matter to myself, that he could have sold three times the amount, *if he had the output.*

The local record of the *Dorking and Leatherhead Advertiser* shews that a member of the Leatherhead U.D.C. informed the Council that he *swept the board* at Bookham Flower Show in 1938 with produce fertilised by the L.U.D.C. Manure. Wonderful results were claimed by others with roses and strawberries and with all manner of root vegetables, but especially onions, parsnips and potatoes. Onions were even found to double their size, when treated with the compost in experiments carried out by another member of the Council. As to Mr. Davies himself, he records experiments in his own garden, where he used his product as a top dressing for lawns and roses, passing it first through the crusher for repulverisation. Of this finely crushed material, in which Mr. Davies observed a close resemblance to peat moss, he tells us that it gave him grass of exceptional thickness and a vivid green, which survived the hottest and driest periods of summer without becoming burnt up, as had been the case on previous occasions; and he noticed the superior condition of his own lawn to others that had been treated with expensive artificial fertilisers. Regarding his roses, Mr. Davies tells us that he found their growth strong, their colour improved and at least three crops were obtained, the last one lingering until Christmas.

Concerning Whitehall and the Indifference of its Officials.—From this cheerful account of two wasteful and costly systems of *disposal* transmuted into a combined scheme of *utilisation,* profitable to the local authority and of inestimable value to the community at large, Mr. Davies turns to less hopeful signs. The author, he writes, has received no official assistance or encouragement from the officials dealing with the disposal of such waste matter at the various Ministries. *The attention of the appropriate officer has been drawn to the scheme from time to time with negative results.* Mr. Davies adds that he has *very definitely been given the impression that he is a crank.* The Ministry of Agriculture has proved no more enterprising than the Ministry of Health, as may be seen from the evasive character of the Ministry's reply to a question in the year 1941 respecting the use of composts of this kind, and whether they should be encouraged in other boroughs. These questions were asked with regard to the work at Maidenhead; yet such is the apathy of the Ministry of Agriculture, which claims to be making the necessary enquiries, that it has made no attempts to examine the work which has been in progress for over five years at Leatherhead, with numerous practical tests and experiments.

The Record of Maidenhead.—Such is the record of Leatherhead. That of Maidenhead is even older, though less of an example to other boroughs, because the work here has been carried out by contractors, and not by the Borough and its own employees. The history of the Maidenhead experiment is told in an article contributed to the *Journal of the Institution of Municipal and County Engineers* (June 24th, 1941) by the Maidenhead Engineer and Surveyor, Mr. C. T. Read. In this article the writer refers to two very excellent contributions to the proceedings of the Royal Society of Arts, that of Lt.-Col. F. C.

Temple on *Municipal Manufacture of Humus from Habitation Wastes,* and that of Mr. G. V. Jacks on *Humus and the Farmer.* These writings, says Mr. Read, will explain some of the intricacies involved in this question of composting waste matter, so that pitfalls may be avoided and the material used to best advantage.

Once the early difficulties and the conservatism of local farmers had been overcome, the scheme was found to fulfil what Mr. Read holds to be the dream of every Sewage Works Manager; for (so he tells us, and such indeed is their unbelievable attitude to National Wealth) they dream of a *simple pipe through which sludge may be pumped never to be seen again.* For them this is the value of the system, but for all who value the health of the people the stress is not upon the satisfactory disposal of the unwanted waste matter, but its return at last to the natural cycle.

Where there is no Vision, the People perish.—A committee of five municipal engineers was recently set up by the Non-County Boroughs' Association to investigate and report upon the merits of the method of composting refuse and sludge at Maidenhead under the Sams Patent No. 251885. An interim report was presented by this committee, which was published in the Official Circular of the Non-County Boroughs Association (No. 5 of Vol. LI, dated November 1941), and I had hoped to learn from this of some definite recommendations. Yet in spite of the years of trial and the success shewn by the company operating this scheme, I find nothing but the most cautious and reserved statements, as though the whole affair were some new-fangled and untried system, together with the astonishing statement that *it is impossible to do anything in war-time.* The committee, having thus rejected action in the present emergency, when it is most needed, adds, however, that it is *strongly of the opinion that when normal conditions of life return an effort might well be made by local authorities to assist agriculture.*

A Call to Action.—So ends, for the moment, the story of the most important innovation of our time, destined (as I am convinced) to save humanity if human stupidity and inertia can be overcome, and subject to the proviso that humanity does not first destroy itself by other means. But if salvation is to be achieved, the small number of sanitary engineers who are equipped with sufficient vision to see that their mission is, in fact, *salvation* and not *destruction,* must be fortified and strengthened in their work by all that the ablest agriculturists can say and do to assist them. Left to engineers alone, this work can never progress with sufficient speed; it requires the fullest pressure from agricultural interests and the deliberate stimulation of public opinion, which must be continued in spite of all the vast interests opposed to reform and in the teeth of their violent opposition. Indeed, I am credibly informed (and offer it as an example to be followed by others) that Dr. Henry Gillett of Oxford prayed for the Borough Engineer to such good effect that the *Divine Grace* is now (it is said) working in the Engineer towards the adoption of a new sewage system in keeping with the principles we have advocated.

Of Aspirations and Prophecies.—Once the principles upon which the cycle of life rests are truly understood and recognised, we may expect and prepare for the most far-reaching changes in our social organisation and way of living. In place of those sewage-laden craft, such as *The Mancunian* and *The Salford City,* which still sail down the Manchester Ship Canal to deposit their burdens in the ocean, or those grim barges at Erith, we shall see vast fleets of ships bearing back, to the lands from which our food comes to us, their loads of compost. But even more probable is the future redistribution of population to avoid such distant transactions, the drift back from the towns to the countryside, the de-congestion of over-populated lands such as our own, the return to an economy where the people of little towns eat the produce of neighbouring fields in all its freshness, and unspoilt by preservative processes, returning to these same fields their rich heritage of fertile humus.

Then at last will Ajax return to the proper dignity which ancient heraldry afforded him, when it attributed to the great Alexander the arms described by Shakespeare in a passage which we have already noticed; and I do not mean where it is written *this love is as mad as Ajax: it kills sheep;* for the metamorphosed Ajax will nourish them, and you may have the wool and the mutton. But I speak of the painted cloth where the lion holds his pole-axe sitting on a close-stool; and if this was a good enough device for one of the Nine Worthies, and a conqueror at that, the British Lion might find a worse seat and a new world to conquer into the bargain. And below we will inscribe the stately lines of Byron, which my friend the Antiquarian has this moment recited for my pleasure (together with the Duke of Bedford's reply and further backchat, which we will omit as unseemly and unworthy of so great a subject), this quatrain that gives such a decorous quality to a necessary and useful function, the lyric of reincarnation and perpetual motion:

> *O Cloacina, Goddess of this place,*
> *Look on thy suppliants with a smiling face,*
> *Soft, yet cohesive let their offerings flow,*
> Not rashly swift nor insolently slow.

What words could better express the even rhythm proper to the Cycle of Nature?

Last Words to the Kindly Critic

The Author humbly admits his own Inadequacy.—To you, gentlemen, the critics and reviewers, these last words are addressed, to lighten perchance by my *Peccavi* the harshness of your censures. Indeed, I propose to shew that most of the things you have in mind to say have already been said, and we will consider them seriatim, with suitable apologies or explanations.

I will begin with my friend the Antiquarian, whom we have this minute left, who comes to me at the very moment when I am finishing a book, some weeks overdue on my contract, with a host of suggestions enough to make my head ache, exposing the pitiful inadequacy of my poor researches by a random display of his own brilliant store of knowledge.

Of certain Mediaeval Practices.—What, he says, have you no note on the use of *mempiria,* those balls of hay with which our mediaeval ancestors completed their toilet? Surely you are familiar with those instructive hexameters upon this subject, where the notable line is found:

Dum paro mempirium, sub gumpho murmurat anus?

But these *mempiria,* as you doubtless know, were only employed for the final polish of perfection. If you search the *Mediaeval Vocabularies* you will find the word for those peculiar instruments, curved like a hockey stick, which were used in the first instance, from which we have the phrase, *to get hold of the wrong end of the stick*. You may well imagine that this was a likely catastrophe on a dark night, and in the North they say *the moocky end of the stick,* which makes the meaning plainer.

That is a grim reflection (said I), but, unless I am mistaken, we may soon be reduced to such methods. For Mr. Unwin has just informed me that he has used all his quarter's ration of paper; and the day may soon come when we shall have to choose between a pound note and a petrol coupon, unless we go back to the Roman sponges or your *mempiria.*

Then I suppose (he continued) that you have searched the *Glossarium Tetraglotton* for the practices of a later date, those useful guides to conduct (for they were frequently revised and re-issued) where you will find the most minute and detailed account of the things that interest you. For I confess, he added, that I too have some curiosity as to these things, and I could never understand the reticence of our own archaeologists in discussing them, though they know well enough that there is no such happy hunting-ground as an old cesspool or rubbish-heap. Why, I can remember a prehistoric cesspool (it was near to Northampton) where, the place being clay-lined, there was such a stench when we opened it up that the first men to go down fainted and those who followed were compelled to wear gas-masks.

The Smell of Prehistoric Man.—Yes, said my friend, I have smelt Prehistoric Man, just as I have smelt a Roman army on the march, when we once boiled some Roman sandals, causing the sweat to come out of them, and I may tell you there was never such a stench known; but this way one is very near to the past. Does not Monsieur Viollet-le-Duc recall in his memoirs how he conducted a

woman of the *ancien régime* through some newly excavated sewers, causing her to remark in a nostalgic
ecstasy: *Ça me rappelle bien le beau temps?* And then,
you have, of course, studied the *Inquisitiones Post Mor-
tem?*

Curious Facts regarding James the First.—I confessed
that I had not, and he continued: Ah, my friend, there
you will find the most interesting material. The number
of lives that were lost through falling into a jakes, it is indeed unbelievable. At London Bridge, for example, where
you might have expected them to fall into the river, they
seem to have preferred to end their lives in a cess-pit. But
our horror of excrement, as you have doubtless noted, is
really a very new-fangled idea. Why, if you will look up
the unpublished portions of the manuscripts of Sir Roger
L'Estrange at the British Museum you will find a most
illuminating commentary upon this fact. He describes
with approval the enthusiasm of King James the First for
hunting, the old rascal being reckless enough in the hunting field, for all his terror of cold steel. And Sir Roger tells
us that such was his absorption in this sport that he would
not leave the saddle even to relieve himself, so that his
servants had a pretty mess to clean up at the day's end.
Now you might suppose such a story would be told to
discredit the monarch; but Sir Roger, as you know, was
the most ardent Royalist, Tory and Jacobite who ever
lived, and he tells this story not to shew that James was a
filthy old man but to demonstrate a truly regal monomania
for venery.

The Mystery of the Royal Closets.—Why, I said, you
have given me enough work for a month at least, if I am
to search out all this, and I shall need a second volume to
take it all in. But while we are discussing this matter, can
you tell me what became of Queen Elizabeth's water-

closet? Was James so wedded to the saddle that the place fell into disuse and disrepair?

As to that, said my friend, I cannot tell you; but I know that James did on occasion descend from the saddle or the throne to relieve himself, because his knight's stool is to this day at Hampton Court, a curious contraption adorned with velvet and brass gilt studs, of which you will find a photograph in *The Connoisseur* for March 1941. But as to your own problem, if any suggestions of mine seem to you of note or value, all that you have to do is to put them into an appendix to your book as *arrières pensées,* or (if you prefer) *derrières pensées,* suggesting to the reader further fields of research. The subject which you have chosen being, in fact, inexhaustible, you cannot expect to say the last word on it. But by throwing out a few hints of unexplored fields you will disarm criticism by your candour; and those who follow your footsteps (I trust they will be many) will thank you for the signposts, rather than sneer at your many omissions. To say too little invites contempt and to say too much courts envy; but tell your readers where more is to be found, and you will avoid both extremes, earning only gratitude.

Of Notable Omissions.—Let me, then, confess that there are many sources which I have not consulted, for one reason or another, which should prove of value to my successors. There is, for example, the *Sérées de Guillaume Bouchet,* beloved of Sir John, and there are the works of Susruta on Aryuvedic medicine (a profitable field, as I am told) and a work known as the *Bibliotheca Scatologica* (very rare). I have not consulted any of these, through no fault of my own—such are the tribulations of scholarship in time of war. Well, as Jack Falstaff said of another matter, Good body, I thank thee. *Let them say 'tis grossly done; so it be fairly done, no matter.* I have done my poor best. And speaking of Falstaff, I wish I could have told you what was in the publican's mind when he said: *Thou art a Castilian king, Urinal!* Surely some dark meaning lurks here, relevant to my theme, but I cannot fathom it. Maybe it was but liquor.

Discoveries of Dr. Edgar Bérillon.—Then there was a clue I wish I had discovered earlier which came to light in a book by Jacques Barzun, on *Race, A Study in Modern Superstition.* The author tells us of the unique researches of Dr. Edgar Bérillon, recorded in the Bulletin of the Society of Medicine of Paris (June 25th, 1915) and expanded in the reports of the French Association for the Advancement of Science (February 4th, 1917). This Dr. Bérillon discovered that Germans—the date of his discovery must be regarded as purely accidental—suffered from polychesia, or excessive defaecation, and bromidrosis, or body odour. These racial defects, he concluded, lead to degenerescence and unnatural crimes. Furthermore I read that the Doctor detected German spies by these tests and by the infallible method of urinalysis, having found that German urine contains 20 per cent non-uric acid, compared with 15 per cent for other races. When these spies had been duly dispatched he performed upon their bodies *post-mortem* examinations revealing the dark secret of the Teutonic large intestine, which (he affirmed) was nine feet longer among Germans than among normal persons. Such abnormalities, the Doctor admitted, occurred sometimes in France, but were always accompanied by a German cast of countenance. Unfortunately these researches were not pursued further after the last war, and they appear to have been overlooked by the propagandists of today.

Of a Book on Old English Easances.—But what I most regret is that I have never yet seen a copy of what should surely have been a remarkable work, published (as I know for a fact) by a well-known London firm of publishers under a fictitious imprint. The title-page of this book bears the following legend:

OLD ENGLISH EASANCES
A Text book by
The Author of
RAMBLES IN RUTLAND
OLD ENGLISH VILLAGE PUMPS
OLD ENGLISH BOWLING GREENS
and other technical
WORKS

This work, published (I understand) in the 'twenties, bears no date of publication, was originally obtainable through a monomark, and is now out of print. In place of the publisher's imprint, the following remarkable address is given:

SITWELL AND WAYTE LTD.
LADIES' LANE, PENNYCOMEQUICK
TELEGRAMS, RUMBLES

All this information I have from the most reliable source imaginable, together with the price, which was five shillings. But I have attempted in vain to obtain a copy and can only offer these details to those who care to pursue the matter further.

Concerning curious Pots de Chambre.—One of my friends whom I used to meet in the Reading Room of the British Museum (it is now open again, I am told—alas, too late to help me much) has a notorious familiarity with the *Special Cupboard,* and from him I learn of other works which he assures me I should have studied. For example, there is *Woman,* he says, by Ploss and Bartel, in three volumes, full of very curious information. And another person asks whether I have any note upon those curious and decorative *pots de chambre* which were carried in carriages in the seventeenth and eighteenth centuries, of which he mentions some royal examples and notably certain of these articles which (he says) had pictures of Cromwell and Monk on the bottom, to express the sentiments of the owners and perhaps to serve as a diuretic.

Indeed, from my own experience, had I been minded to digress further from my moral purpose, I could have told of many strange places I have known, such as the lavatory of a restaurant in Soho, *sur les toits,* for which reason I have always called this place the *Café René Claire.* Or, had I sought merely to entertain, I could have collected innumerable anecdotes, new and old, true and fictitious, such as the celebrated story of the Wesleyan Chapel, or of the Chinese Washing Machine, of the White Chief who sat upon the well; of the Birmingham man who failed to become a lavatory attendant because he was illiterate, and how he made his fortune. Or of that young lady who was by misadventure shut all night in one of those comfortless places to be found on small stations, in the company of a porter who had sought to rescue her; and how she obtained heavy damages from the Company.

Of strange Customs.—And again I might have discussed learnedly the uses of words and phrases, such as the origin of the expression *to shift for one's self,* or the use of the word *dung* for nearly two centuries past, to describe those journeymen tailors who complied with their masters' terms. Or I suppose I could have discussed at length the ways adopted in strange and distant lands; the metal seats used in parts of Australia on account of spiders that hide themselves in wood and emerge to attack (or so I am told); and the experience of a friend of mine, a reverend gentleman, in Newfoundland, during an intense and bitter winter, when he was invited to use a shovel because it was unsafe to venture abroad.

The taunt of *vieux jeu* would never have withheld me

from such narratives and discussions; for every story is old, and one subject is not more trivial than another in Lilliput. Man is tolerable only when he laughs at himself and never so ridiculous as he appears in the solemn moments of pomp and circumstance, when he stands upon his dignity. I could leave the matter there with *je m'en fiche,* were it not that this same capacity for taking ourselves seriously is the true and only Original Sin. How else has it come about that great nations can be governed by cutthroats, pickpockets or even imbeciles? What living statesman could last four and twenty hours in a country where people laughed out loud at his bombastic lies? But though the poorest story that can raise a laugh is worth more than all the speeches made in Parliament in the last twenty years, I will leave that task to others: mine is to provide useful information where it is most needed and most lacking.

Composts will outlive Churchill.—So while your betters (as you are pleased to consider them)

> *Decide all Controversies by*
> *Infallible Artillery*
> *And prove their Doctrine Orthodox*
> *By Apostolic Blows and Knocks,*

I have been busy with this postscript to Harington, in the belief that there is Nothing Like Leatherhead, and confident that compost will be remembered when Churchill is forgotten, just as Ajax has outlived the Armada. Many have helped me, of whom few have known the cause they served, and of these the staff at Chelsea Library should be awarded the first prize, which is my deepest gratitude.

But to return to those whose suggestions I have felt unable or unwilling to follow for one reason or another, there was one who would have had me investigate further the mystery of that peculiar heresy, *Stercoranism,* with which

Humbertus, Bishop of Sylva Candida, charged Nicetas, saying that he believed the consecrated elements did undergo digestion and evacuation. But of this I think I have already said enough. And another has but this day been telling me of a book called *Kabloona,* by a Frenchman who wrote of Eskimos, and how they make do in their igloos, with the aid of a common pot and no false modesty, unmoved by odours which appal the newcomer. Alas, it is too late for me to pursue this new thread: take out your notebook, Posterity! Yet another, a most accomplished lady, greatly anxious to help, recommended that I should spend at least some months in studying *yoga;* because, she said, one of the first signs in this practice is that very little waste is given off, until by degrees it is utterly eliminated; which I do not believe (although it accords so well with the theories of Swedenborg and Jacob Boehme) for I know that *yoga* includes the most ingenious methods of *elimination.*

An historic Document of the present International Riots.—Then my learned friend Dr. Griffiths, to whom I owe so many useful suggestions which have led to fruitful lines of research in this book, would have had me deal with everything from Philo (who wrote something, it seems, on Baal-Peor) to the tensile strength of paper in war-time, offering, as an example of the importance attached to this last question, a letter sent by a certain firm to the Ministry of Supply, complaining of an insufficient allowance of toilet paper. In this letter, the last of many (of which earlier protests would appear to have been milder), much space was devoted to the number of employees, the hours worked, the effect of Sunday shifts, the average number of calls made by an employee in the course of a day, the area in square inches required per occasion, and especially the decline in tensile strength through the use of cheap pulp, making a larger supply necessary. At bottom, said the firm's secretary, this was the problem. But if I am to concern myself with such abstruse and remote contingencies, I can see no end to my subject or to my book. I offer this example only as an illustration of the lengths to which one could go without a firm hand at the helm.

Art consists in drawing the Line somewhere.—Others, again, would have me solve mysteries and propound the most difficult questions. What, asks one, was the true meaning of that advertisement which appeared in (I think) May 1941 in the *Sevenoaks Chronicle,* where a person inserted the enigmatic words: *Wanted, a wooden structure for sitting in. State price?* Another correspondent would have me enumerate and explain the long list of names, proprietary and otherwise, attached to Ajax, giving their history and derivation. To such persons I can only give my answer in the words of Mr. Chesterton: *Art consists in drawing the line somewhere.*

How a Student of these Matters helped a Bishop to prevail, when Spiritual and Temporal Weapons had failed.— Next I must needs reply to two schools of critics, one of which will say that I have treated my subject with overmuch seriousness, while the other will accuse me of too much levity. To the first school I will reply that this is a very serious matter, the importance of which historians and sociologists have greatly under-rated in the past, and in addition to all the evidence already set out in proof of this fact I will offer you a story which may be verified in the *Nuremberg Chronicle.* For there you will find that a certain baron, having defied a proud prelate who was his feudal overlord, was besieged in his castle by the Bishop. And when the Bishop could not prevail either by the temporal means at his disposal or by the powerful weapon of excommunication, he had recourse to a stratagem revealed to him by a page-boy, the servant of the Baron, who (in dread of the ghostly powers of the Church) escaped from the castle to advise the Bishop on this matter. Acting, then, upon information received (as our police are wont to say) the Bishop placed two cross-bowmen in a privy place at an hour indicated by the page; and things falling out as the boy had said, the Baron received a couple of bolts in his posterior what time he made his morning ejestion upon the battlements (being a person of regular habits), for they shot straight up the shaft that led into the Baronial jakes. And this, as I suppose, was an event of some importance to all concerned, and shews that an understanding of my chosen subject may help even a bishop to prevail, where neither temporal power nor spiritual threats have availed him.

Then, on the other hand, it may be supposed by some persons, unacquainted with my serious purpose and unaware of the intricacies and great delicacy of the problems I have chosen to discuss, that in attacking *prudery* I would have myself associated with those libertines who allow neither decency nor reserve to have a place in our daily habits. For it is well known that such persons have a large secret following, such as those old men who are to be seen in the front stalls at what are called *leg-shows,* with their bowler hats on their knees. And the craving of these insatiable *voyeurs* has been epitomised in the words of Sally Rand, the Fan Dancer, who said: *I never made any money until I took off my pants.*

In Praise of Moderation.—But this same authority has warned us against the false logic which assumes that what is desired today (by some) for its rarity should be cultivated promiscuously, as though the Crown Jewels could be in every shop window. And of the heretical doctrines of nudism she observes that the nudists tell you that your moral fibre is made stronger if you go naked; but all the nudists I ever saw (she says) had scratches all over their rear ends where they had been sitting down on thorns. Which reasoning, however feminine, cannot be gainsaid; so that we are reduced to the conclusion in general that the moral fibre should not be indiscreetly exposed, but cultivated by the practice of *moderation in all things*. Or, in plain words, I have attempted to give you enough levity to carry my heavy cargo, and enough cargo to justify and excuse whatever offences I have committed against the conventions of prudery.

A Marxist is rebuked.—But one, a stern Marxist, tells me that I and my subject are both exceedingly decadent, shewing the inherent escapism of the revolting bourgeoisie, of which (he says) I am a hideous example. Why, I replied, are you not dialectician enough to know that if one escapes far enough one comes full circle, approaching Reality by the North-West passage as demonstrated by Galileo and Einstein? For though you may represent truth in a crude, two-dimensional form, like Mercator's Projection, to obtain a better view of it, I assure you that it moves in circles like everything else; and if you go far enough in any direction you will come back to where you started, taking your opponents in the rear. And this, I said, is what I have done; I began this book to escape from a world that wearied me, and believing that the best part of Man went down the drain; but I have come back through space and eternity to expose one of the worst *rackets* in the world, by which I mean the trade in chemical fertilisers. What, said he then, in 1942 and with a war on? And I told him yes, in 1942, and *because* there is a war on. For the neglect of dung was never such a grave matter as it is today.

Our Future must depend upon the Development of our own Resources.—To you, therefore, the future critics, I will say once more that Rome fell because it neglected the worship of Stercutius and Cloacina. The one was mocked by generations of Romans who threw the wealth of Italy and the empire into the Tiber, the other deity was offended by later Romans, who allowed bad drains to breed pestilence. And Spain fell because she preferred foreign tribute to the cultivation of her own soil, where all true wealth is to be found. Is it not therefore sound sense to say that the greatness of this country should lie in the development of its own resources, and particularly in the use of all waste matter as Nature intended it to be used? From the unregenerate Ajax of mediaeval times we have evolved the converted or twice-born Ajax; we have, to a very large extent, achieved the ideal of *sanitation*. But unless we are to be ruined by a system that has the defects of its own good qualities, the ideal of *soil fertility* must be combined with that of hygiene, and this is what I understand by *the further metamorphosis,* the most urgent programme of salvage and salvation. Indeed, I believe that one of our greatest Salvationists once astonished Paris with the admonition, *Tournez vos fesses à Dieu;* and this seems to me to express our present need symbolically, though the wording of the exhortation was unintentional.

The Mysticism of Ajax and its Interpretation.—But if you should think this savours of blasphemy, I swear it is not so intended. Indeed, but we are too restricted in our notions of holiness, and have forgotten too much of what our forefathers did not need to be told. Who now would say with St. Bridget these roaring lines?—

> *I would like to have a great lake of beer*
> *For Christ the King.*
> *I'd like to be watching the heavenly family*
> *Drinking it down through all eternity.*

Do you imagine a religion that could produce so robust a mysticism would have closed the door to Ajax? On the contrary, where Pan and Bacchus participate in the communion, Cloacina will be close at hand and Stercutius busy in the fields.

Or where will you find a better symbol of mortality than in these temples of which I write, where *memento mori* is written in unmistakable language? For here we may well feel with St. Bernard (as Skelton has it) that Man is but a sack of stercory, and shall return unto worm's meat. *Change and decay in all around I see* might well be inscribed upon their walls, or those words of Aristagoras, which I believe were actually written within the lavatories at Merton College: πᾶν ῥεῖ, οὐδὲν μένει; everything passes, nothing remains. (Beneath which some person is said to have written his own version, πᾶν μένει, οὐδὲν ῥεῖ; everything remains, nothing passes; which he signed as Constipagoras.) But these are comforting thoughts at such times as the present, like those verses of Herrick, beginning *All things decay with time,* where he speaks of the fall of Dictators from the same inevitable cause. Therefore a jakes is the best place in the world to consider mortality with relief and eternity with optimism.

Then let us apply ourselves to religion in a proper spirit of humility, such as we should feel in these places and in the exercise of such humble functions; for nothing is so conducive to it. This was known to Antigonus, who, when a poet called him the son of Apollo, replied that the man who emptied his close-stool knew better. Therefore there is no better place to consider the beam in our own eye, and no worse place for the consideration of the mote in our neighbour's, as Mr. Somerset Maugham reminds us in his *Summing Up.* For he says here that he wishes His Lordship at the Old Bailey had, beside his bunch of flowers, *a packet of toilet paper,* which would remind him that he was a man like any other.

We should not judge the Work of Others by our own Shortcomings.—And when (says the poet Donne of another matter) a whirlwind hath blown the dust of the churchyard into the church and the man swept out the dust into the churchyard, who will undertake to sift those dusts again and to pronounce, This is the Patrician, this the noble flour, this the yeomanly, this the Plebeian bran? Aye, who, indeed? And does not a jakes teach us the same lesson of humility? Or again, I have heard that certain lines were found, some say, at Somerset House; though others will have it that the lines were inscribed in the Inns of Court. But whichever it was, a person wrote upon the wall:

> *I do not like this place at all,*
> *The seat is too high and the hole is too small.*

And another, to shew the subjectivity and presumption of this person, wrote beneath his complaint these words of reproof:

> *You lay yourself open to the obvious retort,*
> *Your bottom's too big and your legs are too short.*

Thus we should learn to ask whether we are ourselves at fault before we begin to abuse the handiwork of others; and there is no better place in my opinion for such humble and salutary reflections.

The religion of the future will not despise such paths to perfection, but rather will it especially concern itself with all that we now consider either *ultra vires* or *infra dig*. It will demand in the rebuilding of our cities, after the present rioting, that sanitation and cleanliness should be a first consideration. It will substitute *dirt* for *immodesty* as its principal *taboo*. It will attack the sale of adulterated and devitalised food, demanding that the people should have vitamins, and have them more abundantly. It will be concerned with the needs of the soil, with the limitation of population to a reasonable figure (consistent with the resources of each country) to avoid the evils which we have described; and it will pursue justice and freedom and the Good Life, where men are good because they are happy and satisfied.

A final Exhortation to Humility and Repentance.— *Homo-soi-disant-sapiens* so little deserves the title which he has bestowed upon himself that no exercise is more fitting or more conducive to a state of humility (in which alone we can get wisdom, and with all our getting, get understanding) than the consideration of those functions of which we are most ashamed and of those things we hold most in contempt. Therefore, if Solomon lived today he might send us, not to the ant but to the dung-beetle for instruction; that we, having discovered the use and value of our most humble functions, might learn to use our heads as intelligently as Nature uses our bowels, and to keep our hearts as clean as we shall learn to keep our houses and cities. And having put aside prudery, which is the cloak of false modesty to cover true shame, we shall see ourselves as we are, nearer to the ape than to angels, but all the nearer to repentance and absolution for that very knowledge. For which reason, if there is but one grain of truth in the gospel according to Dr. Groddeck, I, who have written this book, may claim a small footstool, or an even lowlier seat, among the Benefactors of the Race.

Completed and revised at
The College of St. Mark and St. John, Chelsea
upon the *Ides of March*   IMPRIMATUR

Notes and Afterthoughts

AJAX AS LEVELLER (pp. 5–6, 47–50, 52, 228–9, 238–43, 318–21 *et passim*)

Montaigne's words were: *Les Rois et les Papes fientent, et les dames aussi.* Compare C. F. Racot de Grandval:

> *Les derrières des rois et ceux de leurs sujets*
> *Sont égaux pour l'odeur, quand ils ne sont pas nets.*

And Caspar Dornavius, in his *Amphitheatrum Sapientiae,* quotes also:

> *Imo Duces, Reges, summus cum Caesare Papa*
> *Si quando hunc illos imperiosa voco*
> *Adveniunt omnes propere . . .* (etc. etc.).

But bitterest was the complaint of Charlotte Elizabeth of Bavaria, Duchess of Orleans and sister-in-law of Louis XIV. Writing to her aunt she enumerated the great persons subject to a necessity which she (like Swift) found intolerable. (*Ah, que cela serait joli si cela ne chiait pas.*) Ernst Toller, in his autobiography, said he wondered as a child whether the Kaiser suffered this indignity: but, being abused for asking, concluded he did not. Others have taken a happier view of the matter.

> *Là, déroulant avec mystère*
> *Un papier qu'elle ne lit pas*
> *La beauté chaste et solitaire*
> *Dévoile un instant ses appas* (etc.)

Caca-Dauphin was even, at one time, a fashionable colour.

CONVIVIALITY (pp. 30, 50, 67–8, 83, 165–7)

Sir Nathaniel Wraxall in his *Memoirs* cites the Duc de St. Simon as saying that Mme. de Maintenon commonly accompanied Louis XIV on these occasions, and so did his minister Louvois. Ferdinand, King of Naples, maintained the custom when Wraxall visited his court in 1779 (the King's favourite courtiers attended him). Indeed, Wraxall noted that the custom was still general in Italy, and scarcely less so in France. Henry III and IV of France were among further examples mentioned by Wraxall, also Marshal Suvarov, who received his aides-de-camp and staff officers in this manner. The Duc de Vendôme received *the greatest person-ages on public business in the same situation,* according to Cardinal Al-beroni. Like the handshake, this practice may have begun as a reassurance against treachery, for Mr. Norman Douglas informs me of an Arab prov-erb: *Beware of the man who will not —— with you.* D'Aubigné certainly saved the life of Henry IV by his presence on such an occasion, in 1575, before Henry became King of France. An old woman approached him from behind and would have brained him with a billhook but for D'Aubigné, who nevertheless wrote these lines on the tragedy averted:

> *Cy git un roi, grand par merveille,*
> *Qui mourut comme Dieu permet*
> *D'un coup de serpe d'une vieille*
> *Ainsi qu'il chioit dans un têt.*

Herbert Read has some reflections on our own sociable retreats in *Annals of Innocence and Experience.* An American friend asks whether I include telephoning with conviviality, as this is among the amenities of the Savoy Hotel. I notice in contrast that the Benedictines in Lan-franc's time were addicted to *sleeping* in these places, so that it was neces-sary to make provision (*Decr. pro Ord. S. Bened.* Cap. 4) for watch to be kept *ne forte aliquis Frater dormiens ibi remanserit.*

GODS OF THE JAKES (pp. 23, 31–2, 246–50)

The sixteenth chapter of Isaiah concerns Moab; and though Baal-Peor is not specifically mentioned the writer says that his bowels will sound like an harp for Moab and his inward parts for Kir-haresh. Aristophanes said that the god Aesculapius was coprophagous and Pliny that the Egyptians revered the dung-beetle (which I had forgotten when writing the last page of Cap. XV) as the image of the universe, and of Isis and Osiris. Dr. Magnus Hirshfield adds the Assyrians and the Hottentots to peoples who had Privy Gods. But St. Jerome gives the most astonishing instance: *crepitus ventris inflati qui Pelusiaco religio est;* and *Crepitus* was a little godling at Rome, also. Christians maintained the tradition, St. Erasmus being in charge of the belly and the entrails, while St. Phiacre and St. Étanche were invoked to relieve a man *of the emeroids, of those especially which grow in the fundament.* Indeed, some verses published at Antwerp in 1643, *Sur l'enlèvement des reliques de Saint Fiacre,* etc., tell us that these were used to cure Richelieu. According to Usuardus a certain Ster-cutius was among the Christian martyrs at Merida, but I do not know his relationship to the pagan deity. Mr. Percy Smith tells us in *The Lore of the Whare-Wānaga* (Memoirs of the Polynesian Society, Vol. III) that *it is strange how sacred a place the latrine is in all Maori ceremonies.* The altar should be placed near the latrine or near a tomb, which the Maoris consider *the only proper sites;* but the altar is desecrated by *the approach of food. Turuma* signifies among these people a latrine or a place of prayer. . . . The symbolic commode mentioned by Lord Berners in *Sur-*

realist Landscape (a poem addressed to Salvador Dali) may have a similar significance in the unconscious minds of our esteemed contemporaries. Long before their time an Italian poet was perplexed that Jove, who assumed so many forms, did not take that of Ajax.

HOLY DIRT (pp. 2, 42)

The Venerable Bede tells us, among the virtues of the Virgin Queen Ethelrida, that she would rarely wash in a hot bath. And a King of Tara and High King of Ireland owed his prosperity entirely to the good fortune of having drunk from waters sanctified by a clerical closet, thus winning divine approval.

LOUIS XIV AND HIS COURT (pp. 83–4)

The problems of Fontainebleau are movingly described in the letter of Charlotte Elizabeth (see note on *Ajax as Leveller*). The Duchess considered the Electress fortunate in that she could choose her time, for at Fontainebleau one must wait for darkness to use the open spaces. This grieved Her Grace, who preferred privacy and something to sit on. She found the streets of Fontainebleau full of reminders of a human frailty she deplored, and especially of souvenirs of the Swiss Guards, of which she wrote with astonishment. Roger de Rabutin, Comte de Bussy, tells of certain titled ladies in a box at a theatre who behaved in a manner that indicates an absence of accommodation in such places also in the seventeenth century (*Supplément aux Mémoires et Lettres*). This story is extraordinary for the unnecessary offence caused to those in the pit, which led to the enforced and hasty withdrawal of the guilty aristocrats. *Projet utile à tout le monde* is the title of a late eighteenth-century work proposing the erection of public conveniences. I have not seen this work, but suspect it to be a translation of a pamphlet erroneously attributed to Swift and referred to in this book (p. 159).

MOSLEM CLEANLINESS (pp. 63–4, 183–7)

The astonishment shewn by George Sale and Gislenius was common among Europeans until, having themselves at last discovered hygiene, they began to pretend a monopoly of it. Henry Blount, in his *Voyage Into the Levant* (1634), said of the Turks that *he or she who bathe not twice or thrice a week are held nasty:* every time they make water, or other unclean exercise of nature, they wash those parts little regarding who stands by. It is strange to think of a time when Englishmen marvelled or sneered at Moslems and Hindus (to whom I should have added the Sikhs) not for their alleged filthiness but for their fastidiousness.

NICETY OF NATIVES (pp. 69–70 *et passim*)

From a passage in *Purchas, His Pilgrims* (II, vii, 936) I conclude that Amerigo could not have been more disgusted at his islanders than the

Negroes of Guinea were at the habits of the Dutch. These Negroes, who were *curious to keep their bodies clean,* and washed often, were unashamed of nakedness but wondered at the Netherlanders because these could not (or would not) hold their wind, which the natives held to be a shame and contempt done to them. (We also learn of these Guineans that their privies were on the borders of their villages, and when full were burnt to the ground.) This is not the only reference in the *Pilgrims* to the nicety of Negroes and the coarseness of the Hollanders, and perhaps Amerigo's islanders took as poor a view of the gallants in his company. John Bulwer, who quoted the *Pilgrims* in his *Anthropometamorphosis* (1650), coupled the Irish with the Guineans for horror of *crepitus,* saying that they were *much of the same opinion in this point of unnatural behaviour.*

NOTABLE DEATHS IN THE JAKES (pp. 22–3, 52, 239–40)

The death of Arius was long a favourite subject for ingenious comment. *Viscera ejus repente simul cum vita effusa sunt,* says one old writer, though Matthew of Westminster takes first prize with *he suddenly left his bowels, his life and his heresy at the same time and place.* There is another reference in *The Phylacteries of Presbytery* (*Harleian Miscellany*, ed. by Oldys, VIII 77). St. Gregory of Tours in his *History of the Franks* tells of a wicked priest who persecuted Sidonius, Bishop of Clermont; visiting a jakes he gave up the ghost in that place (*ingressus autem in Secessum suum, dum ventrem purgare nititur, spiritum exhalavit*). Here his servant found him: *Reperit Dominum super cellulam Secessus defunctum.* St. Gregory draws the proper Arian parallel. In 1683 a servant of Lord Essex, peeping through a keyhole, found his master in a similar situation. As to murders, I notice that Matthew of Westminster follows William of Malmesbury in his account of Ironside's death, adding that the weapon was left in his bowels by Eadric's son. James I of Scotland was killed in a jakes (A.D. 1437, in the Black Monastery at Perth) and so was Henry III of France, who was fatally stabbed in the belly like Eglon, and in the same circumstances. (*Sic transit gloria mundi.*) We have already noted the narrow escape of Bruce, and of Henry of Navarre, *étant allé faire ses affaires dans un têt à cochons.* Joannes Ravisius the Weaver, in the sixteenth century, is said to have made a list of these cases, but I have not seen it. Charles of Spain, the Holy Roman Emperor, was the only monarch *born* in a privy, to the best of my knowledge.

PSYCHOLOGY AND THE BOWELS, ETC. (pp. 177–8, 230–1)

Pète qui a peur, says the old proverb. The influence of fear on our functions was discussed by Aristotle, also by Schurig in his *Chylologia,* to which Francis Grose in his *Lexicon Balatronicum* adds further wisdom from old stories and sayings. I cannot recall that Groddeck, Freud or Theodore Reik anywhere explains why women are, on the average, more costive than men, but suspect a psychological origin. The prospect of food had a strange effect upon that Duchess of Orleans of whom Mlle. de

Montpensier tells us that the mere announcement of a meal would send her running *pour se placer sur la chaise percée*. In the seventeenth century Paul Scarron seems to have known that avarice caused constipation, for he wrote of his stepmother:

> *Cy git qui se plut tant à prendre*
> *Et qui l'avait si bien appris*
> *Qu'elle aimait mourir que rendre*
> *Un lavement qu'elle avait pris.*